Sedgwick

THE SONGS THAT MADE AUSTRALIA

WARREN FAHEY

Omnibus Press

First published 1984

Exclusive Distributors:
Omnibus Press
139 King Street
Sydney NSW
Australia 2000

Music Sales Limited
78 Newman Street
London WIP 3LA UK

Music Sales Corporation
24 East 22nd Street
New York NY10010 USA

Designed by Cozzolino Hughes, assistant Megan Stone

Cover illustration by Ray Condon

Individual illustrators are credited on page 236

Set in Franklin Gothic and Trade Gothic by
A G Markby – The Typesetting Studio Pty Ltd

Made and printed in Australia at
Impact Printing (Vic) Pty Ltd, Brunswick, Victoria

Fahey, Warren.
Eureka – the songs that made Australia.

Includes index.
ISBN 0 949789 04 6.

1. Songs, English – Australia – Texts. I. Title.

784′.0994

Contents

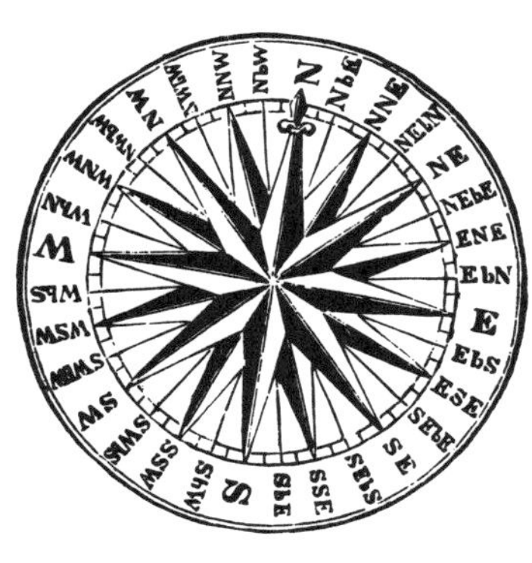

The one hundred and six songs in this *Eureka* Omnibus offer a rare key to the treasure chest of Australia's past and present. The songs are mainly the old traditional songs composed by disgruntled bush workers, optimistic gold seekers, men and women who tramped the old bush tracks during the lean times of the 1890's and 1930's and there are the later songs of industrial growth on the coalfields, songs about love, about leisure and songs about the future.

It is a collection to be sung, for these songs are not the workings of some ardent writer commissioned by Tin Pan Alley, but rather the creative works of the men, women and children who built Australia. These are the songs that made Australia!

A salute must be made to the people who made this collection a reality. Firstly, a word of praise for the song carriers – in this modern age of hustle, bustle and the ever-present media, it is encouraging to know that the old songs are still remembered and treasured. Singing can isolate all of us from the turmoil of this crazy world and the songs, like magic, can transport both the singer and the listener to another time space. To those people who have given their songs, I offer a toast "Long may their songs be sung!" To the song collectors of Australia and of the international folk song revival, we all owe a debt of gratitude. To Dave de Hugard, that fine singer of bush songs, I offer my thanks for musical arrangements. Finally, in the words of the late "Swagman" Jack Pobar, "You know, these old songs smack of the real Australia. After a couple of verses you can almost smell the gum-leaves and hear the billy boiling – fair dinkum!"

Warren **F**ahey

CONVICTS, TRANSPORTATION AND SEA SHANTIES

Introduction

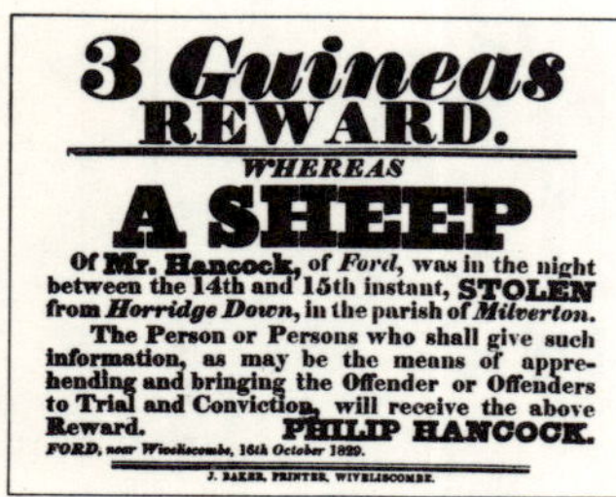

3 Guineas
REWARD.

WHEREAS

A SHEEP

Of Mr. Hancock, of *Ford*, was in the night between the 14th and 15th instant, STOLEN from *Horridge Down*, in the parish of *Milverton*.

The Person or Persons who shall give such information, as may be the means of apprehending and bringing the Offender or Offenders to Trial and Conviction, will receive the above Reward.

PHILIP HANCOCK.

FORD, near Wiveliscombe, 16th October 1829.

J. BAKER, PRINTER, WIVELISCOMBE.

Australia grew up the hard way. The first white settlers were a ragged mob of transported pick-pockets, poachers, political activists and "persons who stole goods over the value of five shillings". The British social system was in obvious decay and the gaols and prison hulks were swollen to their limits. Court reports show unjust verdicts such as the hanging of a thirteen-year-old lad in 1801 for stealing a teaspoon, and in 1816, a boy of ten was given the death sentence for shoplifting. In the early 1800's there were more than two hundred offences punishable by death. The unlucky ones were sent to Botany Bay.

Captain Cook, RAN, had landed in Australia in 1770, and in August of 1787, the British Government declared the establishment of the penal colony of New South Wales. A year later eleven small vessels, to be known as the First Fleet, assembled off Portsmouth, under the command of the retired naval officer, Captain Arthur Phillip. One thousand people, three-quarters of them convicts, set sail in the belief that Botany Bay was the new land for colonisation.

It was a "new land" but one with little joy. The Aboriginal population were, understandably, hostile to the intruders, the scorching climate was certainly nothing like Europe, and news and supplies came rarely. It was, in fact, a very large and ill-equipped gaol.

The transportation era spanned seventy-two years and ended as late as 1868. During these blood-stained years some one hundred and forty thousand males and twenty-five thousand females found themselves part of one of the most inhumane prison systems ever devised.

Perhaps the most renowned of our convict ancestors were six of the Tulpuddle Martyrs. These were village workers in Dorsetshire who on hearing their wages had been cut from nine shillings to seven shillings a week, protested by attempting to form a primitive trade union. They were charged with "administering unlawful oaths" and in 1834 they were transported for seven years on a charge of "seditious conspiracy".

However, it was from Ireland that the majority of so-called "political prisoners" originated. That is if one considers their desperate action as criminal! Before the great Irish potato famine the typical family lived solely on dried potatoes. Their English absentee landlords were no better than slave-masters. When the potato crop failed the British Redcoats moved in to "teach the starving Irish a lesson" – they destroyed their farm houses, took the farm animals and forced the Irish people to live in caves and peat-bog shelters. It is no surprise that thousands of Irish men, women and children planned and plotted to rid themselves of the British.

The convict population of Botany Bay exploded and further penal settlements were established in Van Diemen's Land, Moreton Bay, Norfolk Island, Port Macquarie and Fremantle. The transports arrived in ships crammed to the gills. The voyage was long and conditions were filthy with disease rife. There were shipwrecks, fights, murders and near starvation. It was a journey of torment, torture and tempest.

Life in the convict settlement depended on so many variables. Some officers were compassionate but the majority were unpredictable and keen on "setting an example". Lord Melbourne, annoyed that crime in England was increasing, made a statement that one of the main reasons was "that criminals regarded transportation somewhat like a relaxing sea voyage". Lord Stanley, his Secretary of State for the colonies, promised him that transportation to Australia would become a sentence "more dreaded than death itself".

And "dreaded" it did become. As a nation we have inherited an untidy past that opens with ghastly tales of men being flogged to death, women being cruelly treated and small children being made to work at labour not even fit for a work-horse. Deprivation was an accepted part of convict life and it comes as a surprise to learn that these are the people who helped build our country into the twentieth century.

After years of bloodshed and convict labour the colony boasted fine homes, cottages, shops and roadways. Slowly, the colony came around to its senses. There was a realisation that the times had changed and that this was, in fact, the new land. The air smelt sweet, the climate felt comfortable, emigrants were arriving to swell the social ranks and there was always the opportunity to select your own piece of land – the pioneering spirit had arrived. Times had changed.

Transportation to Van Diemen's Land went on until 1853 and to Botany Bay until 1857, but the terrible wounds of the system were felt for generations afterwards. This common "come all ye" relates the story of the young transported Englishman including the trial, family shame, the sentence and voyage to Australia, and, eventually, contrition and the inevitable warning to others to avoid the temptations of breaking the law.

From a broadside held in the Mitchell Library, Sydney.

I was bred and born in London town,
A place you all know well,
And brought up by honest parents,
The tale to you I'll tell.
Brought up by honest parents
And reared so tenderly
Until I became a roving blade
At the age of twenty-three.

My character soon was taken
And I was sent to gaol.
My friends and parents did their best
To get me out on bail.
But the jury found me guilty
And the judge to me did say,
I sentence you to twenty years
In a place called Botany Bay.

My poor old father stood at the bar
His head was bowed with care.
Likewise my poor old mother
Who tore out her grey hair.
My son, my son what have you done,
I heard my mother say,
They've sentenced you to twenty years
In a place called Botany Bay.

They put me aboard a sailing ship
One cold December morn,
And I never will forget the time
We passed around Cape Horn.
The captain as he passed me by
These words to me did say,
You'll rue the transportation, me lad,
Now you're bound for Botany Bay.

There is a lass in London town,
A place I know quite well,
And when I gain my freedom
With her I'm going to dwell,
And when I gain my freedom
I'll marry her one day.
No more I'll be a roving blade
And adieu to New South Wales.

Now you that have your liberty
Pray keep it if you can,
And don't go midnight rambling
Or break the laws of man.
For if you do you're sure to rue
And the judge to you will say,
I sentence you to twenty years
In a place called Botany Bay.

Am Em F C Dm G B♭

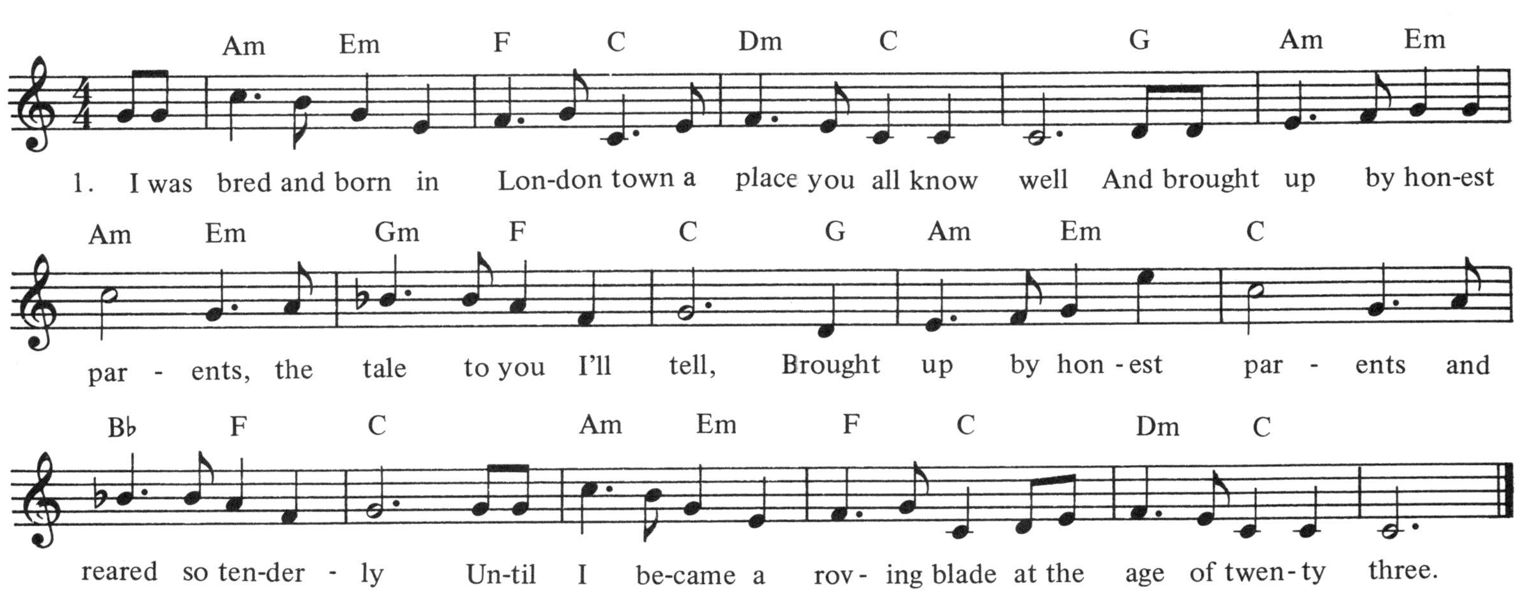
Am Em F C Dm C G Am Em
1. I was bred and born in Lon-don town a place you all know well And brought up by hon-est
Am Em Gm F C G Am Em C
par - ents, the tale to you I'll tell, Brought up by hon-est par - ents and
B♭ F C Am Em F C Dm C
reared so ten-der - ly Un-til I be-came a rov- ing blade at the age of twen-ty three.

Australia

"It was when the trial was ended, when those who were found guilty were brought out of the courthouse to be taken back to prison. The sentenced men came out looking eagerly at the people until they recognised their own and cried out to them to be of good cheer. "'Tis hanging for me", one would say. Then another: "Don't go on so, old mother, 'tis only for life I am sent." And yet another: "Don't you cry, old girl, 'tis only fourteen years I've got and maybe I'll live to see you all again." Then off they filed to the transports in Portsmouth and Plymouth harbours waiting to convey their living freights to that hell on earth so far from home. Not criminals but good, brave men were these." (A Shepherd's Life, *W. Hudson published 1910, in London).*

From Bob Hart and collected in the late 1960's. The song seems to be related to another equally rare song telling of transportation to "Virginny" (Virginia, USA) which was collected in 1907 by George Gardiner.

When I was a young man, my age seventeen,
I ought ha' been serving Victoria our Queen,
But those hard-hearted judges,
O how cruel they've been,
To send us poor lads to Australia.

I fell in with a damsel, she was handsome and gay,
I neglected my work more and more every day,
And to keep her like a lady I went on the highway
And for that I was sent to Australia.

Now the judges they stand with their whips in their hand.
They drive us like horses to plough up the land.
You should see us young fellows working in that gaol-yard.
How hard is our fate in Australia.

Australia, Australia, I would ne'er see no more,
Worn out with fever, cast down to death's door,
But should I live to see, say seven years more,
I would then say adieu to Australia.

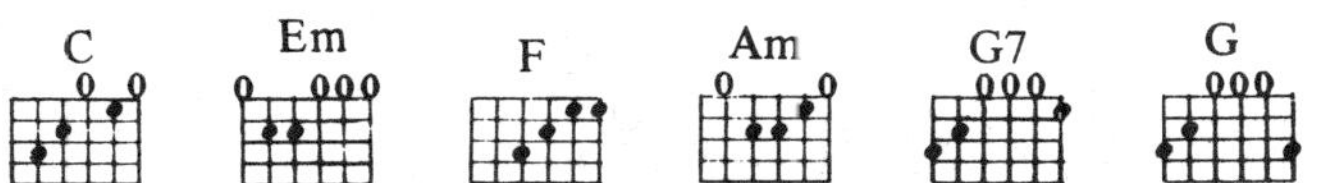
C
Em
F
Am
G7
G

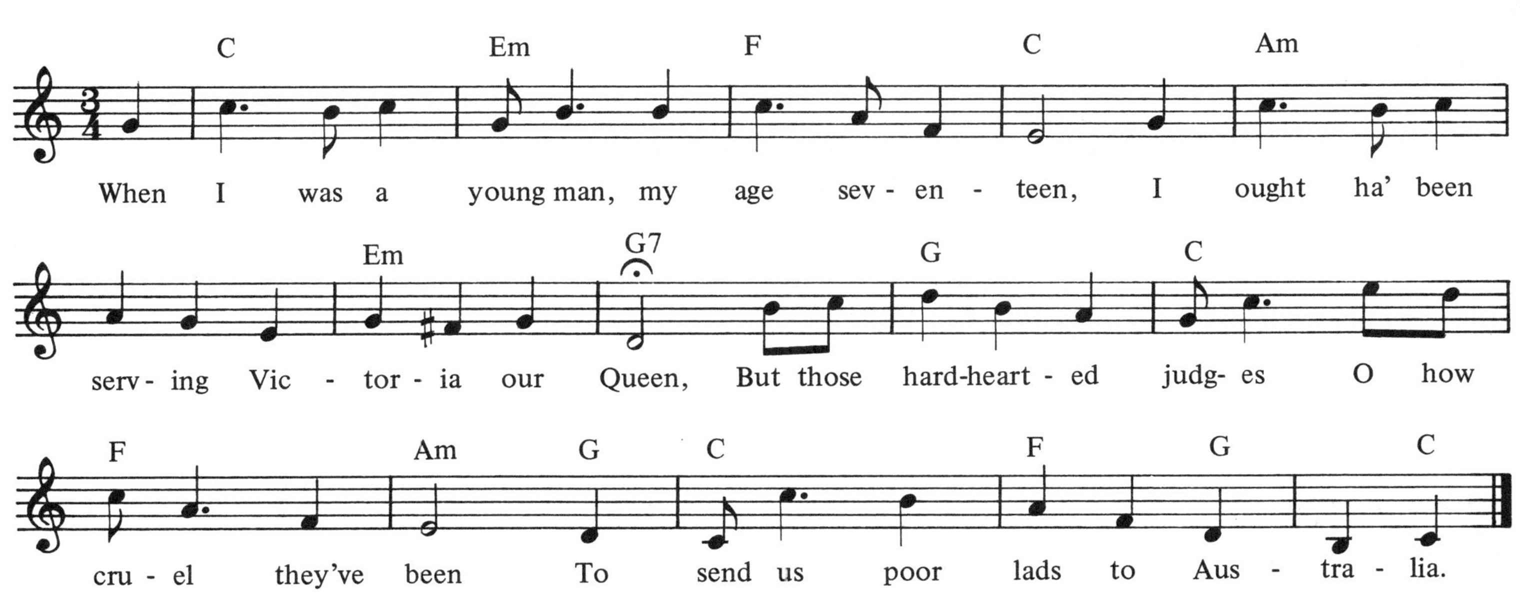
C Em F C Am
When I was a young man, my age sev - en - teen, I ought ha' been
Em G7 G C
serv - ing Vic - tor - ia our Queen, But those hard-heart - ed judg- es O how
F Am G C F G C
cru - el they've been To send us poor lads to Aus - tra - lia.

The Rigs of the Time

Life in nineteenth century England turned sour for the labouring class. They were exploited, misjudged and suffered no lack of lords or masters. Those who owned and held the land believed that the land belonged to the rich man only, that the poor man had no part nor lot in it, and had no sort of claim on society. As the age-old saying has it:

"The King he governs all,
The Parson prays for all,
The Lawyer pleads for all,
The ploughman pays for all
And feeds all!"

From the repertoire of John Salmond, Norfolk, and collected in 1947 by E. J. Moeran (B.B.C. Library). One line of the text has been collated with the broadside of the same title. This version adapted by Roy Palmer from Cambridge University Press The Painful Plough, *1973.*

Oh, 'tis of an old butcher, I must bring him in,
He charges two shillings a pound, he think it no sin;
Clap his thumb on the scales and makes them go down:
He swears it's good weight, when it lacks half a pound.

CHORUS:
Singing honesty's all out of fashion,
These are the rigs of the time, time, me boys,
These are the rigs of the times.

Now the next is a baker, I must bring him in,
He charge fourpence a loaf, he think it no sin;
When he do bring it in, it's not bigger'n your fist,
And the top of the loaf is popped up in the dish.

Now no wonder that butter be a shilling a pound –
See the new farmers' daughters as they ride up and down –
If you ask them the reason, they'll say, bonny lad,
There's a French war and our cows has no grass.

Oh, the next is a publican, I must bring him in,
He charge fourpence a quart, he think it no sin;
When he do bring it in, the measure is short:
The top of the pot is popped up with the froth.

Now the very best plan that I can find
Is to pop them all up in a high gale of wind;
And when they get up the cloud it will bust
And the biggest old rascal come tumbling down first.

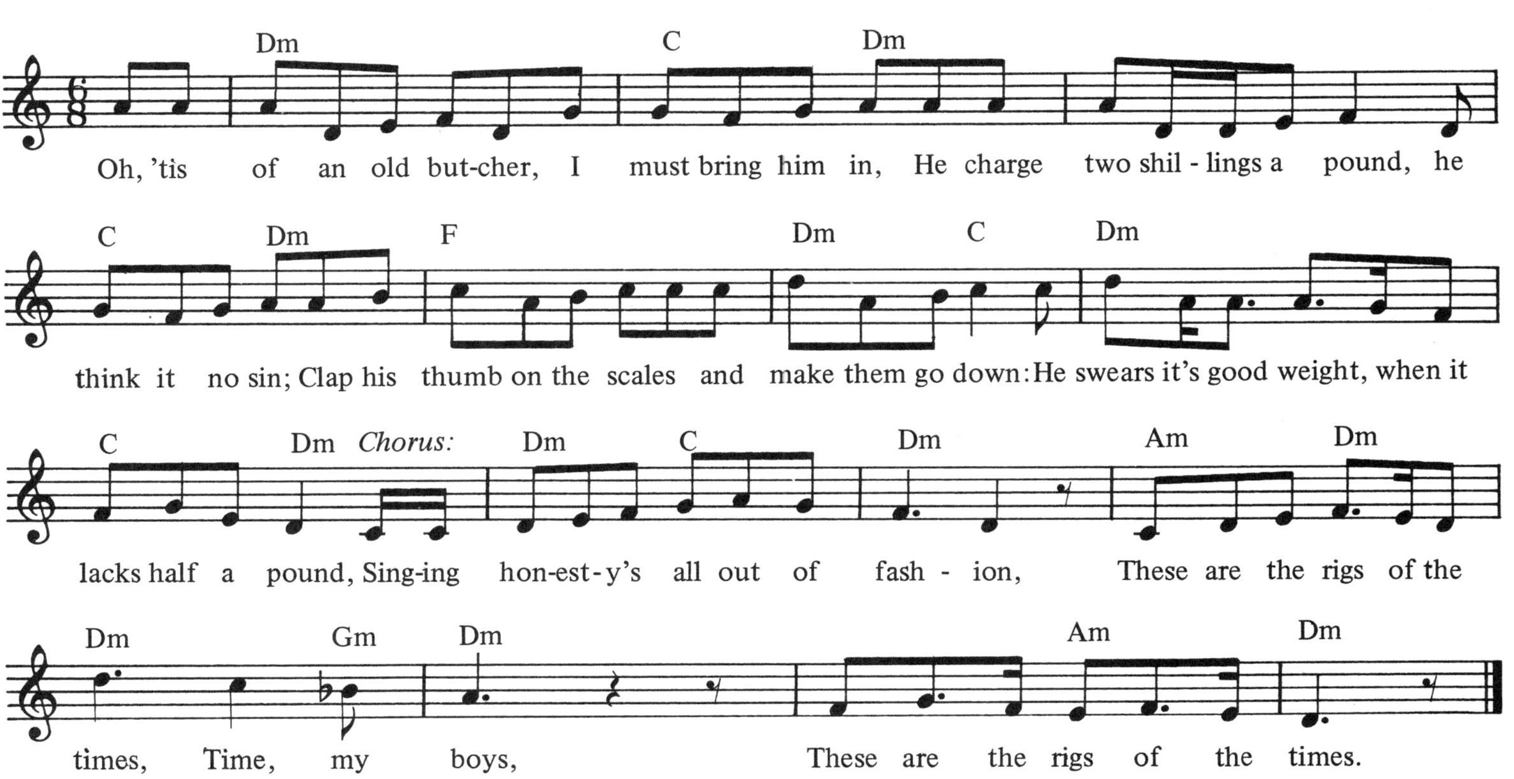

Dm
C
F
Am
Gm
Dm
C
Dm
Oh, 'tis of an old but-cher, I must bring him in, He charge two shil - lings a pound, he
C
Dm
F
Dm
C
Dm
think it no sin; Clap his thumb on the scales and make them go down: He swears it's good weight, when it
C
Dm
Chorus:
Dm
C
Dm
Am
Dm
lacks half a pound, Sing-ing hon-est-y's all out of fash - ion, These are the rigs of the
Dm
Gm
Dm
Am
Dm
times, Time, my boys, These are the rigs of the times.

Henry's Downfall

The poor of yesteryear had a literature of their own — although they seldom read they created an unwritten literature that correctly represented their feelings and ways of thinking. The straightforward story of "Henry's Downfall" was popular because it is both narrative and emotional.

From a ballad broadsheet in the Mitchell Library, Sydney. The tune has been adapted from the collected British version by Warren Fahey.

Come all you wild and wicked youths
Wherever you may be,
I pray you give attention
And listen unto me.
The fate of our poor transports
You shall understand,
The hardships they do under-go
Upon Van Diemen's Land.

CHORUS:
Young men all now beware
'Lest you are drawn into a snare.

I and five more went out one night
To Squire Dunhill's park
To see if we could get some game,
But the night it proved too dark.
And to our sad misfortune
They hemmed us in with speed,
And sent us off to Warwick Gaol
Which caused our hearts to bleed.

And at the March assizes
At the bar we did appear.
Like Job we stood with patience
To hear our sentence there.
We being old offenders
It made our case more hard.
Our sentence was for fourteen years
And I got sent on board.

The ship that bore us from the land
Speedwell was by name.
For about six months and upwards
We ploughed the raging main.
No land nor harbour could we see,
Believe me it is no lie,
Beneath us one black water,
Above us one blue sky.

I often looked behind me
To see my native shore.
That cottage of contentment
That I should see no more,
Nor yet my poor old father,
He tore his old grey hair,
Likewise my aged mother,
In her womb she did me bear.

On the fifteenth of September
Was where we made the land,
At four o'clock next morning,
All chained hand to hand.
To see my fellow sufferers,
I'm sure I can't tell how,
Some were chained to a harrow
And others to a plough.

No shoes nor stockings had they on
No hats had they to wear.
Leather breeches and linen drawers,
Their feet and heads were bare.
They drove about in two and two
Like horses in a team.
The driver he stood over them
With his malacca cane.

As we marched into Sydney Town
Without no more delay,
A gentleman he bought me
His book-keeper to be.
I took the occupation —
My master loved me well.
My joys were out of measure
I'm sure no tongue could tell.

He had a female servant,
Rosanna was by name,
For fourteen years a convict,
From Wolverhampton came.
We often told our tales of love
While we were blest at home,
But now the rattling of our chains
In a foreign land to roam.

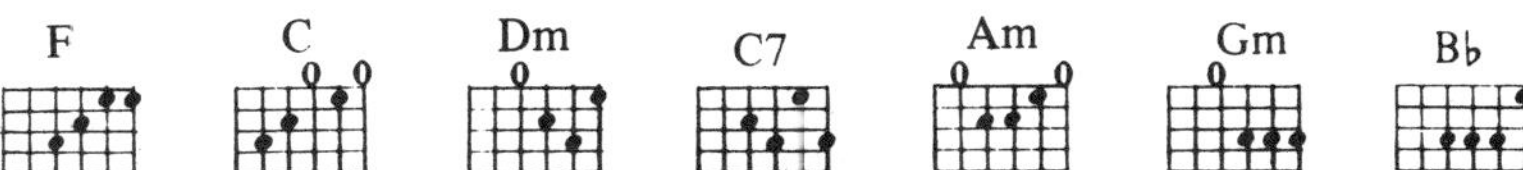

F C Dm C7 F Dm

Come all you wild and wick-ed youths where - e-ver you may be, I pray you give at -ten- tion _ And

Am C7 F Am C7 Am C7

lis - ten un to me. The fate of our poor trans - ports You shall un - der - stand, The

Dm Am Dm Gm C7 *Chorus:*

hard-ships they un - der - go U - pon Van Die - men's Land. _____ Young men

F B♭ Am C7 F

all now be - ware Lest you are drawn in - to a snare.

VISKA

"The rich man in his castle, the poor man at his gate, God made them, high or lowly, and order'd their estate." (From a hymn of the Victorian age.)

It is a fact of history that the working men of Britain and Ireland lived little better than slaves. They worked endless hours for landlord and church with very little return. If they begged to voice their opposition to this unfair system they were treated like criminals. It is no surprise that starving men and women would risk the horrors of transportation to steal what they felt rightfully belonged to all.

A transportation song as published in Roy Palmer's excellent book The Painful Plough *(Cambridge University Press, 1973). Text is from a broadside in the Modern Collection and the tune is based on "The Ploughman" as sung by Mr Henry Burstow and collected in 1904 by Ralph Vaughan Williams.*

You sons of old England, now listen to my rhymes,
And I'll sing you a short sketch of the times.
Concerning poor lab'rers we all must allow,
Who work all day at the tail of the plough.

CHORUS:
Oh, pity poor lab'rers, oh, pity them all,
For five or six shillings they work the whole week.

There's many poor lab'rers to work they will go
Either hedging or ditching, to plough or to sow,
And many poor fellows are used like a Turk:
They do not get paid fair for half a day's work.

And many poor lab'rers, I'm sorry to say,
Are breaking of stones for eighteen pence a day.
Bread and water's the fare of the poor lab'ring man,
While the rich they can live on the fat of the land.

Some pity the farmers, but I tell you now,
Pity poor lab'rers that follow the plough.
Oh pity poor children half-starving and then
Divide every great farm up into ten.

There's many young fellows you'll see every day
For snaring a hare they are banished away
To Van Diemen's Land or to some foreign shore
And their wives and their children are left to deplore.

There's many a farmer that's making a fuss,
While the poor and the starving can scarce get a crust.
Do away with their hounds and their hunters so gay,
And give the poor lab'rers a little fair play.

Fair play is a stranger these many years past
And pity's bunged up in an old oaken cask,
But the time's fast approaching, it's very near come,
When we'll have the farmers all under our thumb.

Em C D G
Em C Em D
You sons of old Eng - land, now list to my rhymes, And I'll
G Em C
sing you a short sketch of the times. Con - cern - ing poor lab - 'rers we
Em D G D
all must al - low, Who work all day at the tail of the
Em Chorus: C Em C Em
plough. Oh pi - ty poor lab - 'rers, oh pi - ty them all, For
G Em C D Em
five or six shil - lings they work the whole week.

Van Diemen's Land

Songs about poaching were extremely common, because poaching itself was so widespread. As the people were unable to procure fresh meat honestly, they took to stealing or poaching. Poaching became so prevalent that it was hardly an exaggeration to say that every other man you met was a poacher! It was generally thought that those men were justified in their actions; "They had by hook or by crook to obtain food somewhere, in order to enable their wives and children to live at all, to keep the breath in their bodies" (extracted from the autobiography of Joseph Arch, 1826-1919, edited by Roy Palmer, 1972). In 1828 the penalties for poaching became three months imprisonment for the first offence, six for a second, and seven years transportation for a third. But if three or four men, one of whom carried a gun or bludgeon, were found in a wood, all were liable for transportation for fourteen years to Van Diemen's Land.

This song had widespread circulation through Australia, Ireland and the British Isles. This version from the broadside printed by Catnach of London and held in the Birmingham Library. The tune has been assembled by Warren Fahey. Colin O'Lochlainn prints another version in the 1952 edition of his Irish Street Songs.

Come all you gallant poaching boys that ramble free of care,
That rove out on a moonlit night with gun and dog and snare.
The hare and lofty pheasant you have at your command,
Never thinking of your last career upon Van Diemen's Land.

Poor Tommy Brown from Nenagh Town, Jack Murphy and poor Joe,
We was three daring poachers as the gentry well do know.
One night we were trepanned by the keepers hid in the sand,
Who for fourteen years transported us into Van Diemen's Land.

The first day that we landed here upon the fatal shore,
The settlers came around us, some twenty score or more;
They ranked us up like horses and they sold us out of hand,
And they yoked us up to ploughing-frames to plough Van Diemen's Land.

The hovels that we're living in are built of mud and clay,
With rotten straw for bedding, and to that we daren't say nay.
They fence us in with raging fire, and we slumber as we can,
But it keeps away the wolves and tigers upon Van Diemen's Land.

There was a girl from Newport, Susan Somers was her name,
And she had been transported for playing of the game;
But she took the captain's fancy and he married her out of hand,
And she gives us all good treatment upon Van Diemen's Land.

It's often when in slumber I have had a pleasant dream;
With my sweetheart I've been sitting down beside a crystal stream;
Through Ireland I've gone roaming with my sweetheart by the hand;
Then I wake up broken-hearted upon Van Diemen's Land.

So all you lively poaching lads, this warning take from me:
I'd have you quit night walking and avoid bad company,
And throw aside your guns and snares, for let me tell you plain;
If you knew of our misfortunes you would never poach again.

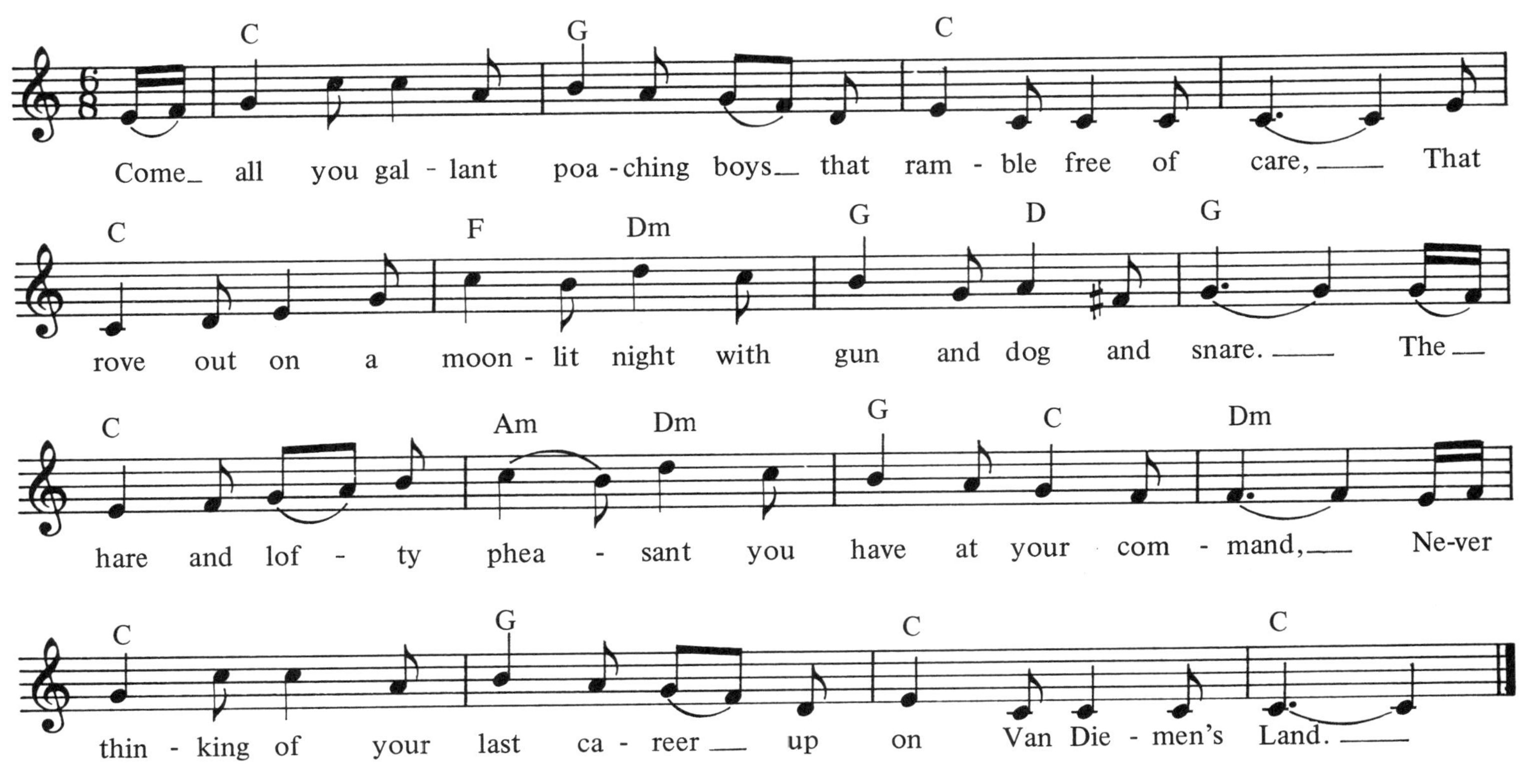

C G F Dm Am
Come all you gal - lant poa - ching boys that ram - ble free of care, That
rove out on a moon - lit night with gun and dog and snare. The
hare and lof - ty phea - sant you have at your com - mand, Ne-ver
thin - king of your last ca - reer up on Van Die - men's Land.

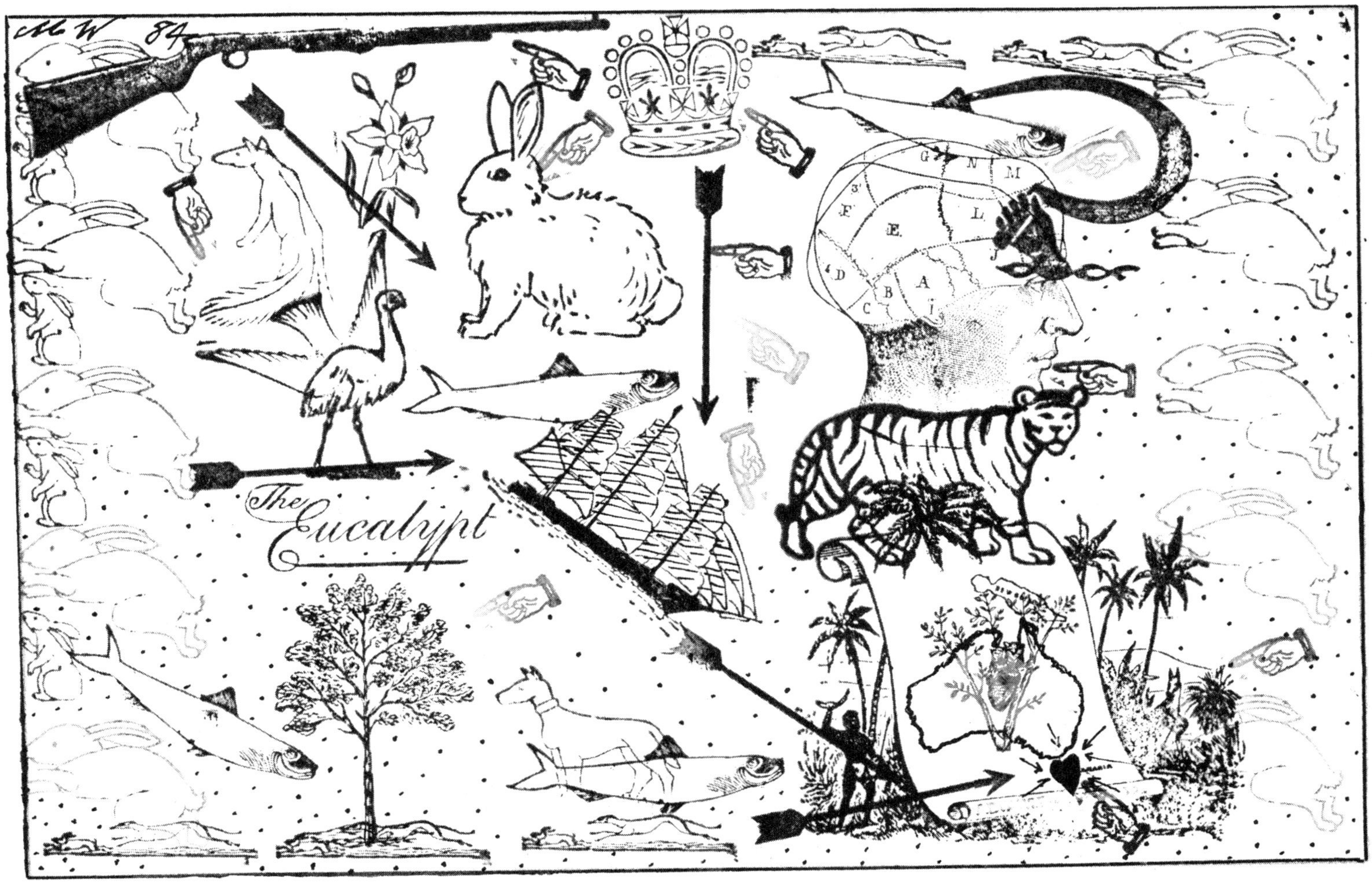
The Eucalypt

The Gaol Song

The treadmill, one of the cruellest yet most overlooked methods of convict punishment inflicted in recent centuries, consisted of a large revolving cylinder to which was attached a circular iron frame. This was fitted with steps rather like the paddle-wheels of the early steamships. The drum could be either filled with stones or connected to a flour mill or water pump. When the convict stepped, the drum revolved forcing the convict to continue his upward stride. It was cruel torture and punishment continued hour upon hour until the prisoner was reduced to a state of physical collapse. The first two Sydney treadmills were erected in 1823. The wry wit of the convicts nicknamed the treadmills "The Dancing Academies".

A popular broadside commenting on life on the treadmill in British gaols. A similar version appears in the Penguin Book of English Folk Songs.

"**S**tep in, young man, I know your face,
It's nothing in your favour.
A little time I'll give to you:
Six months unto hard labour."

CHORUS:
To me Hip! fol the day, Hip! fol the day,
To me Hip! fol the day, fol the digee, oh!

At six o'clock our turnkey comes in,
With a bunch of keys all in his hand.
"Come, come, my lads, step up and grind.
Tread the wheel till breakfast time."

To me Hip! etc.

At eight o'clock our skilly comes in,
Sometimes thick and sometimes thin,
But devil a word we must not say –
It's bread and water all next day.

To me Hip! etc.

At half past eight the bell doth ring.
Into the chapel we must swing,
"Down on our bended knees to fall.
"The Lord have mercy on us all."

To me Hip! etc.

At nine o'clock the jangle rings.
All on the trap, boys, we must spring.
"Come, come, my lads, step up in time,
The wheel to tread and the corn to grind."

To me Hip! etc.

Now Saturday's come, I'm sorry to say,
Sunday is our starvation day.
Our hobnail boots and tin mugs too,
They are not shined nor will not do.

To me Hip! etc.

Now six long months are over and past,
I will return to my bonny, bonny lass,
I'll leave the turnkeys all behind,
The wheel to tread and the corn to grind.

To me Hip! etc.

Dm Am Gm F C

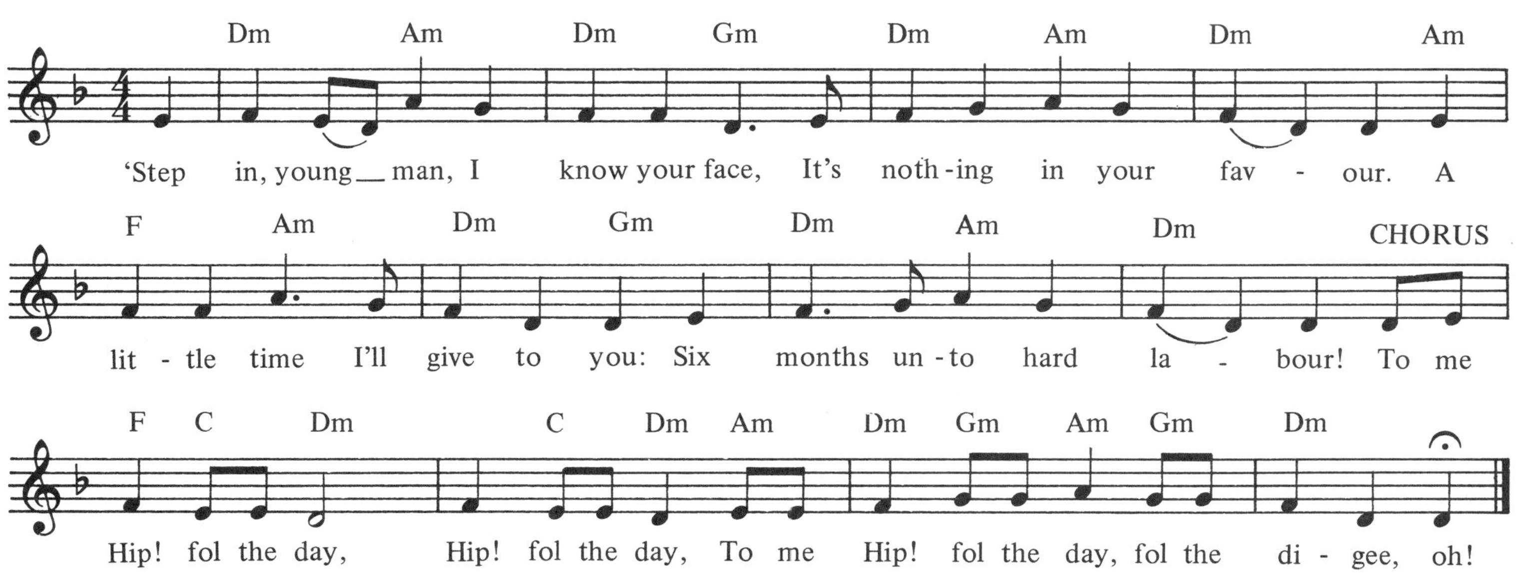

Dm Am Dm Gm Dm Am Dm Am
'Step in, young — man, I know your face, It's noth-ing in your fav - our. A
F Am Dm Gm Dm Am Dm
CHORUS
lit - tle time I'll give to you: Six months un-to hard la - bour! To me
F C Dm C Dm Am Dm Gm Am Gm Dm
Hip! fol the day, Hip! fol the day, To me Hip! fol the day, fol the di - gee, oh!

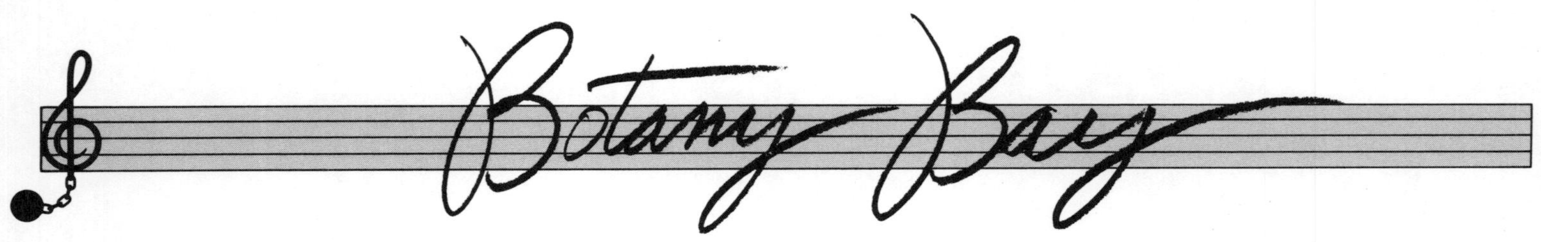

Desperate convicts, men and women carrying on the old fight against English authority, had little to "make merry" in song. Although a product of the Music Halls, rather than the prison hulks, this song does have some credentials as a popular folk song. It certainly tells the story of those who would cross the law-makers complete with a warning to others "... or you'll end up in Botany Bay!"

From the British musical comedy Little Jack Sheppard, *1885. The musical proved very popular and a year later it was staged in Melbourne.*

Farewell to old England for ever,
Farewell to my rum culls as well,
Farewell to the well-known Old Bailey,
Where I used for to cut such a swell.

CHORUS:
Singing, too-ral, li-ooral, li-addity,
Singing, too-ral, li-ooral, li-ay.
Singing, too-ral, li-ooral, li-addity,
Singing, too-ral, li-ooral, li-ay.

There's the captain as is our commander,
There's the bo'sun and all the ship's crew,
There's the first and the second-class passengers,
Knows what we poor convicts goes through.

'Tain't leaving old England we care about,
'Tain't cos we misspells wot we knows,
But because all we light-fingered gentry,
Hop round with a log on our toes.

For fourteen long years I have ser-vi-ed,
And for fourteen long years and a day,
For meeting a bloke in the area,
And sneaking his ticker away.

Oh had I the wings of a turtle-dove,
I'd soar on my pinions so high,
Slap bang to the arms of my Polly love,
And in her sweet presence I'd die.

Now, all my young dook-ies and duch-ess-es,
Take warning from what I've to say –
Mind all is your own as you touch-es-es,
Or you'll meet us in Botany Bay.

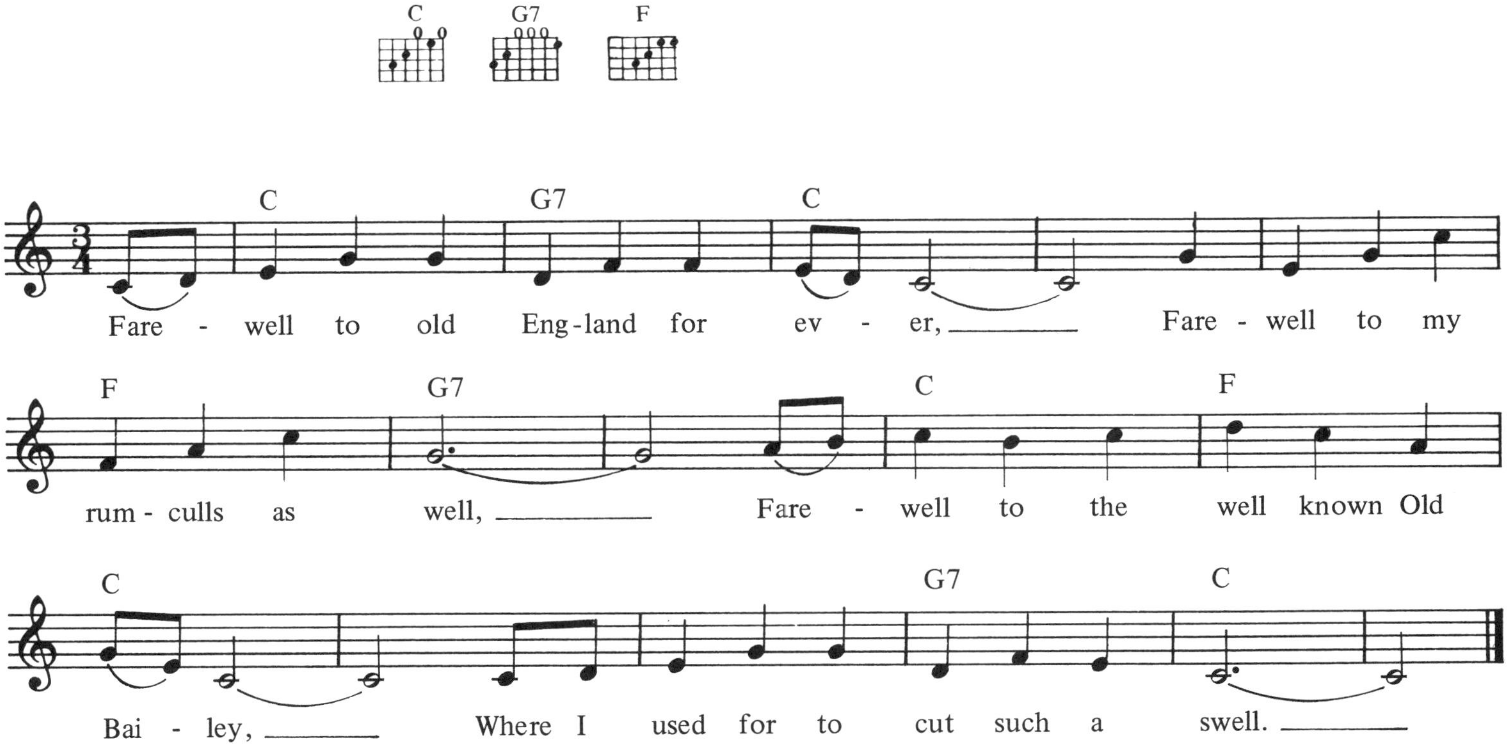

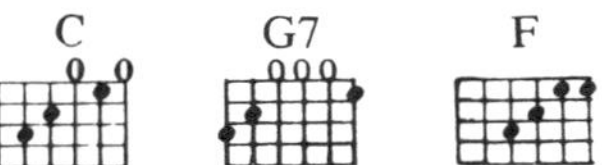

C G7 C

Fare - well to old Eng-land for ev - er, ——— Fare - well to my

F G7 C F

rum - culls as well, ——— Fare - well to the well known Old

C G7 C

Bai - ley, ——— Where I used for to cut such a swell. ———

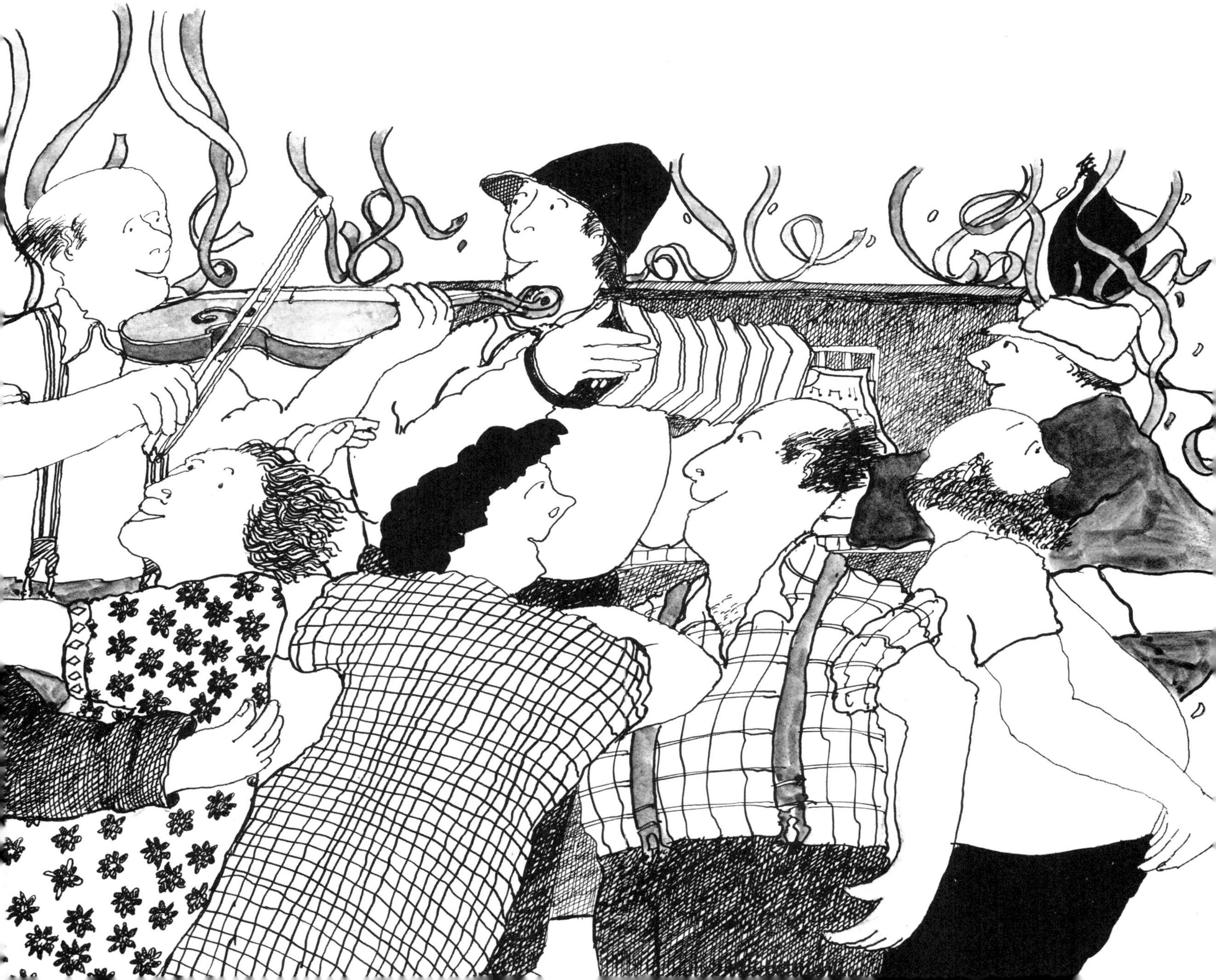

The Convict Maid

Women were treated no better than men. Nearly 25,000 were sentenced to New South Wales and Van Diemen's Land, mostly during the 1830's and 1840's. Records show that about half came from Ireland, most of the remainder from England, and a few from Scotland. In gaol they were treated harshly, often cruelly. The voyage to Australia was full of fear and when the Amphitrite *was wrecked on the French coast in 1833, all 106 female prisoners and a dozen children aboard were drowned. The* Neva *from Cork in 1835, was wrecked on reefs near Tasmania drowning nearly all the 150 female convicts and their fifty-five children on board. The stories back in England were true and the transports had sound reason to fear.*

From a widely distributed broadside from the Seven Dials print shop operated by Birt.

You lads and lasses all attend to me,
While I relate my tale of misery;
By hopeless love was I once betrayed,
And now I am, alas, a convict maid.

To please my lover did I try so sore,
That I spent upon him all my master's store,
Who in his wrath did so loud upbraid
And brought before the judge this convict maid.

The judge his sentence then to me addressed,
Which filled with agony my aching breast:
"To Botany Bay you must be conveyed,
For seven long years to be a convict maid."

For seven long years I toil in pain and grief,
And curse the day that I became a thief,
O, had I stuck by some honest trade,
I ne'er had been, alas, a convict maid.

to Botany Bay you must be conveyed.
curse the day

Jim Jones at Botany Bay

The sentenced convict had good reason to fear transportation to the penal colonies. Language can only give a pale imitation of the grisly reality of blood-soaked flesh being lashed away by a cat-o-nine-tails whip or some other hideous punishment. Despite the terrible pain, some men took pride in uttering no sound during the flagellation and would refer to their flogging as "getting a present of a new red shirt".

From "Old Pioneering Days in The Sunny South" *by Charles MacAlister. The tune appears as the Irish air "Irish Mollie, Oh!".*

O listen for a moment lads,
And hear me tell my tale –
How o'er the sea from England's shore
I was condemned to sail.
The jury says, "He's guilty, Sir,"
And says the Judge, says he –
"For life, Jim Jones, I'm sending you
Across the stormy sea."

"**A**nd take my tip before you ship
To join the iron gang,
Don't be too gay in Botany Bay
Or else you'll surely hang –
Or else you'll surely hang," says he.
"And after that Jim Jones,
It's high upon the gallows tree,
The crows they'll pick your bones."

"**Y**ou'll have no need for mischief there,
Remember what I say,
They'll flog the poaching hide off you
Out there at Botany Bay!"
The waves were high upon the sea,
The wind blew up in gales,
I would rather drown in misery
Than come to New South Wales.

The waves were high upon the sea
And the pirates came along,
But the soldiers on our convict ship
They were five hundred strong.
They opened fire and somehow drove
That pirate ship away,
I'd have rather joined the buccaneers,
Than come to Botany Bay.

For night and day the irons clang,
And like poor galley slaves,
We toil and toil, and when we die
Must fill dishonoured graves.
But by and by I'll break my chains
And to the bush I'll go,
And I'll join the bold bushrangers there –
Jack Donahoe and Co.

And late at night when everything
Is quiet in the town,
I'll kill the tyrants one and all,
I'll shoot the bastards down,
I'll give the law a little shock;
Remember what I say,
They'll yet regret they sent Jim Jones
In chains, to Botany Bay.

F Gm Dm

F Gm Dm
Oh lis - ten for a mo - ment lads and hear me tell my tale___ How
F Gm Dm
o'er the seas from Eng land's shore I was con-demned to sail___ The
F Gm Dm
ju - ry says 'He's guil - ty sir' and says the judge says he___ 'For
Gm Dm Gm Dm
life Jim Jones I'm send - ing you a - cross the storm - y sea.'___

It seems as if Ms May had been sentenced to Botany Bay once before. In the final verse of the song we find her once more bound for the penal settlement – or as the song so tactfully puts it: "They paid her passage back to Botany Bay."

The streets of convict Sydney were certainly known to the likes of Maggie May, however, the scene of this crime takes place around the London dock area. A not unusual tale – sailor meets streetgirl and she plies him with cheap liquor and eventually robs him of his money.

From the singing of Mr Jim Cargill, of Randwick, New South Wales. Collected in 1973 by Warren Fahey. This song seems to retain its widespread popularity and is common to almost every seafarer's repertoire.

Oh gather round, you sailor lads, and listen to my song,
And when you hear my tale you'll pity me;
I was a goddam fool, in the port of Liverpool,
The first time that I came home from sea.

I was paid off at the Hove from a trip to Sydney Cove,
Two pound ten a quarter was my pay;
I jingled of my tin . . . I was very soon taken in
By a little girl they all call Maggie May.

CHORUS:
Oh, Maggie Maggie May, they have taken you away
To slave upon that cold Van Diemen's shore,
For you robbed so many sailors and dosed so many whalers,
You'll never cruise down Lime Street any more.

'**T**was a damned unlucky day when I first met Maggie May
Cruising up and down old Canning Place;
She had a figure fine like a trimmer of the line,
And me being a sailor, I gave chase.

In the morning when I woke, stiff and sore and stony broke,
No shirt, trousers, waist-coat could I find.
The landlady said, "Sir, I can tell you where they are:
They'll be down in Stanley's hock-shop, number nine."

To the bobby on his beat at the corner of the street,
To him I went, to him I told my tale;
He asked, as if in doubt, "Does your mother know you're out?"
But agreed the lady ought to be in jail.

To the hock-shop I applied, but no trousers there I spied,
So the bobbies came and took that girl away;
The jury guilty found her of robbing a homeward-bounder,
And paid her passage back to Botany Bay.

C C7 F G7 D7

C C7 F C
Ho gath - er round you sail - or boys and lis - ten to my song And when you hear my

G7 C C7
tale you'll pi - ty me I was a god - dam fool in the

F G7 C
port of Liv - er - pool the first time that I came home from sea

(& CHORUS) C7 F C
I was paid off at the Hove from a trip to Syd - ney Cove Two pound ten a

D7 (G7) C C7
quar - ter was my pay I jin - gled of my tin, I was

F G7 C
ve - ry soon taken in By a lit - tle girl they all call Mag - gie May.

Ten Thousand Miles Away

This song, although lighthearted compared to the majority of transportation songs, points to the terrible fear of separation from family and loved ones. To some convicts transportation to the new penal settlements was better than imprisonment in the hell-holes of the British convict hulks or community prisons. Here, at least, they had fresh air, sunshine and exercise.

Sung by Jack Pobar, Toowoomba, Queensland, and collected by Warren Fahey, in 1973. Russell Ward first located a version in Songs of American Sailormen *edited by J. Colcard, and another version appears in* The Scottish Student's Song Book *published in Glasgow, 1891. As Mr Pobar's version was incomplete this version has been adapted by the collector.*

Sing ho, for a brave and gallant ship
And a fair and favouring breeze,
With a bully crew and a captain, too,
To carry me over the seas.
To carry me over the seas, my boys,
To my true love far away;
I'm taking a trip on a government ship
Ten thousand miles away.

CHORUS:
Then blow ye winds, heigh ho!
A-roving I will go,
I'll stay no more on England's shore
To hear the music play.
I'm off on the morning train
To cross the raging main;
I'm taking a trip on a government ship
Ten thousand miles away.

My true love she was beautiful,
My true love she was young,
Her eyes were like the diamonds bright,
And silvery was her tongue,
So silvery was her tongue, my boys,
Though she's now far away –
She's taken a trip on a government ship
Ten thousand miles away.

Oh, dark and dismal was the day
When last I seen my Meg;
She'd a government band around each hand,
And another one round her leg.
And another one round her leg, my boys,
As the big ship left the bay;
"Adieu," said she, "remember me,
Ten thousand miles away!"

I wish I were a bo'sun bold,
Or even a bombardier,
I'd build a boat and away I'd float,
And straight for my true love steer.
And straight for my true love steer, my boys,
Where the dancing dolphins play,
And the whales and the sharks are having
their larks
Ten thousand miles away!

The sun may shine through a London fog,
Or the river run quite clear;
The ocean's brine be turned to wine,
Or I forget my beer.
Or I forget my beer, my boys,
Or the landlord's quart a day,
Before I forget my own sweetheart
Ten thousand miles away.

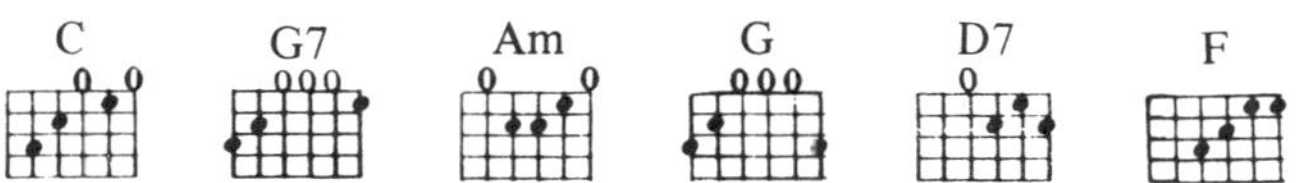

C G7 C
Sing ho, for a brave and gal - lant ship And a fair and fav'- ring breeze, With a
C Am G D7 G C
bul - ly crew and a cap-tain too To car-ry me ov - er seas, To car-ry me ov- er seas, my boys, To my
F G7 C F C G7 C
true love far a - way; — I'm ta-king a trip on a gov'ment ship, Ten thou-sand miles a - way.

Chorus:
C F C
Then blow ye winds heigh ho! A - rov -ing I will go, I'll stay no more on En-gland's shore To
F G7 C F
hear the mu- sic play, I'm off on the mor-ning train To cross the rag - ing main. I'm
C G7 C
ta - king a trip on a gov'ment ship, Ten thou- sand miles a - way.

Here's Adieu to All Judges and Juries

This song seems to be the original "Botany Bay" transportation ballad complete with the flying eagle and sweet Polly's arms. It is probably from a stage melodrama with the first verse sung from the women's view and the remainder from the convicted transport. It is interesting to note how these songs were used to "warn" others of the dangers of leading a criminal life. Today we have television, radio and newspapers!

From a British broadside c. 1815. Widely circulated.

Here's adieu to all judges and juries,
Justice and Old Bailey too;
Seven years you've transported my true love,
Seven years he's transported you know.

How hard is the place of confinement,
That keeps me from my heart's delight,
Cold irons and chains all bound round me,
And a plank for my pillow at night.

If I'd got the wings of an eagle,
I would lend you my wings for to fly,
I'd fly to the arms of my Polly love,
And in her soft bosom I'll lie.

And if ever I return from the ocean,
Stores of riches I'll bring to my dear,
And it's all for the sake of my Polly love,
I'll cross the salt seas without fear.

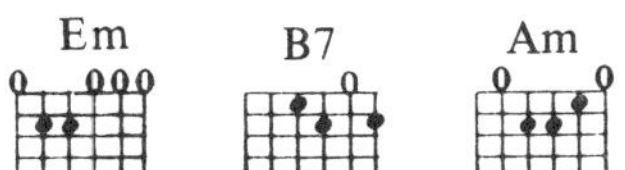

Em
B7
Am

Em B7 Em
Here's a - dieu to all jud - ges and ju - ries,
Am Em
Jus - tice and Old Bai - ley too; Sev - en
Am Em
years you've trans - por - ted my true love, Sev - en
Am B7 Em
years he's trans - por - ted I know.

The Exile of Erin

This song is also known as the "Plains of Emu" and refers to the agricultural convict settlement of Emu Plains which was situated some thirty-five miles west of Sydney. As the convict and military population increased there was a continual demand for foodstuffs, and the Emu Plains settlement was part of the network of agricultural prison farms servicing the colony.

Better known as "The Plains of Emu". From the Sydney Gazette, *1829.*

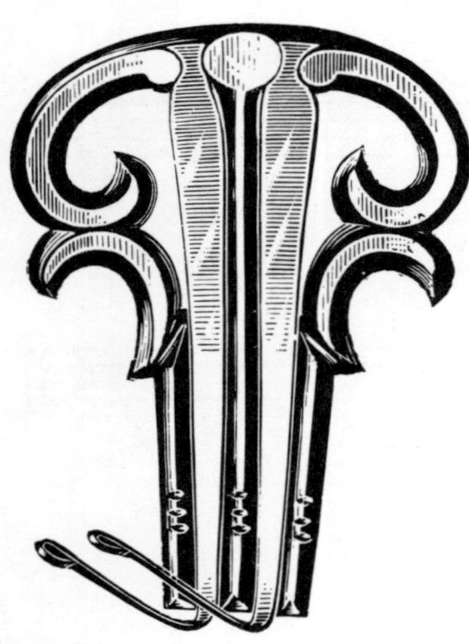

O, farewell my country, my kindred, my lover,
Each morning and evening is sacred to you,
While I toil the long day without shelter or cover,
And fell the tall gums, the black-butted and blue.
Full often I think of and talk of thee Erin,
Thy heath-covered mountains are fresh in my view,
Thy glens, lakes and rivers, Loch-Con and Kilkerran,
While chained to the soil on the Plains of Emu.

The ironbark, wattle, and gum-trees extending
Their shades under which rests the shy kangaroo,
May be felled by the blessed who have hope o'er them bending,
To cheer their rude toil, though far exiled from you.
But alas, without hope, peace, or honour to grace me,
Each feeling was crushed in the bud as it grew
Whilst "never" is stamped on the chains that embrace me,
And endless my thrall on the Plains of Emu.

Hard, hard was my fate, far from thee to be driven,
Unstained, unconvicted, as sure was my due,
I loved to dispense of the freedom of Heaven,
But force gained the day, and I suffer for you.
For this land never broke what by promise was plighted,
Deep treason, this tongue to my country ne'er knew,
No base-earned coin in my coffer e'er lighted,
Yet enchained I remain on the Plains of Emu.

Dear mother, thy love from my bosom shall never
Depart, but shall flourish untainted and true,
Nor grieve that the base in their malice should ever
Upbraid thee, and none to give malice her due.
Spare, spare her the tear, and no charge lay upon her,
And weep not, my Norah, her griefs to renew,
But cherish her age till night closes on her,
And think of the swain who still thinks but of you.

But your names shall still live, though like writing in water,
When confined to the notes of the tame cockatoo,
Each wattle-scrub echo repeats to the other
Your names, and each breeze hears me sighing anew.
For dumb be my tongue, may my heart cease her motion,
If the Isle I forget where my first breath I drew;
Each affection is warmed with sincerest devotion,
For the tie is unbroken on the Plains of Emu.

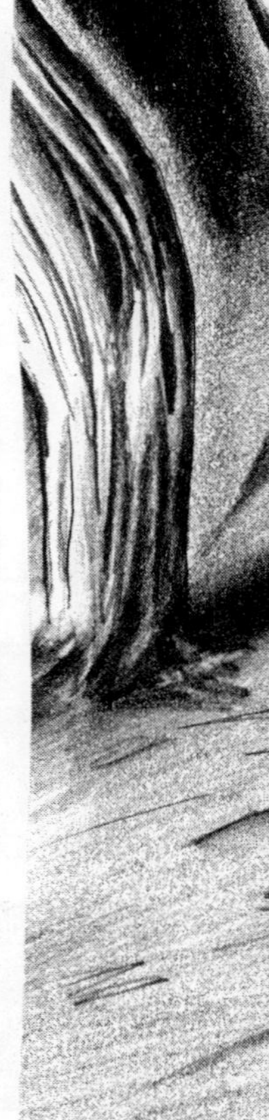

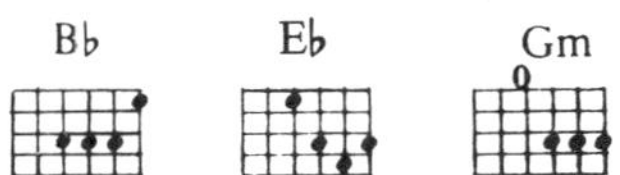

B♭ E♭ B♭

O, fare-well my coun-try, my kind - red,my lov - er, Each morn-ing and eve - ning is

E♭ B♭ Gm

sa - cred to you, while I toil the long day_ with-out shel - ter or co - ver, and

B♭ E♭ B♭

fell_ the tall gums, the black but-ted and blue. Full of - ten I think of and

E♭ B♭ E♭ B♭

talk of thee Er - in, Thy heath cov-ered moun-tains are fresh_ in my view, Thy

Gm B♭ E♭ B♭

glens, lakes and ri - vers, Loch-Con_and Kil-ker-ran, While chained_to the soil_ on the Plains_of Er- in.

Moreton Bay

By all accounts the penal settlement of Moreton Bay, Queensland, was recognised as one of the most fearful. Under the harsh command of Captain Patrick Logan the death rate ran higher than one man in ten each year: no questions asked. This powerful song celebrates the death of Logan in 1830 by an Aborigine's spear. It was considered a fitting death for the monster of Moreton Bay who had tried to create a hell on earth.

Printed in Will Lawson's Australian Bush Songs and Ballads *published Sydney, 1944.*

One Sunday morning, as I went walking,
By Brisbane waters I chanced to stray;
I heard a convict his fate bewailing,
As on the sunny river bank I lay:
"I am a native of Erin's island,
But banished now from my native shore,
They stole me from my aged parents,
And from the maiden whom I do adore.

"**I**'ve been a prisoner at Port Macquarie,
At Norfolk Island and Emu Plains,
At Castle Hill and at cursed Toongabbie,
At all these settlements I've been in chains;
But of all places of condemnation
And penal stations in New South Wales,
To Moreton Bay I have found no equal,
Excessive tyranny each day prevails.

"**F**or three long years I was beastly treated,
And heavy irons on my legs I wore,
My back with flogging was lacerated,
And oft-times painted with my crimson gore.
And many a man from down-right starvation
Lies mouldering now underneath the clay;
And Captain Logan he had us mangled
All on the triangles of Moreton Bay.

"**L**ike the Egyptians and ancient Hebrews,
We were oppressed under Logan's yoke,
Till a native black lying there in ambush
Did deal this tyrant his mortal stroke.
My fellow-prisoners be exhilarated
That all such monsters like death may find,
And when from bondage we are liberated
Our former sufferings will fade from mind."

C F Am Dm G G7

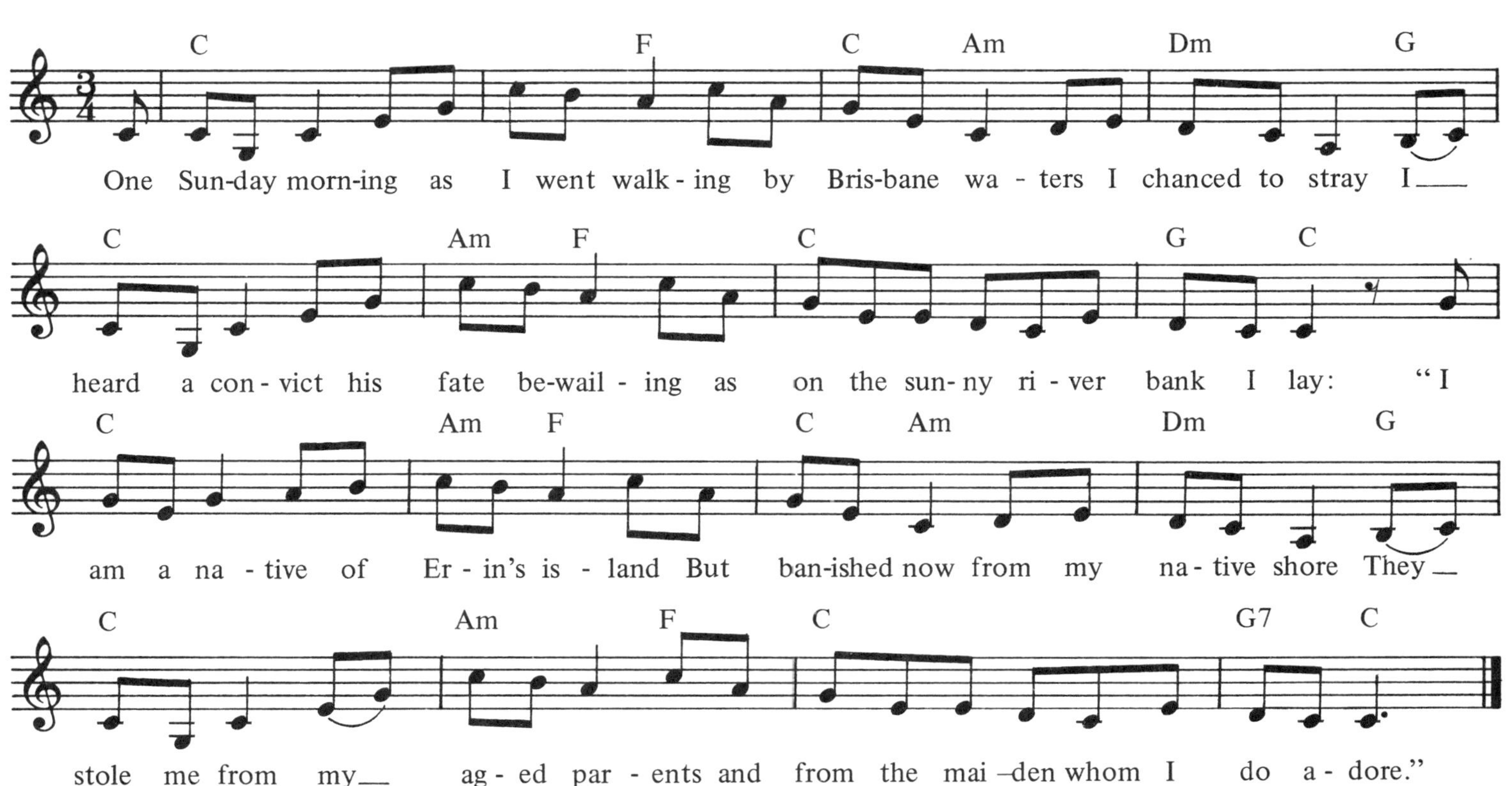
C F C Am Dm G
One Sun-day morn-ing as I went walk-ing by Bris-bane wa-ters I chanced to stray I
C Am F C G C
heard a con-vict his fate be-wail-ing as on the sun-ny ri-ver bank I lay: "I
C Am F C Am Dm G
am a na-tive of Er-in's is-land But ban-ished now from my na-tive shore They
C Am F C G7 C
stole me from my ag-ed par-ents and from the mai-den whom I do a-dore."

The Girls of the Shamrock Shores

One of the terrors of transportation was certainly the fear of being totally separated from family and loved ones. This song is similar to many heart-rending songs from Ireland – a tradition that continued well into the days of emigration when Irishmen were forced by famine to leave Ireland for America and Australia. It was said that Ireland's greatest export product was Irishmen.

From Sister Mary O'Loughlin, Convent of Mercy, South Australia. Collected in 1974 by Warren Fahey.

It was early in the spring when the small birds sing
And the lambs they sport and play
I entered as a passenger
To New South Wales sailed o'er,
And I'll bid farewell to all that dwell
And the girls of the Shamrock shore.

The ship that we set sail upon
The *Speedwell* was her name,
For full five months and longer
We sailed the foaming main;
Neither land nor harbour could we see,
Or the girls of the Shamrock shore.

On the fourteenth of September
We then did reach the land.
We went on shore at Sydney Cove
All chained hand to hand.
My sentence is for fourteen years —
Farewell to the Shamrock shore.

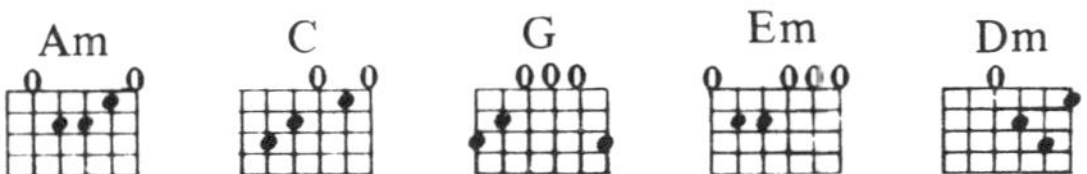
Am C G Em Dm

Am C G Am Em Am Dm
It being in the spring when the small birds sing And the lambs_ they_
Am Em Am C G Am Em
sport and_ play_ I_ en - tered as a_ pass - en -
Am G Am Em Am
- ger To New South Wales_ sailed_ o'er._ And I'll bid fare -
C G Am Em Am Dm Am Em Am
- well to_ all that dwell And the girls_ of the sham - rock_ shore.

The sailor of yesteryear led a pretty hard life with long voyages, bad rations, tedious work and long periods of "off duty". Singing provided escapism for both the working and relaxing sailor. "According to the Act" or "Limejuice and Vinegar", as it was often called, was a well known fo'c's'le or forebitter song that referred to the rations of limejuice and vinegar used to ward off scurvy. It was from this practice that English sailors earned the nickname of "Limeys".

Collected from Jim Cargill, of Randwick, New South Wales, in 1973, by Warren Fahey. This song is also known as "Limejuice and Vinegar" and appears in an excellent recorded version on the Wattle Recording "Traditional Singers of Victoria" collected by Norm O'Connor and Mary Jean Officer.

Now if you want to join an English ship, you must roam about at large,
If you want to join an English ship, you must have a good discharge
Signed by the board of trade and with everything intact,
Or else there's no advance aboard, for it's contrary to the Act.

CHORUS:
So, shout boys, hurrah, I'll tell you it's a fact,
There's nothing done aboard the ship contrary to the Act.
So lay aft, boys, lay aft, and see you get your whack,
Limejuice and vinegar, according to the Act.

Now when you've signed your articles, of course you've heard 'em read,
They'll tell you of the beef and pork, the butter and the bread,
The sugar and the marmalade and, with quantity exact,
Limejuice and vinegar, according to the Act.

Now when you join the ship, my boys, your heads are always sore,
And you expect a watch on watch, just as you have before,
But the mate he cries, "Lay aft, and do as I say exact,
For watch on watch the first day out's contrary to the Act."

Now slack away your weather main-braces and haul upon the lee,
Swell up your jib-halliards and let your sheets go free.
And bring along the watch tackle to board the stout main tack,
For I want to see the main-sail set according to the Act.

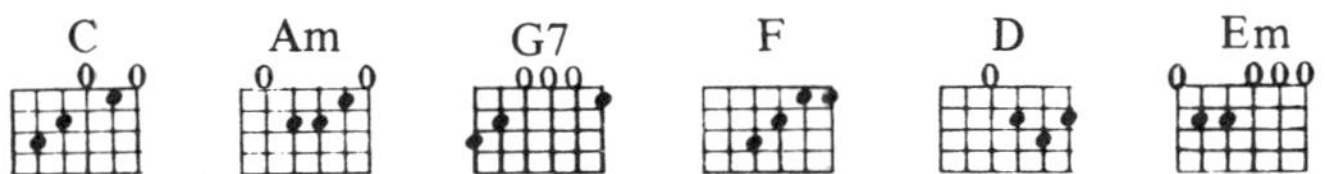

C Am G7 C
Now if you want to join an En - glish ship, you must roam a- bout at large, — If you

F C D G
want to join an En - glish ship, you must have a good dis - charge, — Signed

Am Em G7
by the board of trade and with eve - ry - thing in - tact, — Or

C G7 C
else there's no ad - vance a - board it's con - tra - ry to the act. — So

Am G C
shout boys hur - rah — I'll tell you it's a fact, — there's

F C D G
noht - ing done a - board a ship con - tra - ry to the Act. So lay

F Em G
aft boys lay aft, — and see you get your whack,

C Am G7 C
Lime - juice and vin - e - gar ac - cord - ing to the Act.

This is one of Australia's erotic folk songs chock full of good old-fashioned imagery. "The bush of Australia" is not to be found on the map! When the singer of this song was performing for the collector he carefully closed all the windows "just in case the landlady heard any of the verses".

Collected from Jim Cargill, of Randwick, New South Wales, in 1973, by Warren Fahey. Compare the known British version of Sam Larner where opening refers "One day as I walked near those Oxeborough Banks".

One day as I strolled by the Hawkesbury banks,
Where the maids of Australia, they play their wild pranks,
Near a palm-shaded tree I laid myself down,
To admire the young damsels who gather around
The banks of that stream in Australia,
Round the banks of that stream in Australia,
Where the maids are all handsome and gay.

Soon a charming young damsel before me appeared,
She came for to bathe in the streams close by here,
With kissing and caressing she then said to me:
"Can't you see it's the dress kind nature gave me,
On the morn I was born in Australia,
On the morn I was born in Australia,
Where the maids are all handsome and gay."

Soon exhausted by swimming she swam to the brink,
"Come and save me kind sir, I'm afraid that I'll sink",
Like lightning I sprang and got hold of her hand,
I tried for to rise but fell back on the sand,
And I entered the bush of Australia,
And I entered the bush of Australia,
Where the maids are all handsome and gay.

Soon the eighth month was over and the ninth month had come,
And the charming young damsel brought forth a fine son.
She looked for his dad but nowhere could be found —
It's then she remembered that fall on the ground,
On the banks of that stream in Australia,
On the banks of that stream in Australia,
Where the maids are all handsome and gay.

A E7 F♯m

One day as I strolled by the Hawkes-bu - ry banks, Where the

A D E7 A

maids of Aus - tra - lia they play their wild pranks, Near a

A F♯m E7 A C♯m

palm shad - ded tree I ___ laid my - self down to ad - mire the young

F♯m E7 A

dam - sels who gath - er a - round, ___ The banks of that stream in Aus -

D A D A

- tral - ia round the banks of that stream in Aus - tra - li -

F♯m E7 A

- a, Where the maids are all hand - some and gay. ___

Leave Her, Jollies, Leave Her

A good seafarer's song full of gripes and salted humour. This is the type of song that the sailors would sing when they were homeward bound after a long voyage at sea.

From the singing of Captain Watson of Melbourne. Collected by Norm O'Connor, R. Bailey and Maryjean Officer in 1960.

Captain H. R. Watson

Oh! I thought I heard our old man say,
Leave her jollies, leave her,
Oh! I thought I heard our old man say,
Oh, it's time for us to leave her.

Oh! the times were hard and the wages low,
Leave her jollies, leave her,
Oh! the times were hard and the wages low,
Oh, it's time for us to leave her.

Oh! the seas were high and the gales did blow,
Leave her jollies, leave her,
Oh! the seas were high and the gales did blow,
Oh, it's time for us to leave her.

Oh! she would not stay nor would she wear,
Leave her jollies, leave her,
She shifted green and made us swear,
So it's time for us to leave her.

So tomorrow we will draw our pay,
Leave her jollies, leave her,
Tomorrow we will draw our pay,
For it's time for us to leave her.

Oh! the rats have gone and the grub has too,
Leave her jollies, leave her,
So we'll pack our bags and we'll go too,
For it's time for us to leave her.

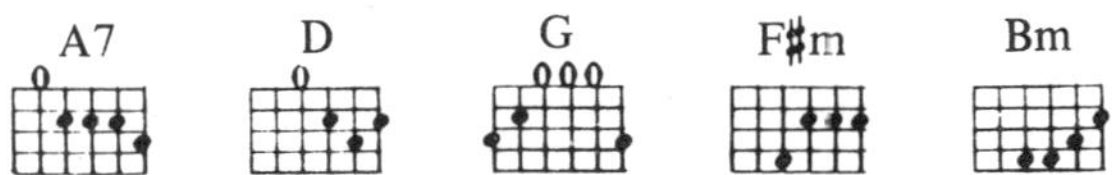
A7
D
G
F♯m
Bm

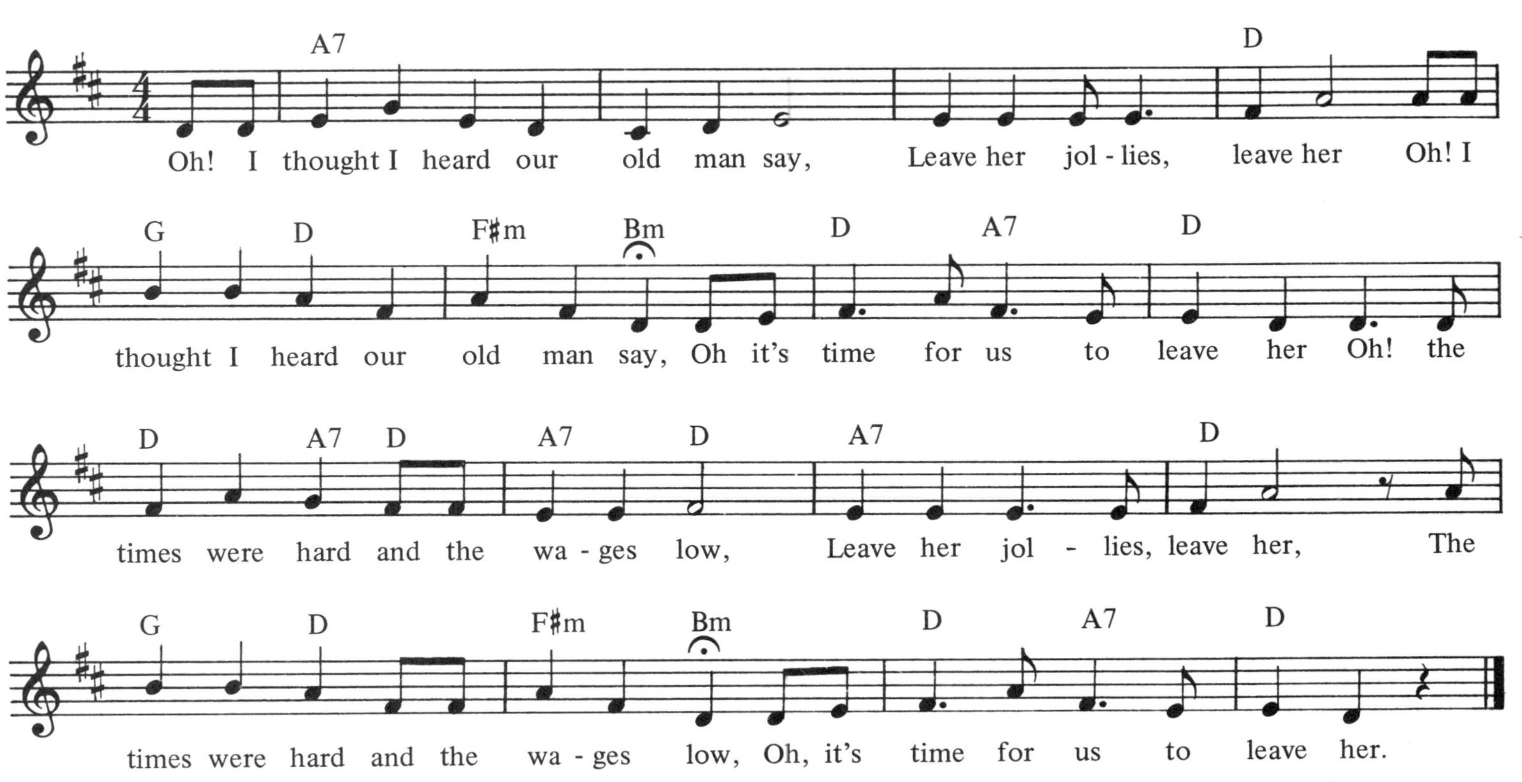
Oh! I thought I heard our old man say, Leave her jol-lies, leave her Oh! I
thought I heard our old man say, Oh it's time for us to leave her Oh! the
times were hard and the wa-ges low, Leave her jol - lies, leave her, The
times were hard and the wa-ges low, Oh, it's time for us to leave her.

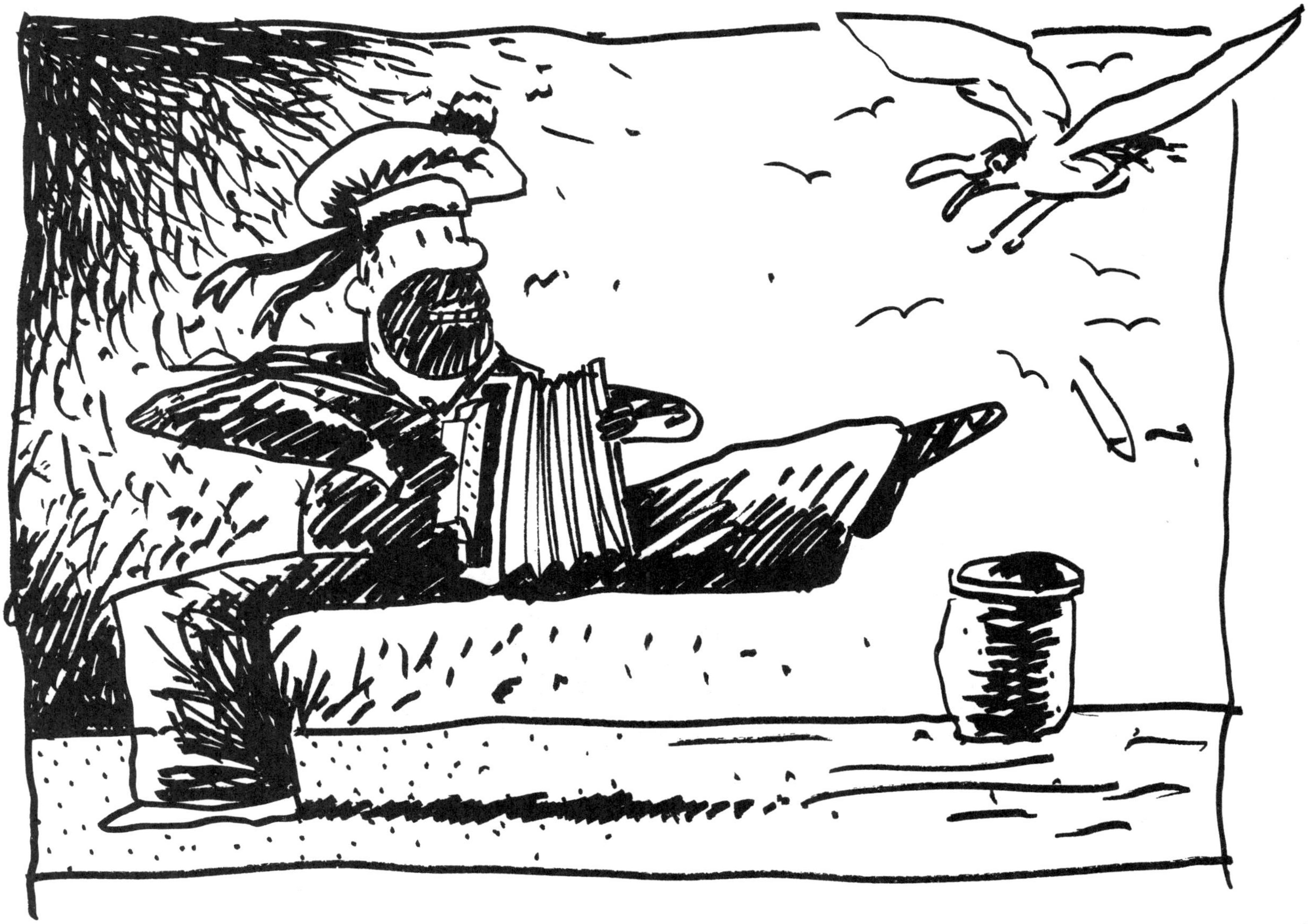

The Black Velvet Band

Will Lawson, writing in the Bulletin *magazine makes comment that the early Tasmanian whaling crews had a song known as "The Hat with The Velvet Band". Apparently, they used the song as a rhythmic work-song, but Lawson adds that they also used the song for drinking and fighting. Times were tough!*

Collected from Mr Arthur Stacey of Bathurst, New South Wales, by Warren Fahey, in 1975. This song had widespread circulation with the colour of the ribbon appearing as blue, black or brown.

'**T**was in the city of London,
In apprenticeship I was bound,
And many's the gay old hour,
I've spent in that dear old town.
One day as I was walking,
Along my usual beat,
A pretty little young maiden
Came tripping along the street.

CHORUS:
Oh, her eyes, they shone like diamonds,
I thought her the pride of the land;
The hair that hung down on her shoulder
Was tied with a black velvet band.

One day as we were walking,
A gentlemen passed us by;
I could see she was up to some mischief
By the rolling of her dark blue eye.
Gold watch she picked from his pocket
And slyly placed into my hand.
I was taken in charge by a copper —
Bad luck to that black velvet band!

Before the Lord Mayor I was taken:
"Your case, sir, I plainly can see,
And if I'm not greatly mistaken,
You're bound far over the sea."
Then it's over the dark and blue ocean,
Far away to Van Diemen's Land,
Far away from my friends and relations,
And the girl with the black velvet band.

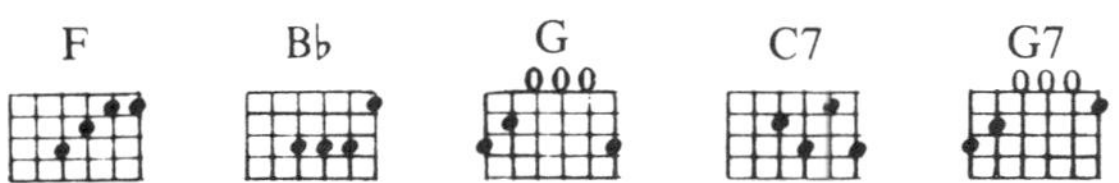
F
B♭
G
C7
G7

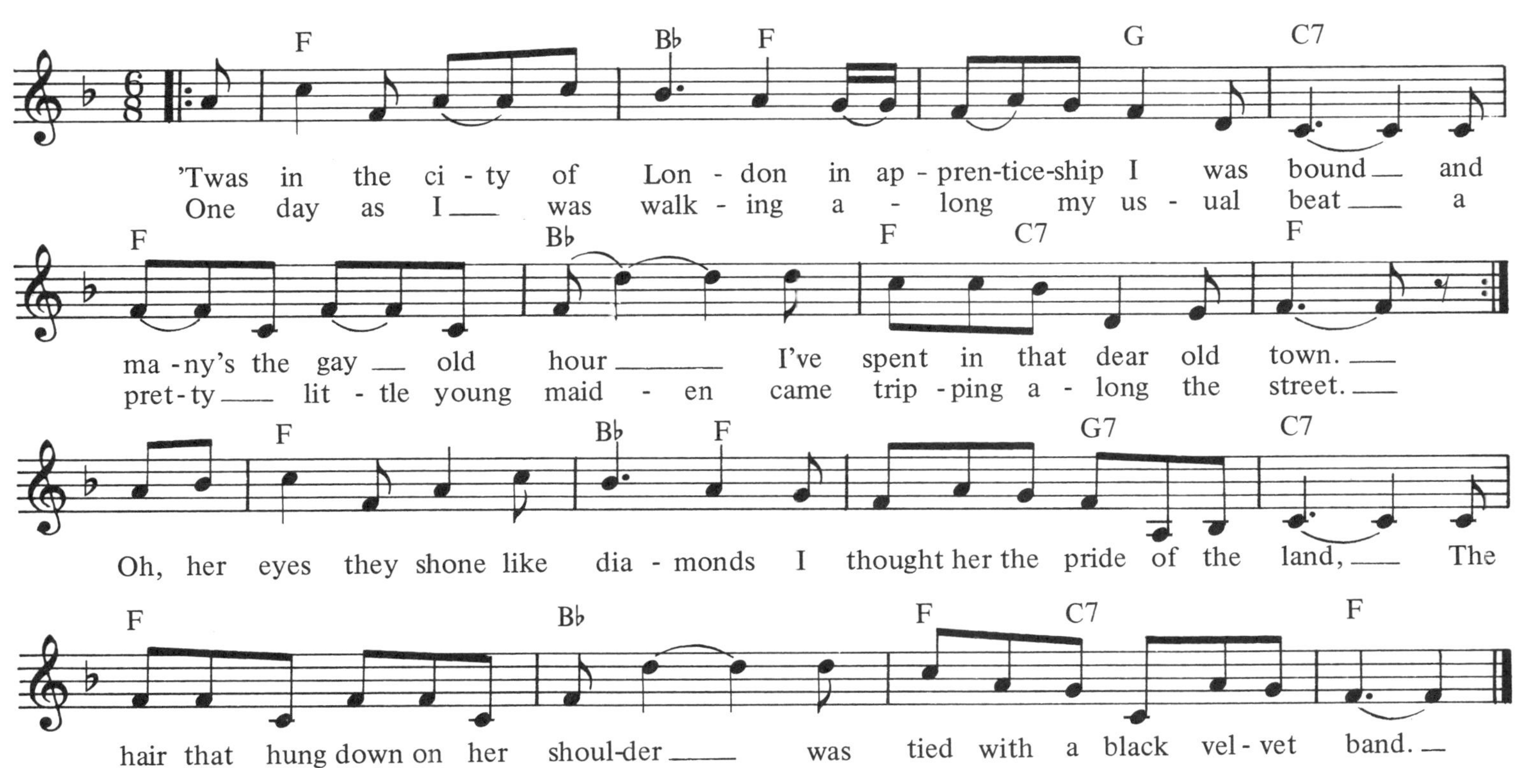
F B♭ F G C7
'Twas in the ci - ty of Lon - don in ap - pren-tice-ship I was bound and
One day as I was walk - ing a - long my us - ual beat a
F B♭ F C7 F
ma - ny's the gay old hour I've spent in that dear old town.
pret - ty lit - tle young maid - en came trip - ping a - long the street.
F B♭ F G7 C7
Oh, her eyes they shone like dia - monds I thought her the pride of the land, The
F B♭ F C7 F
hair that hung down on her shoul-der was tied with a black vel - vet band.

John Kanaka

This halyard song was well established with those sailors working the trade routes of the South Pacific. Such songs were by no means restricted to this area as sailors, being itinerants, moved from ship to ship taking their songs, stories and lore with them. Stan Hugill, a noted expert on seafaring songs, says this shanty was always rendered with a wild yelp where the "ooh" appears in the third solo.

From Sea Shanties, *Stan Hugill (Barrie & Jenkins, 1977). This version seems to have Samoan connections and was recorded by Hugill from a seaman in Barbados, in the West Indies.*

I heard, I heard the Old Man say,
John Kanaka-naka, tulai-e!
Today, today is a holiday,
John Kanaka-naka, tulai-e!
Tulai-e, ooh! tulai-e!
John Kanaka-naka, tulai-e!

We'll work termorrer, but no work terday,
John Kanaka-naka, tulai-e!
We'll work termorrer, but no work terday,
John Kanaka-naka, tulai-e!
Tulai-e, ooh! tulai-e!
John Kanaka-naka, tulai-e!

We're bound away for Frisco Bay,
John Kanaka-naka, tulai-e!
We're bound away at the break o' day,
John Kanaka-naka, tulai-e!
Tulai-e, ooh! tulai-e!
John Kanaka-naka, tulai-e!

We're bound away around Cape Horn,
John Kanaka-naka, tulai-e!
We wish ter Christ we'd niver bin born,
John Kanaka-naka, tulai-e!
Tulai-e, ooh! tulai-e!
John Kanaka-naka, tulai-e!

A Yankee ship wid a Yankee crew,
John Kanaka-naka, tulai-e!
Oh, we're the buckos fer ter push 'er through,
John Kanaka-naka, tulai-e!
Tulai-e, ooh! tulai-e!
John Kanaka-naka, tulai-e!

A Yankee ship wid a Yankee mate,
John Kanaka-naka, tulai-e!
If yer stop ter walk he'll change yer gait,
John Kanaka-naka, tulai-e!
Tulai-e, ooh! tulai-e!
John Kanaka-naka, tulai-e!

Oh, haul away, oh, haul away!
John Kanaka-naka, tulai-e!
Oh, haul away, an' make yer pay!
John Kanaka-naka, tulai-e!
Tulai-e, ooh! tulai-e!
John Kanaka-naka, tulai-e!

CH.
I heard, I heard the Old man say, John Ka -
- na - ka - na - ka tulai - e! To - day, to - day is a hol - a -
CH.
day. John Ka - na - ka - na - ka tu - lai - e! Tu - lai
e - oh! tu - lai - e! John Ka - na - ka - na - ka tu - lai - e!

Radcliffe Highway

This is one of the classic forebitter songs and tells of the inevitable wayward sailor who meets the inevitable girl-of-the-streets. The details of the meeting and the results are told in wry nautical sexual imagery. "Radcliffe Highway" was "much sung around the traps" in London's docking area. Maybe the girl was related to the infamous "Maggie May".

Collected from Jim Cargill of Randwick, New South Wales, by Warren Fahey, in 1973. Learnt during his days of whaling out of Scotland.

Oh as I went a-walking down Radcliffe Highway,
To me, whay-hay, blow the man down,
As I was a-walking down Radcliffe Highway,
Oh give me some time to blow the man down.

A charming flash clipper come sailing my way,
To me, whay-hay, blow the man down,
A charming flash clipper come sailing my way,
Oh give me some time to blow the man down.

I hailed her in English, she answered, "Yar Volt."
To me, whay-hay, blow the man down,
I hailed her in English, she answered, "Yar Volt."
Oh give me some time to blow the man down.

I hove her my tow line and got her in tow,
To me, whay-hay, blow the man down,
I hove her my tow line and got her in tow,
Oh give me some time to blow the man down.

Yard arm to yard arm down the street we did go,
To me, whay-hay, blow the man down,
Yard arm to yard arm down the street we did go,
Oh give me some time to blow the man down.

When the yard she goes up, the block they'll come down,
To me, whay-hay, blow the man down,
When the yard she goes up, the block they'll come down,
Oh give me some time to blow the man down.

Oh, up a-loft this old yard she must go,
To me, whay-hay, blow the man down,
Oh, up a-loft this old yard she must go,
Oh give me some time to blow the man down.

Oh, another pull and we'll belay,
To me, whay-hay, blow the man down,
Oh, another pull and we'll belay,
Oh give me some time to blow the man down.
Belay there!

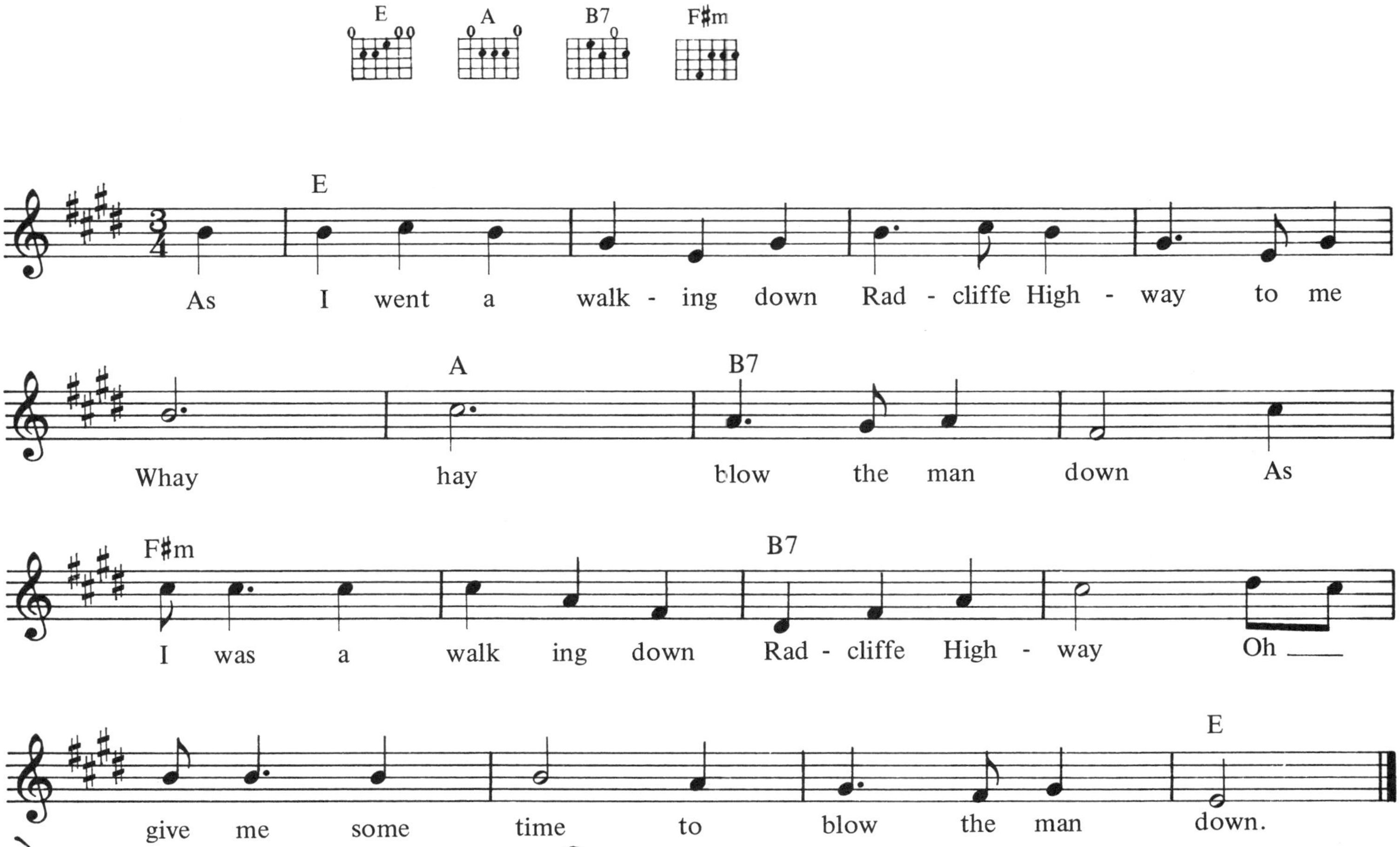

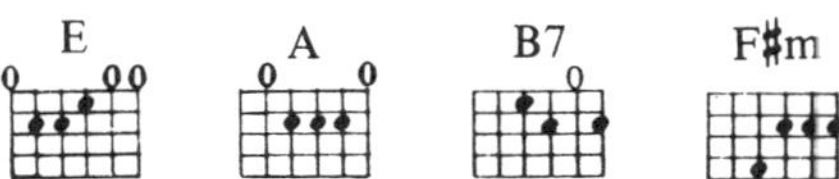

E

As I went a walk - ing down Rad - cliffe High - way to me

A B7

Whay hay blow the man down As

F♯m B7

I was a walk ing down Rad - cliffe High - way Oh ___

E

give me some time to blow the man down.

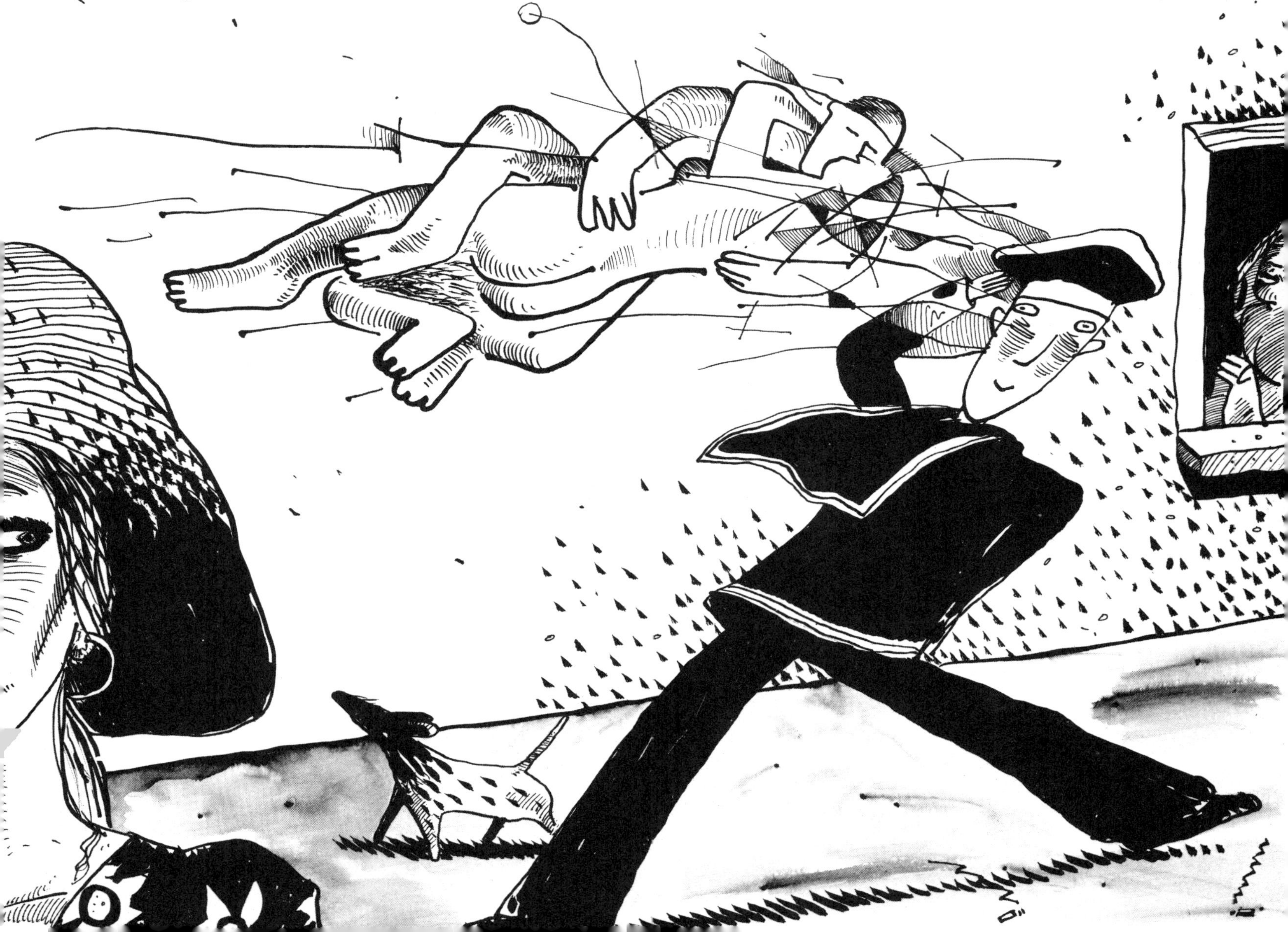

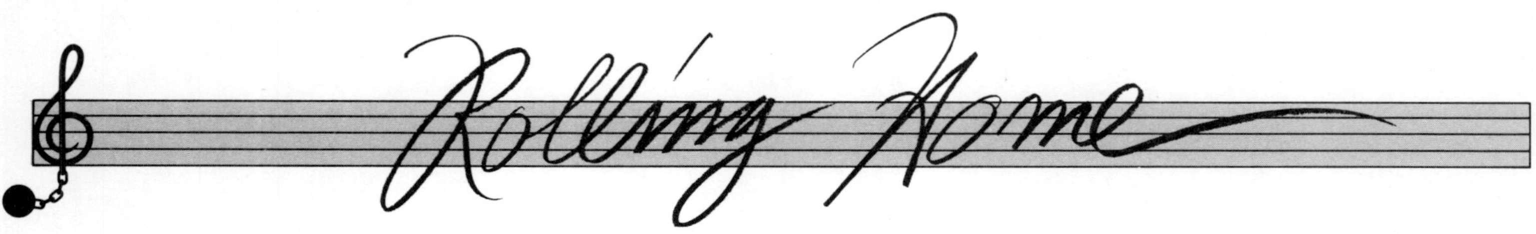

Rolling Home

This is a good steady sea song used to work the capstan. It was extremely popular and many old-timers recall how it was sung when the ships docked out of the Australian ports, headed for England and home. The "Heads" could be Sydney Harbour or Melbourne's Port Phillip.

Collected from Jim Cargill of Randwick, New South Wales, by Warren Fahey, in 1973. Mr Cargill had an extensive repertoire of sea-related songs. Refer Australian Folklore Unit Index, 1974, National Library, Canberra.

Call all hands to man the capstan,
See the cable flaked down clear;
Now we're sailin' homeward bound, boys,
For the Channel we will steer.

CHORUS:
Rollin' home, rollin' home,
Rollin' home across the sea,
Rollin' home to dear ol' England,
Rollin' home, fair land, to thee.

See yer tacks an' sheets all clear, boys,
Lead down now yer buntlines all;
Clear all gear upon the sheerpoles,
Stand by to haul on the catfall.

Now Australia we are leavin',
For old England give a cheer;
Fare-ye-well, ye dark-eyed damsels,
Give three cheers for English beer.

Goodbye, Heads, we're bound to leave you,
Haul the towrope all inboard,
We will leave old Aussie sternwards,
Clap all sail we can afford.

Round Cape Horn on a winter's mornin',
Now among the ice an' snow,
Ye will hear our shellbacks singin',
Sheet 'er home, boys, let 'er go!

Eighteen months away from England,
Only fifty days, no more,
On salt-horse an' crackerhash, boys,
Boston beans that make us sore.

Now, we're low beneath the Islands,
The lee riggin's hangin' slack,
She's a-reelin' off her knots, boys,
Hear the main t'gallant crack.

Now the Lizard Light's a-shinin',
An' we're bound up to the Nore,
With the canvas full an' drawin',
Soon we'll be on England's shore.

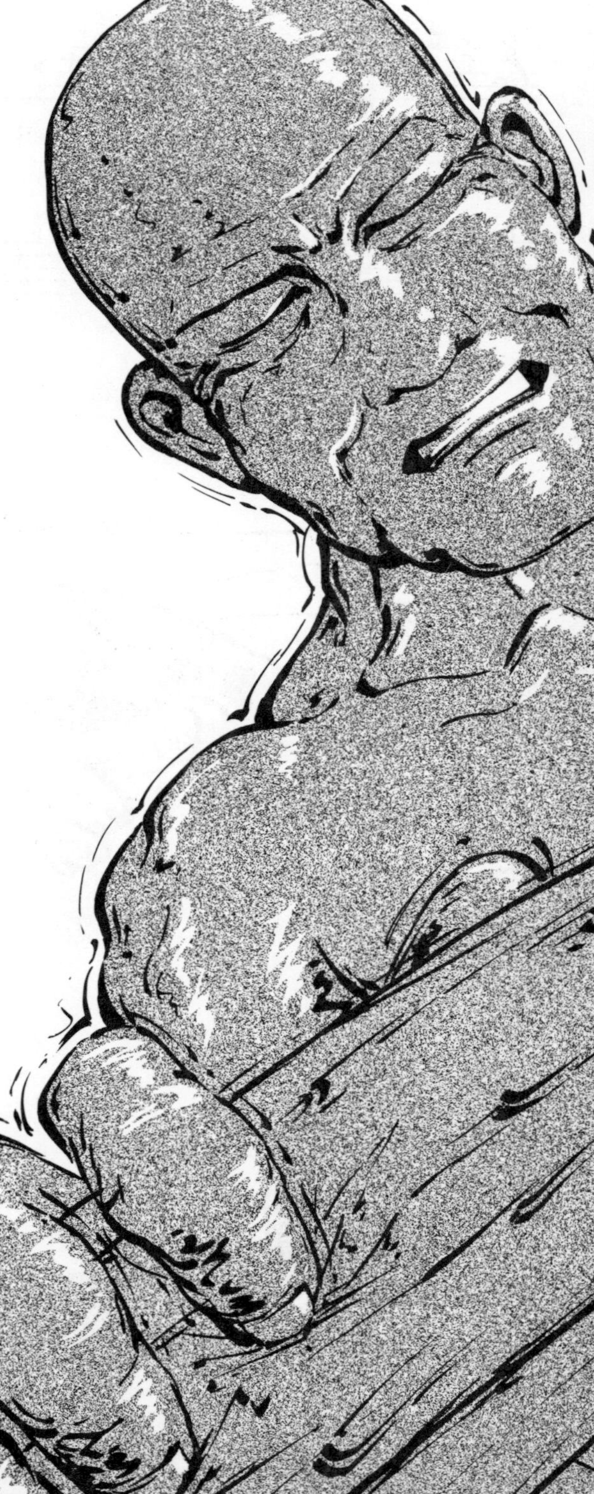

Call all hands to man the cap - s'n, See the ca - ble flaked down clear, Now we're
sailin' home - ward - bound boys, For the Chan - nel we will steer.
CH.
Rol - lin'
home, rol - lin' home rol - lin' home a - cross the sea, Rol - lin'
home to dear ol' Eng - land, Rol - in' home, fair land to thee.

The Catalpa

On April 17, 1876, six Fenian prisoners rowed out of the Western Australian port of Fremantle where they met up with a whaling ship, the Catalpa. *Part of a daring escape plan, the* Catalpa *"stole" away in sight of the government vessel the* Georgette. *The* Catalpa *arrived safely in America in August of 1876 complete with its cargo of six Irish political prisoners. Free men again! The irony of this escape was that it took place on the same day as the annual Perth Regatta.*

A popular adaption of the ballad "The Fenian's Escape". This version collected by Russell Ward from Mr Victor Courtney as published in the Sunday Times, *Perth. Our tune is related to "Judges and Juries".*

A noble whale ship and commander
Was called the CATALPA, they say;
She came out to Western Australia
And took six poor Fenians away.

CHORUS:
Come all you screws, warders and jailers,
Remember Perth Regatta Day,
Take care of the rest of your Fenians,
Or the Yankees will steal them away.

For seven long years they had served here,
And seven long more had to stay,
For defending their country, Old Ireland,
For that they were banished away.

You kept them in Western Australia
Till their hair had begun to turn grey,
When a Yank from the States of America
Came out here and stole them away.

Now all the Perth boats were a-racing,
And making short tacks for the spot,
But the Yankee tacked into Fremantle
And took the best prize of the lot.

The *Georgette,* armed with bold warriors,
Went out the poor Yanks to arrest,
But she hoisted her star-spangled banner,
Saying, "You will not board me, I guess."

So remember those Fenians colonial,
And sing these few verses with skill,
And remember the Yankee that stole them
And the home that they left on the hill.

And now they're safe in America,
And there will be able to cry,
"Hoist up the green flag and shamrock,
Hurrah! for Old Ireland we'll die!"

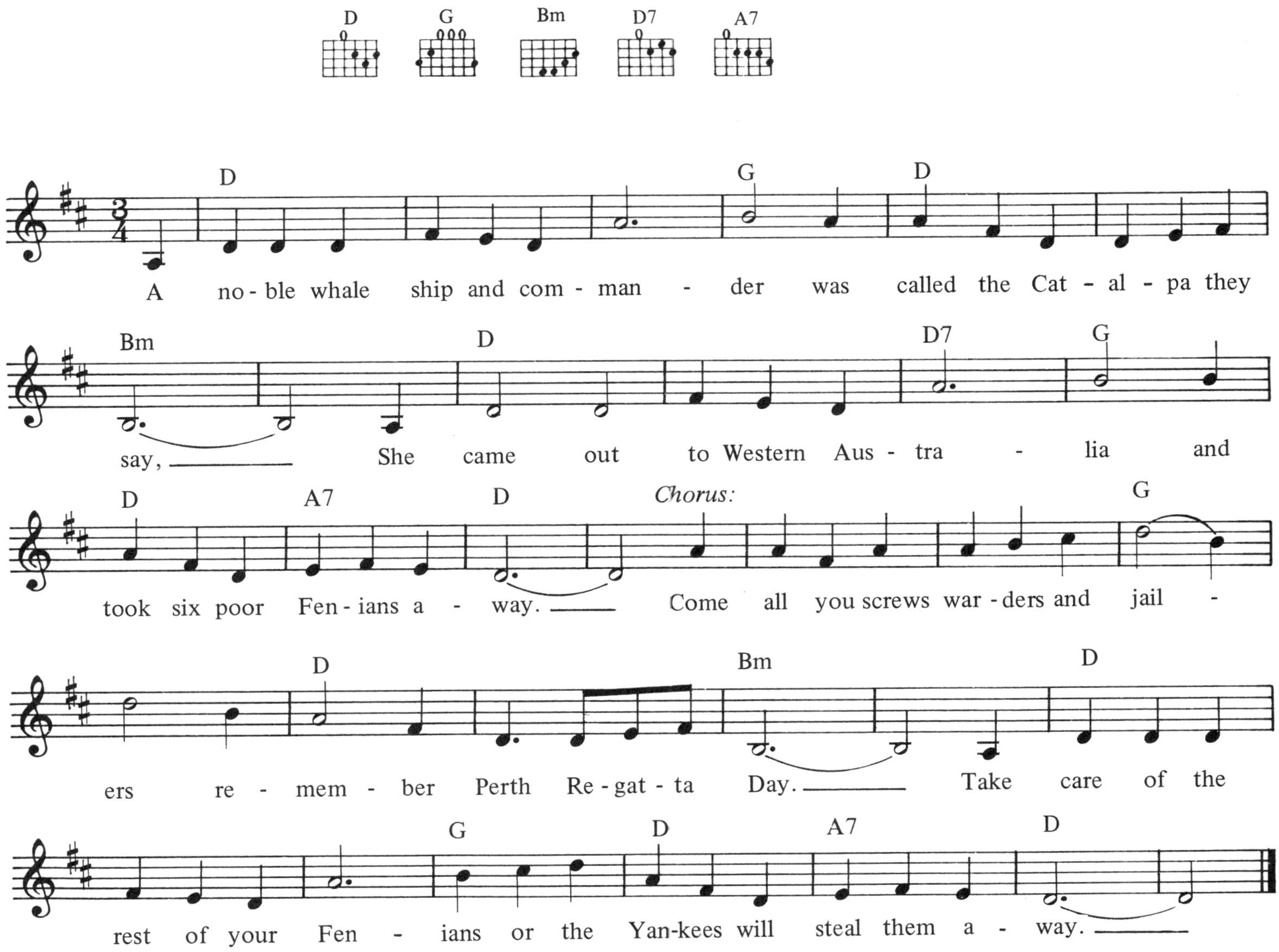

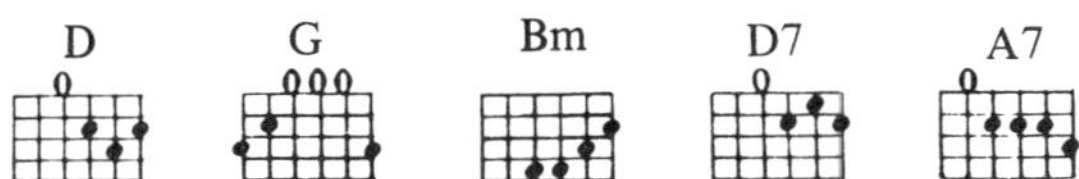

D G D
A no-ble whale ship and com-man - der was called the Cat - al - pa they

Bm D D7 G
say, She came out to Western Aus-tra - lia and

D A7 D
took six poor Fen-ians a - way.

Chorus:

G
Come all you screws war-ders and jail -

D Bm D
ers re - mem - ber Perth Re-gat-ta Day. Take care of the

G D A7 D
rest of your Fen - ians or the Yan-kees will steal them a - way.

South Australia

Life at sea meant endless hours of tedious work and rest. Singing was considered an integral part of life at sea and many old-time sailors were found to have massive repertoires of all types of songs ranging from the usual seafaring ballads through to sentimental popular songs and bawdy ditties. This ever-popular song seems to have been an amalgamation of a number of seafaring stories involving the inevitable combination of girls, whisky and walloping around Cape Horn! There is an American goldrush version with the refrain of "Heave Away, Haul Away, And we're bound for California".

Widely distributed song. This version collated by Warren Fahey offers the standard texts. Compare version printed in Bandicoot Ballads *collected by Ron Edwards.*

SOLO:
In South Australia I was born –
CHORUS:
Heave away! haul away!
SOLO:
South Australia round Cape Horn
CHORUS:
Bound for South Australia.

CHORUS:
Heave away you ruler kings –
Heave away, haul away,
Heave away, you'll hear me sing,
We're bound for South Australia.

There's only one thing that grieves my mind –
It's leaving Nancy Bloom behind.

I'll tell you the truth and tell you no lie –
I'll love that girl till the day I die.

As I was walloping around Cape Horn –
I'd wished to God, I'd never been born.

And now I'm bound for a foreign land
With a bottle of whisky in my hand.

I'll drink one glass to the foreign shore –
And another to the girl that I adore.

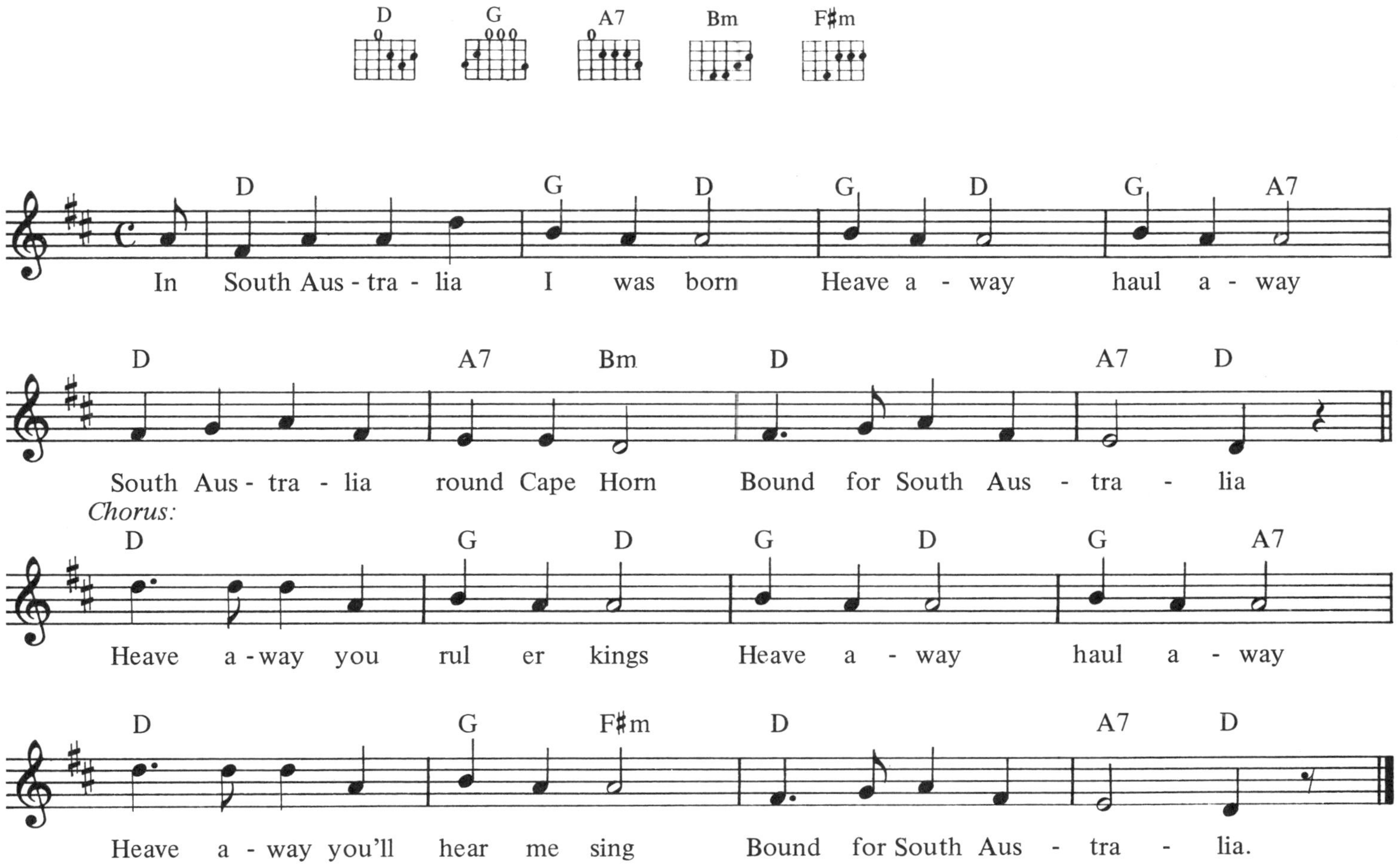

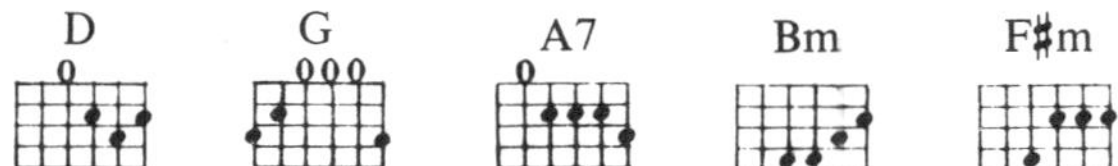

D G A7 Bm F♯m
D G D G D G A7
In South Aus - tra - lia I was born Heave a - way haul a - way
D A7 Bm D A7 D
South Aus - tra - lia round Cape Horn Bound for South Aus - tra - lia
Chorus:
D G D G D G A7
Heave a - way you rul er kings Heave a - way haul a - way
D G F♯m D A7 D
Heave a - way you'll hear me sing Bound for South Aus - tra - lia.

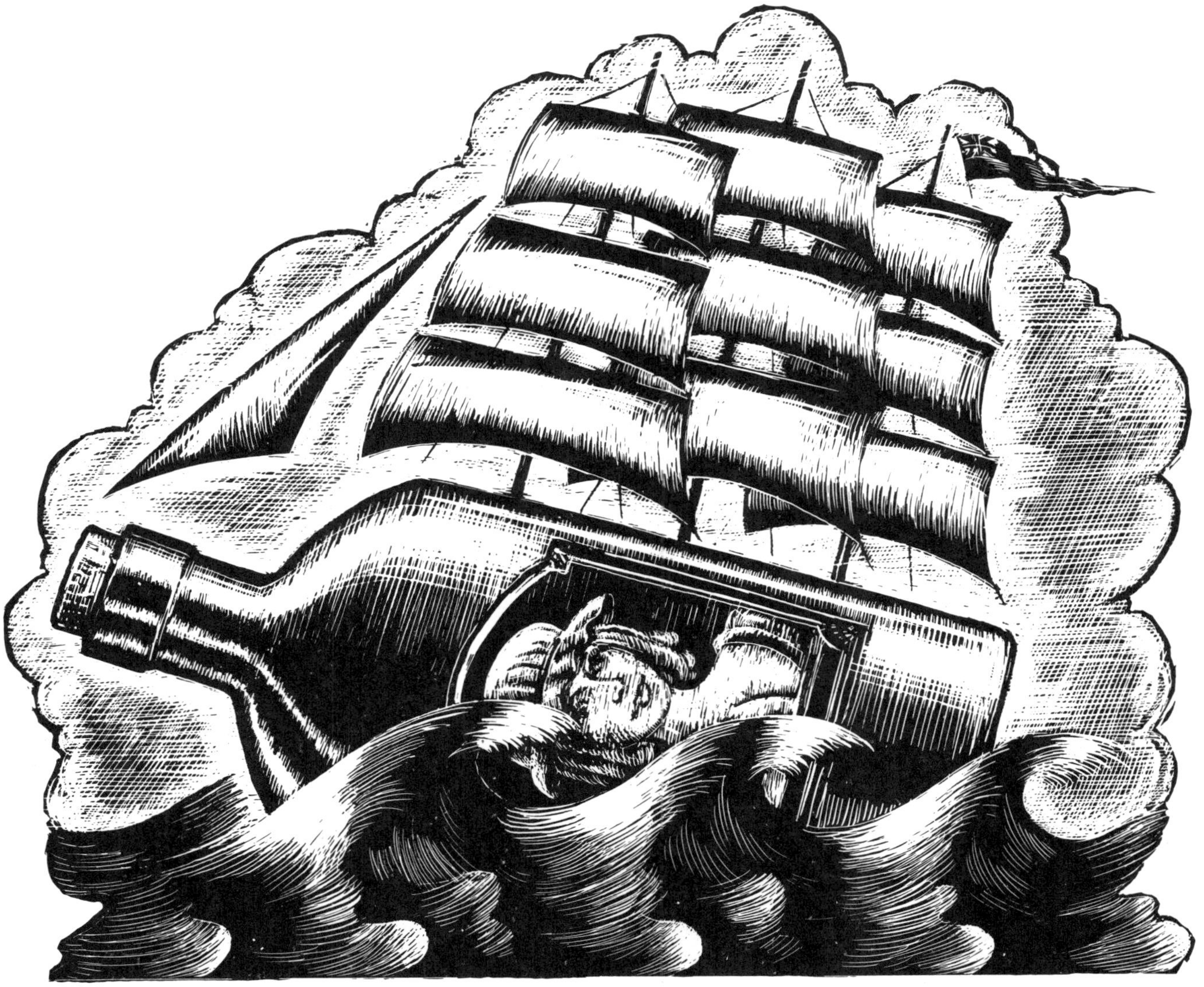

Colonial Experience

With the growth of the colony came merchants, farmers, the military and the confused. The new Victorian Age Sydney covered some two thousand acres and claimed nearly twenty thousand inhabitants. Year by year the colony expanded and the population exploded with emancipists, freeborn and new arrivals. The new land was certainly the scene of hustle and bustle but also of rather unexpected climate, insect life and deprivation. England was never like this!

From the Colonial Songster *with a note providing the tune as "So Early in The Morning". The text is attributed to "a new chum". This version re-worked by Warren Fahey.*

When first I came to Sydney Cove
And up and down the streets did rove,
I thought such sights I ne'er did see
Since first I learnt my ABC.

CHORUS:
Oh! it's broiling in the morning,
It's toiling in the morning,
It's broiling in the morning,
It's toiling all day long.

Into the park I took a stroll –
I felt just like a buttered roll.
A pretty name "The Sunny South!".
A better one "The Land of Drouth!".

Next day into the bush I went,
On wild adventure I was bent,
Dame Nature's wonders I'd explore,
All thought of danger would ignore.

The mosquitoes and bulldog ants
Assailed me even through my pants.
It nearly took my breath away
To hear the kooka's laugh so gay!

This lovely country, I've been told,
Abounds in silver and in gold.
You may pick it up all day,
Just as the leaves in autumn lay!

Some say there's lots of work to do.
Well, yes, but then, 'twixt me and you,
A man may toil and broil all day –
But the big, fat man gets all the pay.

Perhaps such good things there may be,
But you may have them all, for me,
Instead of roaming foreign parts
I wish I'd studied the Fine Arts!

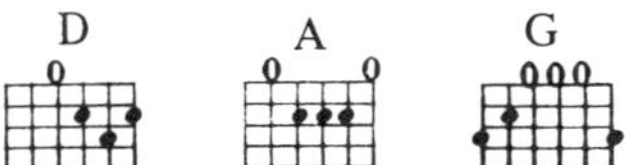

D A D
When first I came to Syd-ney cove And up and down the streets did rove I

D A D
thought such sights I ne'er did see since first I learnt my A. B. C. Oh! it's

D A D
broil-ing in the morn-ing ___ It's toil-ing in the morn-ing ___ it's

G D A D
broil-ing in the morn-ing ___ it's toil-ing all day long. ___

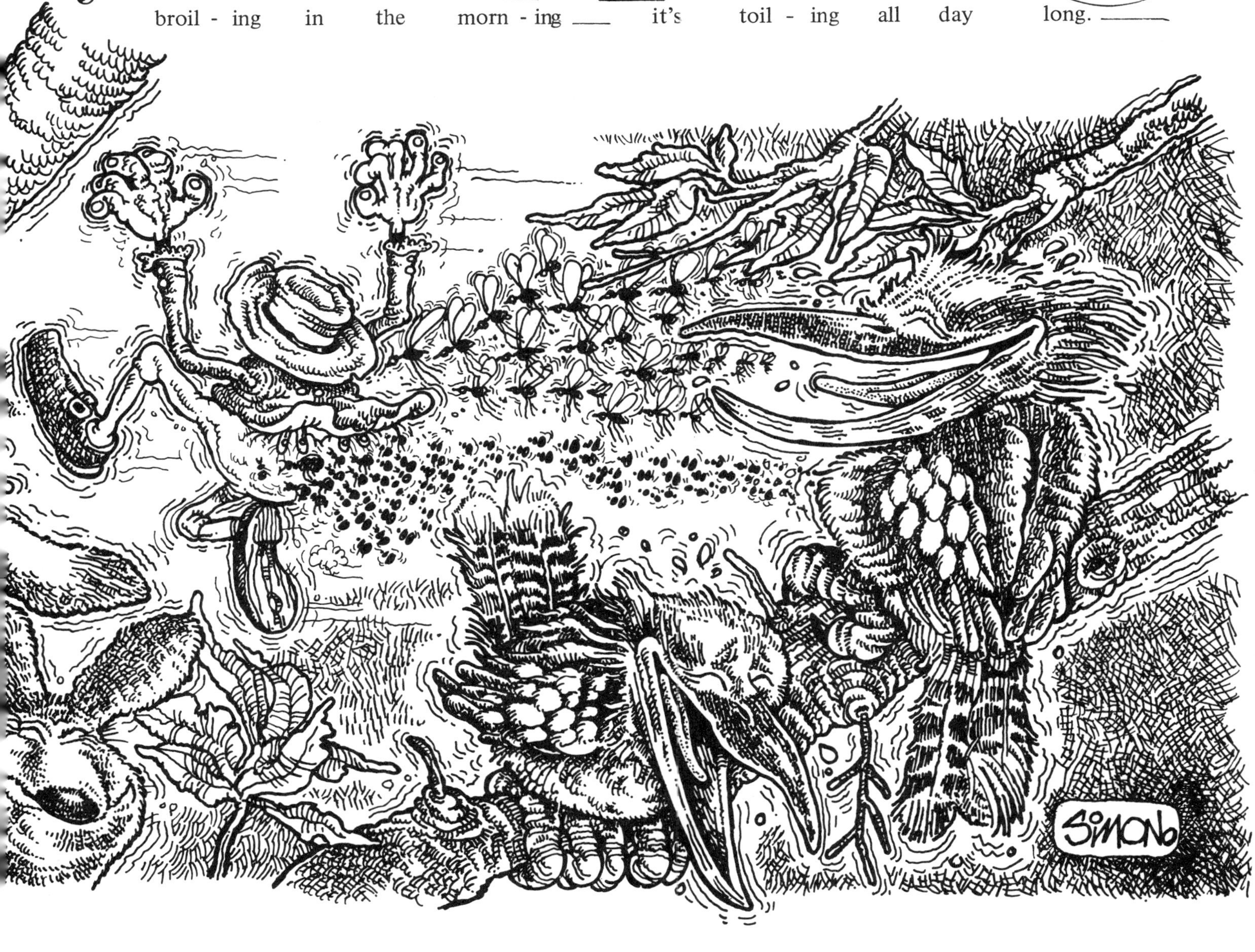

PIONEERING, GOLDRUSH DAYS AND BUSHRANGERS

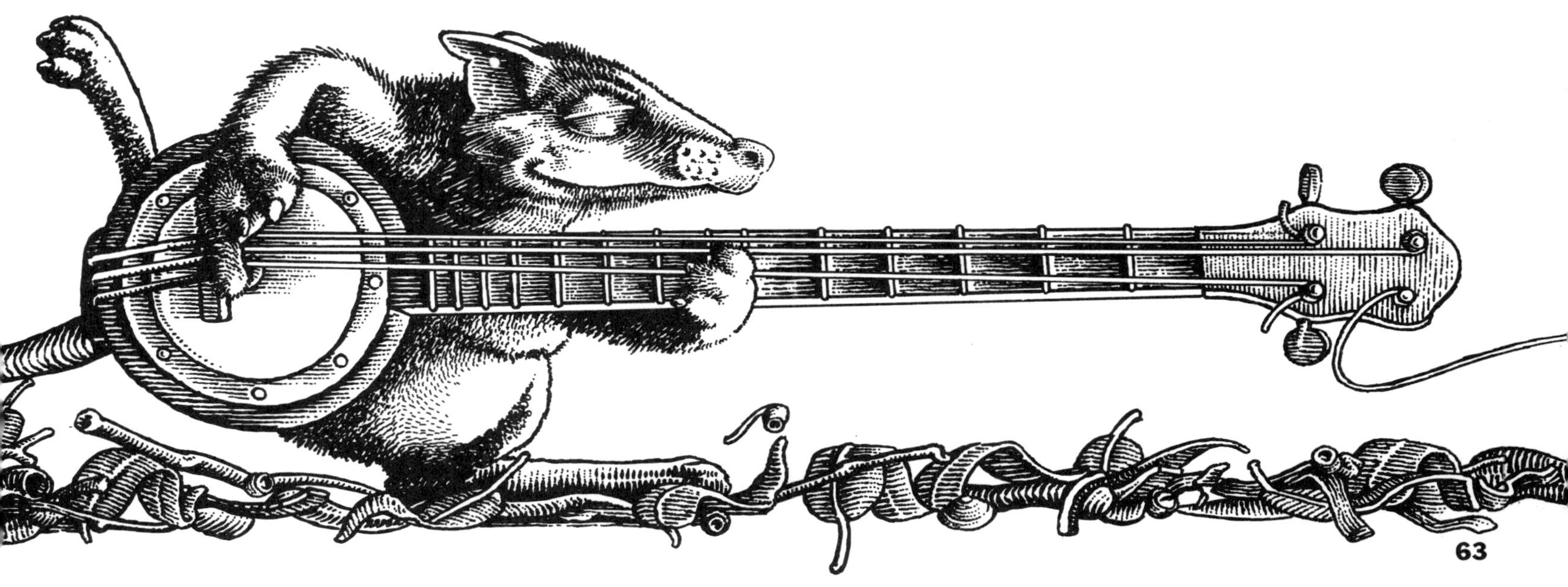

Introduction 2

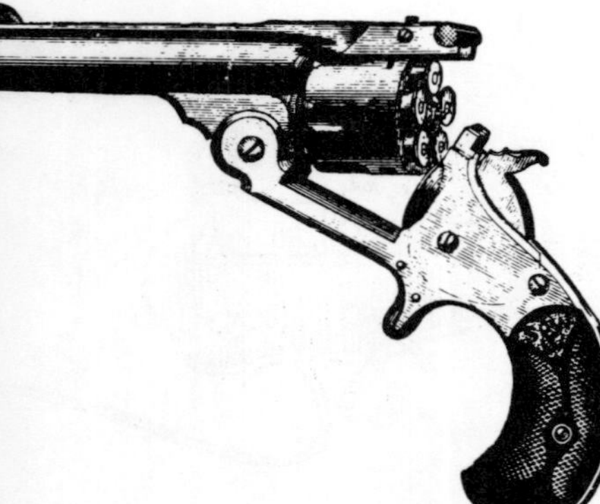

Australia – born of the convict chain-gang and blood-stained back soon realised that the penal colony of New South Wales also had the potential to offer a new life. By the 1830's the colony of Sydney had developed into a thriving trading post. Convict labour had established respectable roadways and had even commenced to painfully wind the macadamised roadway westward into the bushland past Parramatta.

Exploration teams gallantly pushed westward, then to the North and South. Convicts were now becoming settlers as "ticket of leave" holders. In 1836, Governor Burke decided to "throw the country open" and introduced a policy of squatter settlement whereby any "respectable person" could pay ten pounds a year, and a half-penny for every animal, and take out a "squatting licence" to run stock on Crown lands within a limit of twenty square miles.

James Macarthur had successfully introduced sheep-farming to the colony and by the 1840's Australia found itself in the midst of a "wool fever". Originally the sheep-barons thought the fortune was all theirs but it was soon agreed that anyone could make a bid for wool wealth and subsequent independence.

The rest of the continent started to awake. Perth had been settled in 1829 by a small group of farmers; Adelaide declared itself a "free colony" in 1836 stating a policy never to admit transported convicts. Van Diemen's Land, well established as a convict settlement, was now experiencing moves for free settlement. By 1837 the only British stronghold was Brisbane with its notorious penal settlement of Moreton Bay.

In 1834, a squatter, Thomas Henty, moved from Perth and settled illegally in Portland to become Victoria's first settler. Others soon followed including an enterprising young grazier, John Batman, who laid the plans for the growing settlement which later became Melbourne.

Here we had the dawning of a new Australia with the tail-end of a horrific convict heritage and a new pioneering future. Wool was all the word and when Charles Darwin visited Australia he commented: "The whole population, poor and rich, are bent on acquiring wealth. Amongst the highest orders, wool and sheep-grazing form the constant subject of conversation".

On the 12th February, 1851, the subject of conversation changed dramatically when a top-hatted, well dressed young adventurer named Edward Hargreaves discovered gold near Bathurst. The colony went wild. Gold fever had hit and the face of Australia changed.

No longer a relic of the convict system Australia was now the "New Land", the Eldorado, where a smart young fellow could become a rich man – almost overnight! Some did but most left the goldfields in despair, seeking new avenues of enterprise in the new bustling cities and outback farms.

Thousands of city dwellers left for the bush. Inland streams became home and the roadways were jammed with would-be fortune seekers – a passing parade of eager faces. They came on horseback, bullock dray and on foot, each with a variety of tools for digging.

Like a giant cobweb the call of a new rush moved the evergrowing population from one area to another. It was "Rush Away!" and off they would go, ever hopeful. The harbours of Port Phillip Bay, Geelong and Sydney were crowded with the traffic of ships arriving and departing. Gold fever was all the rage!

With gold came new settlements, new laws, new ideas and bushrangers. The highwaymen tradition was not new, but in Australia it was generally considered a "brave and daring" thing to do. Not only did the outlaw have to worry about the law he also had to face the Australian bush with all its dangers. The deeds of such men as Ned Kelly, Ben Hall and Frank Gardiner are all well documented in the official and in the unofficial histories. Australia born of bureaucracy tended to smile as the bushrangers outsmarted the law. The songs, stories and poems from these pioneering days are the myths that nations are built on.

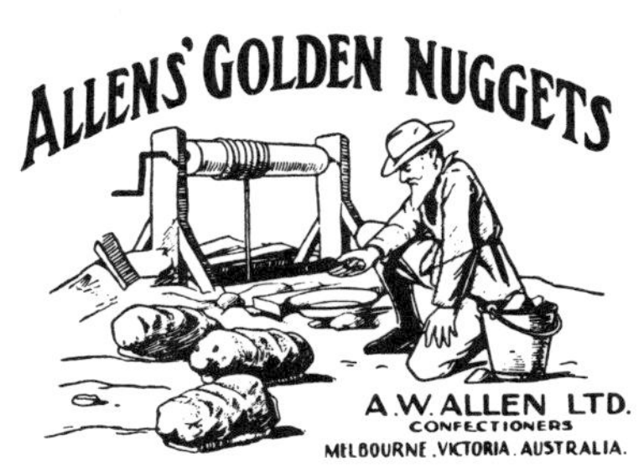

The Old Bullock Dray

As the colony expanded and worked its way inland through the bush, settlers employed all types of transport to shift their sometimes dubious belongings "up the country". The most practical being the heavy but dependable bullock-drawn wagons that could plod their way through overgrown tracks and sometimes no tracks at all. This is a much sung and loved old song that captures the pioneering spirit of the times. It makes reference to the "depot" which was the name given to the notorious "female factory" at Parramatta. It was here that pioneers could select and engage a wife from the register of female convicts.

A much performed song that appears in many bush singers' repertoire. This complete version from swagman Jack Pobar was collected in Toowoomba, Queensland, by Warren Fahey, in 1973.

Jack Pobar, Swagman, 1973

Now the shearing is all over, and the wool is coming down,
I mean to get a wife, me boys, when I go to town,
For everything that's got a mate that brings itself to view,
From the little paddy-melon to the big kangaroo.

CHORUS:
So roll up your bundle and let us make a push,
I'll take you up the country and show you the bush,
I'll be bound such a chance you won't get another day,
So roll up and take possession of the old bullock dray.

I'll teach you the whip and the bullocks how to flog,
You'll be my off-sider when I'm fast in the bog,
Hitting out both left and right and every other way,
Making skin and blood and hair fly round the old bullock dray.

There'll be lots of piccaninnies, you must remember that,
There'll be Buckjumping Maggie and Leather-belly Pat,
There'll be Stringybark Peggy and Green-hide Mike,
Yes, my colonial, as many as you like.

Now that I am married and have piccaninnies five times three,
No one lives so happy as my little wife and me;
She goes out a-hunting to while away the day
While I take down the wool upon the old bullock dray.

C F G7 C7

C F
Now the shear-ing is all ov-er and the wool is com-ing down, I
G7 C C7
mean to get a wife boys when I go to town For eve-ry-thing has got a mate that
F C G7 C
brings it-self to view From the lit-tle pad-dy me-lon to the big kan-ga-roo.

WIFE

Originally titled "Botany Bay Courtship" and printed in the Sydney Gazette *1832, as part of the "Botany Bay Eulogies". The tune used is the "Irish Washerwoman".*

"The real interest of most of the convict women lay not in visits from preachers, not in their work, their babies or feeding arrangements, but in their ultimate fate outside the walls of the Female Factory. Most wished to marry and there was a regular 'courting day' when the women washed themselves, brushed their hair, and stood in a long line." (Australia As It Is, *Rev. J. Morison, 1867, London.)*

"Some smiling and blushing, 'would look as foolish as all young ladies are supposed to . . . others would avert their faces in a sort of indifference'. When the settler had made his choice the woman was given back her own clothes, and 'dressed again like a free woman', then, with her suitor of one hour to the church. Taken back to her husband's farm, the new wife met her neighbours at a mild celebration which might easily end in a drunken brawl." (A Residence of Eleven Years in New Holland, *J. O'Connell, 1841, Boston.)*

C G7 F

The cur - ren - cy lads may fill ___ their glas - ses And drink to the health of the
cur - ren - cy las - ses But the lass I ad - ore the one for me is a
lass at the fe - male ___ fac - to - ry Oh Mol - ly's her name ___ her
name it is Mol-ly Al-though he was tried by the name ___ of Pol- ly She was tried and was cast for
death at New- ry But the judge was bribed and ___ so was the ju - ry.

The Currency Lads may fill their glasses,
And drink to the health of the Currency Lasses;
But the lass I adore, the lass for me,
Is a lass in the Female Factory.

O! Molly's her name, and her name is Molly,
Although she was tried by the name of Polly;
She was tried and was cast for death at Newry,
But the Judge was bribed and so were the Jury.

She got "death recorded" in Newry town,
For stealing her mistress's watch and gown;
Her little boy Paddy can tell you the tale,
His father was turnkey of Newry jail.

The first time I saw this comely lass
Was at Parramatta, going to mass;
Says I, "I'll marry you now in an hour,"
Says she, "Well, go and fetch Father Power."

But I got into trouble that very same night!
Being drunk in the street I got into a fight,
A constable seized me – I gave him a box –
And was put in the watch-house and then in the stocks.

O! it's very uneasy as I may remember,
To sit in the stocks in the month of December,
With the north wind so hot, and the hot sun right over,
O! sure, and it's no place at all for a lover!

"It's worse than the tread-mill," says I, "Mr Dunn,
To sit here all day in the heat of the sun!"
"Either that or a dollar," says he, "for your folly," –
But if I had a dollar I'd drink it with Molly.

But now I am out again, early and late
I sigh and I cry at the Factory gate,
"O! Mrs Reilly, late Mrs Falloon,
O! won't you let Molly out very soon?"

"Is it Molly McGuigan?" says she to me,
"It is not?" says I, for she know'd it was she.
"Is it her you mean that was put in the stocks
For beating her mistress, Mrs Cox?"

"O! yes and it is, madam, pray let me in,
I have brought her a half-pint of Cooper's best gin,
She likes it as well as she likes her own mother,
O! now let me in, madam, I am her brother."

So the Currency Lads may fill their glasses,
And drink to the health of the Currency Lasses;
But the lass I adore, the lass for me,
Is a lass in the Female Factory.

Australia's on the Wallaby

Not only did gold bring a vigorous and adventurous type of people to the colonies. The "rush" to the new discoveries scattered miners to far-flung areas of the huge land. Without gold, Australia would probably have gone along at snail pace settling the country mile by mile.

"Gold diggers are a very migratory class. If they hear of a discovery of a new goldfield they will frequently leave their old diggings and rush to the new one, often to return deeply disappointed but without having learnt wisdom. Let a new "rush" be proclaimed and they are off again. Gold digging appears to be a never-satisfying employment with the mass of people who frequent diggings. They will give up good opportunities for a mere chance of distance!" (B. A. Heywood, 1863.)

As printed in The Bill Bowyang Reciter, *1933, Mitchell Library, Sydney. Compare with Henry Lawson's later work "Freedom on The Wallaby".*

CHORUS:
Australia's on the wallaby, oh listen to the coo-ee,
The kangaroo he packs his port and the emu shoulders bluey,
The boomerangs are whizzing round, the dingo scratches gravel,
And the possum, bear and bandicoot are all out on the travel.

Our fathers came in search of gold, the claim it proved a duffer,
The syndicates and banks went broke, and so we had to suffer.
We're all for freedom for ourselves, ourselves and mates of toil,
Australia's on the wallaby and the billy's on the boil.

With tiger snakes and damper a-sizzling on the coals,
With droughts and floods and ragged duds and dried-up waterholes,
On sun-scorched plains where shade is not they're asking us to toil,
Australia's sons are weary and the billy's on the boil.

The kooka calls, the bats, and now the black duck and the shag,
The mallee hen and platypus are rolling up their swag,
The curlew waves his last farewell beside some lone lagoon,
The brolga does his last gay waltz to the lyre-bird's mocking tune.

F Dm C7 Am

Chorus:
F Dm C7 F
Au - stra - lia's on the wal - la - by Lis - ten to the coo - ee The
Dm C7 F
kan - ga - roo he packs his port and the e - mu shoul - ders blu - ey The
Dm Am Dm Am C7
boom - er - angs are whiz-zing round the din - go scrat - ches gra - vel and the
F C7 F
pos - sum bear and ban - di - coot are all out on the tra - vel.

Sixteen Thousand Miles from Home

This song comes from Singabout Vol. 3 No. 2 *published by the Bush Music Club, Sydney.*

In the days of clipper transport it was difficult to establish distance. In one transportation song it is "ten thousand miles away" and in this gold fossicker's song it is set at sixteen thousand miles. Whatever the distance the likelihood of overnight fortune was improbable. Many an eager digger arrived fresh-faced on the diggings to discover the combination of intense heat, flies and hard yakka was too much for a European. Our digger in this song even suggests a soldier's life is safer and sweeter!

Oh, I'm sixteen thousand miles from home
And me heart is fairly achin',
To think that I should humble so
To come out here stone breakin'.
The road I took was Bungaroo
An' I met with a sub-contractor,
Who eyed me an' studied me
As a parson or a doctor.
With me hooral dooral,
Tiddy falooral,
Tiddy faloll dee-i-doh.

Now I told him I was out of work
An' wanted some employment.
He sez "You do! You stink with scent,
You've had too much enjoyment.
Go over onto yonder hill,
Get from the boss a hammer,
An' nine an' six is your pay,
An' mind you now, that's grammar."
With me hooral dooral,
Tiddy falooral,
Tiddy faloll dee-i-doh.

So I battered an' whacked the whole of the day,
At evening I grew spiteful;
With the sight I didn't know what to do,
I hadn't broke me hatful.
Just then the boss he came along,
Sez he, "You'll have to alter,
You'll be gettin' no run o' the store, be Gosh,
You'll never make your salt, sir."
With me hooral dooral,
Tiddy falooral,
Tiddy faloll dee-i-doh.

So I chucked me hammer down on the heap,
With that I did consider;
I knocked the dust from off me boots,
An' battered me old black beaver.
Bad luck then to the mam an' dad
That reared me up so lazy,
With a silver spoon I'm a regular loon,
With hunger I'm near crazy.
With me hooral dooral,
Tiddy falooral,
Tiddy faloll dee-i-doh.

(To second half of tune.)

Now I'll go and list the army,
I'll go and lift the rifle,
An' if I get shot I'll forget the lot,
All pastime an' all trifle.
With me hooral dooral,
Tiddy falooral,
Tiddy faloll dee-i-doh.

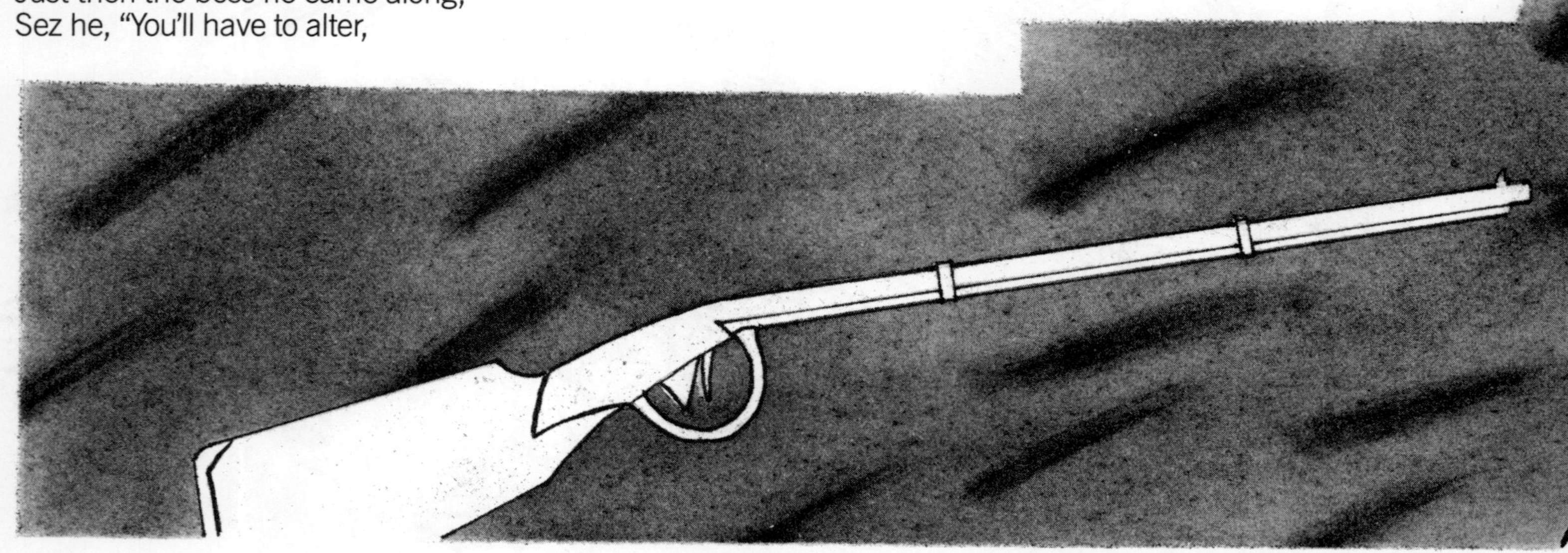

Em D C D
Oh I'm six-teen thou-sand miles from home an' me heart is fair-ly achin' To think

Em G D G
that I should hum-ble so to come out here stone-break ing ____ The

Bm Em C G
road I took was Bun-ga-roo and I met with a sub con-trac-tor who

Am Em Am C D
eyed me and stud-ied me as a par-son or a doc-tor With me hoo-

G *Chorus:* C G D7 G
-ral doo-ral tid-dy fal-oo-ral tid-dy fal-oll dee-dee-i-doh.

The most popular form of mining was the use of the American designed "cradle". However, the search for gold led men and women on a merry chase until eventually they started to dig deep into the ground like rabbits. This popular song tells of the daily life of the pit miner – a familiar tale to many.

"He went and bought a shovel,
And a pick and dish as well,
But every ten minutes' work,
He took a hour's spell.
What! Must I venture down a hole,
And throw up filthy clay?
If my mother could but see me now,
Whatever would she say!"

This song is adapted from a version sung by Mrs Frances McDonald of Broken Hill and was recorded by Warren Fahey, 1973, with the assistance of the Australian Broadcasting Commission, Broken Hill. Mrs McDonald actually commenced to sing "Don't Go Down The Mine" and sung "The Miner" in the middle of the song.

A cradle

The miner, he goes and he changes his clothes,
And then makes his way to the shaft,
For each man well knows he's going below
To put in his eight hours of graft.

CHORUS:
With his calico cap and his old flannel shirt,
His pants with the strap 'round the knee,
His boots watertight and his candle alight,
His crib and his billy of tea.

The platman to the driver will knock four and one,
The ropes to the windlass will strain;
As one shift comes up, another goes down
And working commences again.

He works hard for his pay at six bob a day,
He toils for his missus and kids;
He gets what's left over and thinks he's in clover,
To cut off his 'baccy in quids.

And so he goes on, week in and week out,
To toil for his life's daily bread;
He's off to the mine, hail, rain or shine,
That his dear ones at home may be fed.

Diggin' holes in the ground where there's gold to be found,
And most times where gold it is not!
A man's like a rabbit with this diggin' habit,
And like one, he ought to be shot!

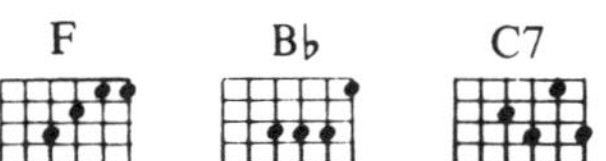
F
B♭
C7

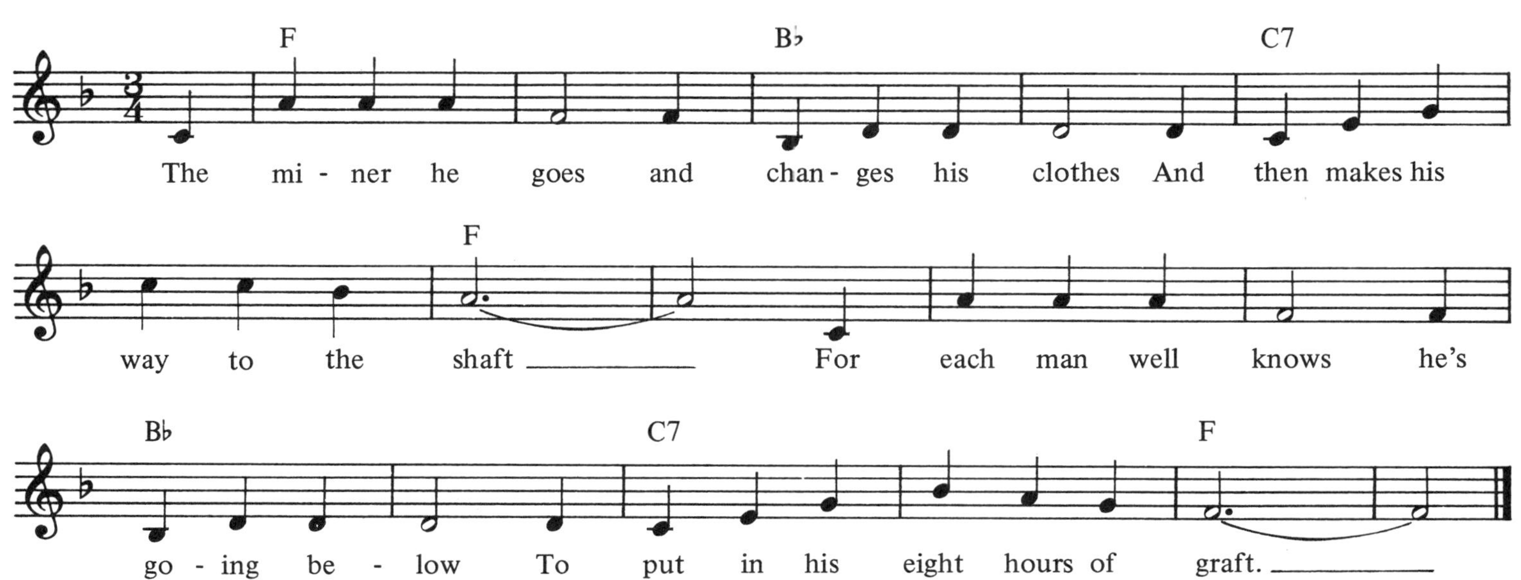
F B♭ C7
The mi - ner he goes and chan - ges his clothes And then makes his
F
way to the shaft ___ For each man well knows he's
B♭ C7 F
go - ing be - low To put in his eight hours of graft. ___

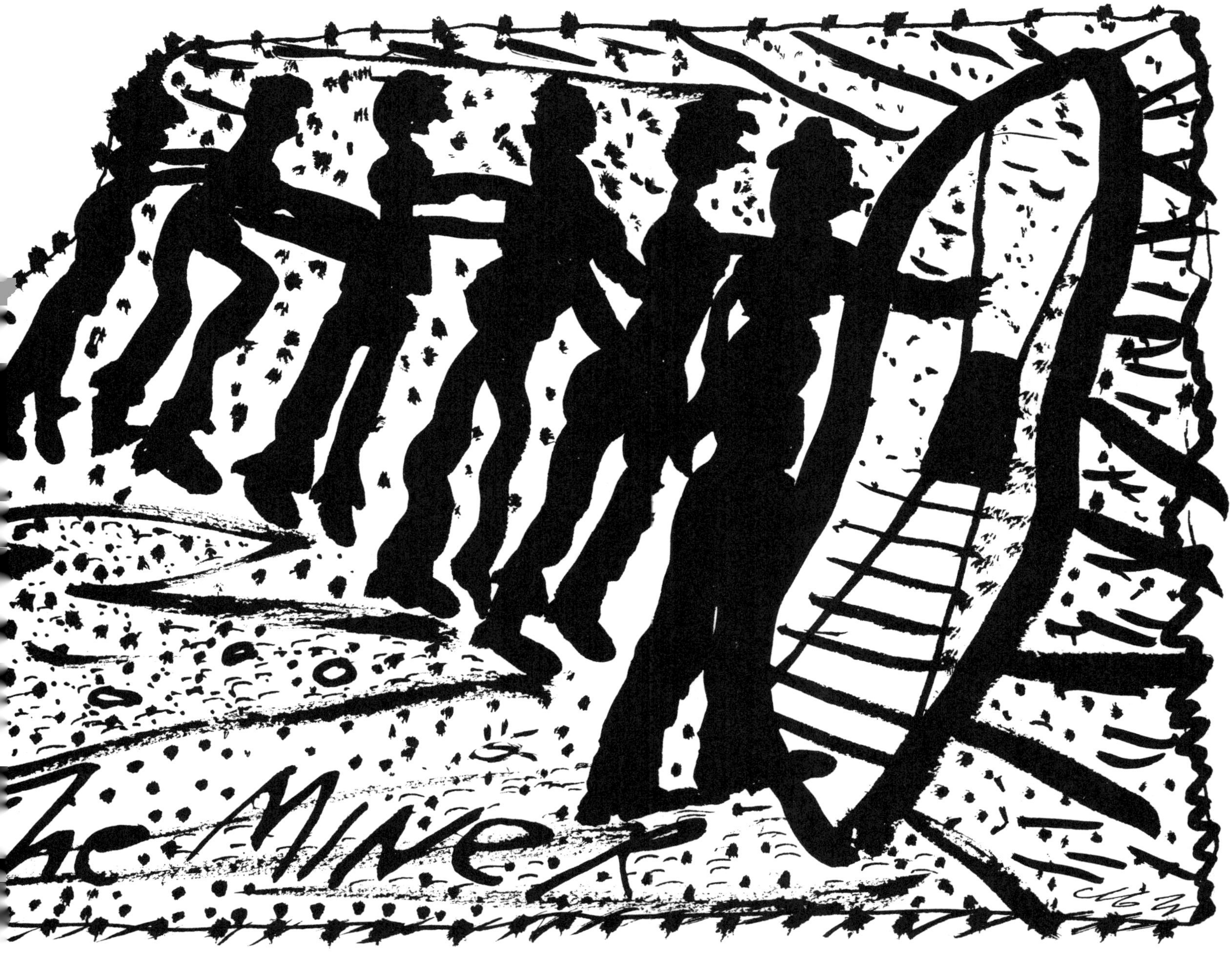

In the 1850's gold was discovered in Australia. Between 1851 and 1861 the population nearly trebled, growing from 405,356 to 1,145,585. The so-called "Australian Madness" spread all around the world and the sea ports of Sydney, and Port Phillip in Melbourne became chaotic as ship after ship arrived crammed with would-be gold hunters. Everyone wanted to strike it rich and their passion was continually fired by reports of "picking up lumps of gold in the streets".

Australia had ceased to be a forsaken territory inhabited by convicts and dangerous blacks ... it was now the "promised land".

Printed in Paterson's Old Bush Songs *as "With My Swag All On My Shoulder". This seems to be the earlier version dealing with the arrival of the eager Irish digger. John Meredith collected the tune from Dr English who recorded a patient in the Royal Prince Alfred Hospital, Sydney. This song seems widely distributed in the folk revival repertoires.*

When first I left old Ireland's shore, the yarns that we were told
Of how the folks in far Australia could pick up lumps of gold!
How gold-dust lay in all the streets and miner's right was free!
"Hurrah!" I told my loving friends. "That's just the place for me."

CHORUS:
With my swag all on my shoulder, black billy in my hand,
I'll travel the bush of Australia like a trueborn Irishman.

When first we reached Port Melbourne we were all prepared to slip,
And bar the captain and the mate all hands abandoned ship.
And all the girls of Melbourne town threw up their arms with joy,
Hurrooing and exclaiming, "Here comes my Irish boy!"

CHORUS:
With his swag all on his shoulder, black billy in his hand,
He'll travel the bush of Australia like a trueborn Irishman.

We made out way into Geelong, then north to Ballarat,
Where some of us grew mighty thin, and some grew sleek and fat.
Some tried their luck at Bendigo and some at Fiery Creek;
I made my fortune in a day and blued it in a week!

CHORUS:
With my swag all on my shoulder, black billy in my hand,
I travelled the bush of Australia like a trueborn Irishman.

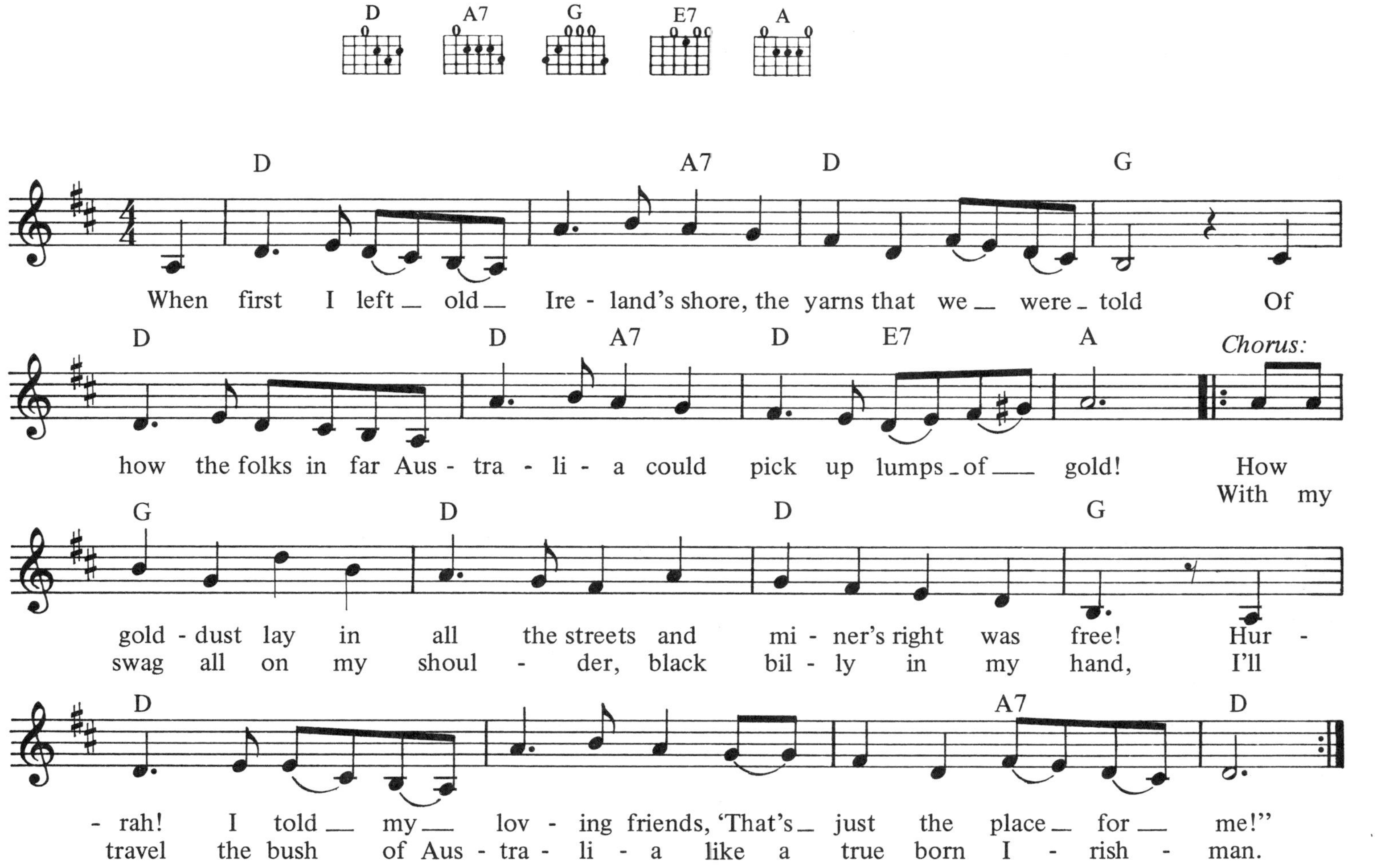

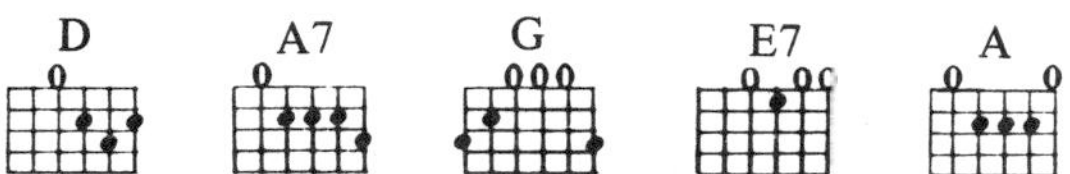

When first I left old Ireland's shore, the yarns that we were told Of how the folks in far Australia could pick up lumps of gold!

Chorus:
How gold-dust lay in all the streets and miner's right was free!
Hurrah! I told my loving friends, 'That's just the place for me!"

With my swag all on my shoulder, black billy in my hand,
I'll travel the bush of Australia like a true born Irishman.

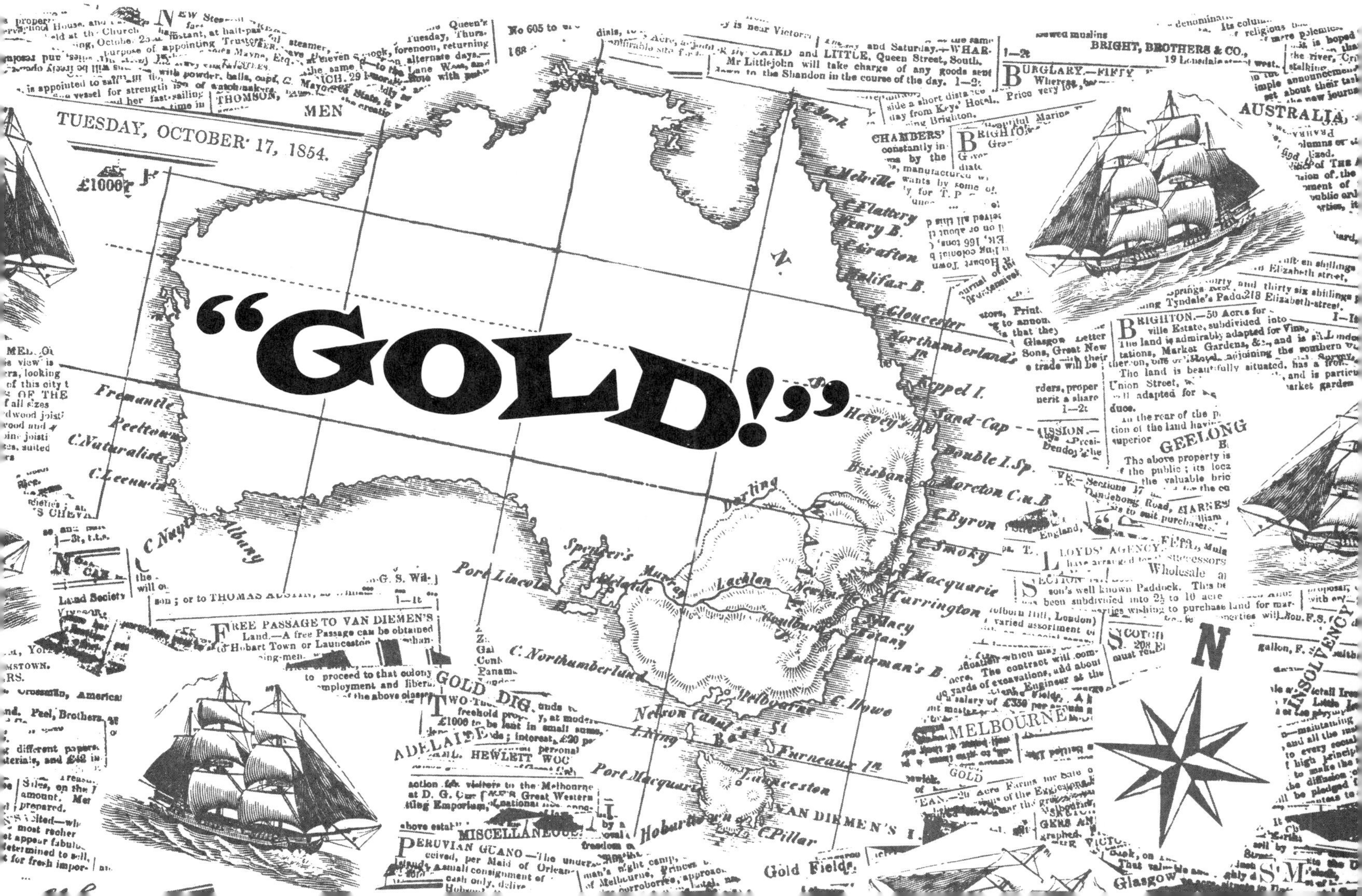

"GOLD!"

The Maryborough Miner

Diggers of all nationalities and backgrounds had to live together on the goldfields. At first there was little violence or crime as the majority of miners were too busy digging to be worried about stealing their neighbour's property. As the goldfields settled down the incidence of violence increased. Claimjumping, bushranging, stealing and fighting became the norm as disappointed fortune-hunters realised that one did not simply "find gold". This classic song relates the story of an obviously "hard bitten" miner who turns sour and ends up in the Cockatoo Island prison in Sydney.

A mining version of the "Murrumbidgee Shearer" which is printed in Paterson's Old Bush Songs. *This version was collected by A. L. Lloyd from Bob Bell, Condobolin, New South Wales, in 1934. It is possible Lloyd would have re-worked the text and tune to make it more singable.*

Come all you sons of liberty and listen to my song,
I'll tell you my observations and it won't take very long —
I've fossicked around this continent, five thousand miles or more,
And many's the time I might have starved, but for the cheek I bore.

I've been on all the diggings, boys, from famous Ballarat,
I've long-tommed on the Lachlan, and I've fossicked Lambing Flat,
So you can understand, my boys, just from this little rhyme,
I'm a Maryborough miner, and I'm one of the good old time.

I came to the Fitzroy River, all with my Bendigo rig,
I had a shovel, a pick and a pan, and for a licence I begged,
But the assay-man called me a loafer, said for work I'd no desire,
And so, to do him justice, boys, I set his office on fire.

Oh yes, my jolly jokers, I've done it on the cross —
Although I carry my bluey now, I've sweated many a horse,
I've helped to rob the escort of many an ounce of gold,
And the traps have been upon my tail more times than I ever told.

Oh yes, the traps have trailed me and been frightened out of their stripes,
They never could have caught me, for they feared my cure for gripes —
And well they knew I carried it, for they had often seen it,
Glistening in my flipper, chaps, my "patent pill machine".

I'm one of the men who cradled on the reef at Tarrangower,
Anxiety and misery my grim companions there;
I puddled the clay at Bendigo, and chanced my arm at Cue,
And I wound up my avocation with ten years on Cockatoo.

So you can understand, my boys, just from this little rhyme,
I'm a Maryborough miner, and I'm one of the good old time.

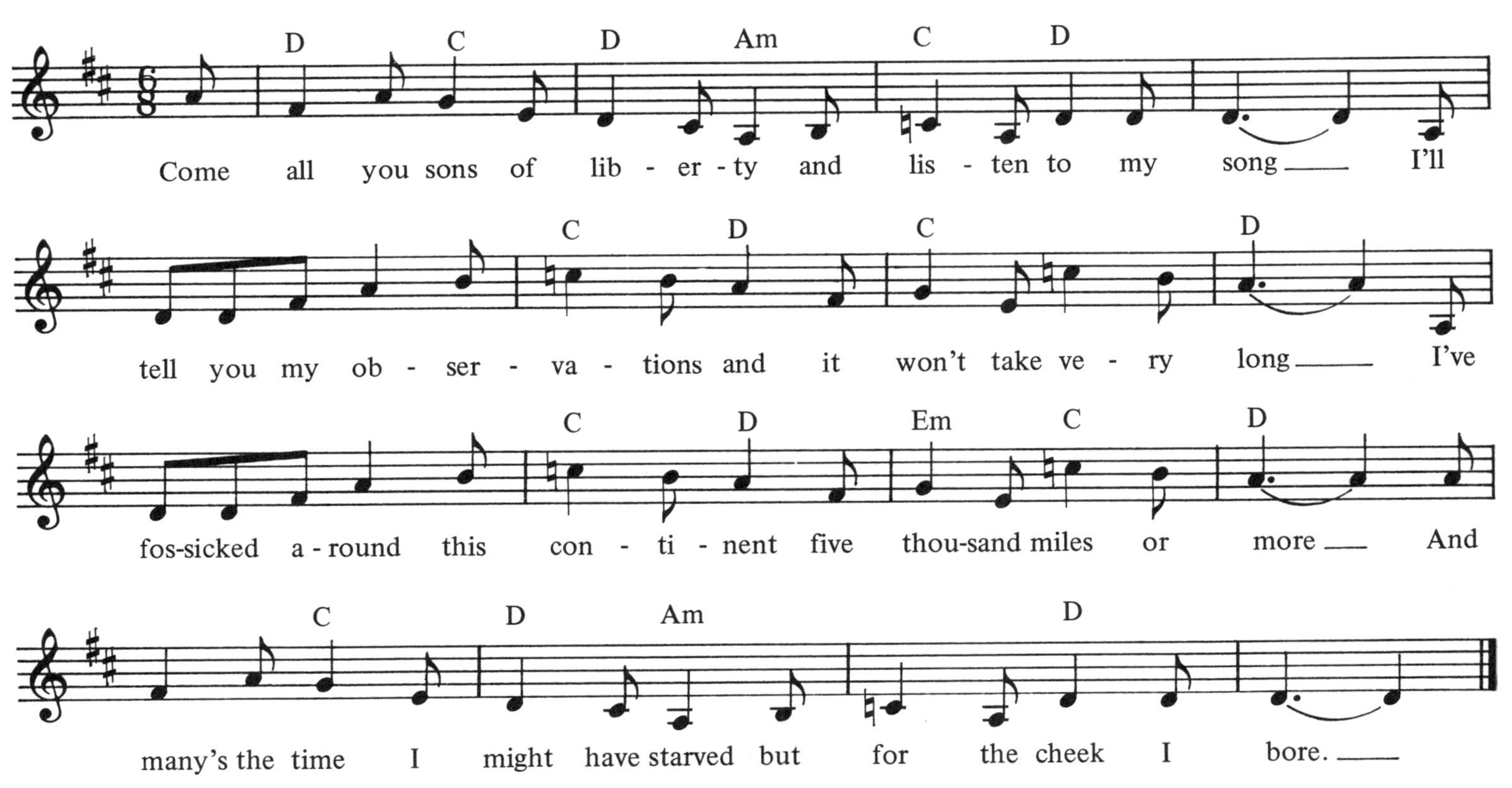
D C Am Em
D C D Am C D
Come all you sons of lib - er - ty and lis - ten to my song I'll
C D C D
tell you my ob - ser - va - tions and it won't take ve - ry long I've
C D Em C D
fos-sicked a - round this con - ti - nent five thou-sand miles or more And
C D Am D
many's the time I might have starved but for the cheek I bore.

Without a doubt the most widely circulated song in Australia's folk song treasure chest. When the ballad first appeared it became the convicts' anthem to annoy and distract their soldier masters. Eventually the song and even the tune were considered treasonous and there are reports of men being lashed for whistling "The Wild Colonial Boy".

There are a number of versions of this song where the bushranger appears as Jack Doolan, Jack Dowling, John Doolin, Jack Donohoe and other names, however, the story of the hold-up and hero's eventual death remain constant. "I'll shoot but not surrender," said the Wild Colonial Boy.

This version from the singing of Mr Herb Green of St Lucia, Queensland. Collected by Warren Fahey in 1973. Herb learnt the song from his workmates and said, "This song was sung by an awful lot of people – it's a very important song!". Herb uses the Jack Dowling text. Australian Folklore Unit Tapes, Australian National Library, Canberra.

I knew a wild colonial boy, Jack Dowling was his name,
He came of honest parents way down in Castlemaine.
He was his father's favourite son, his mother's hope and joy.
The pride of both his parents was the Wild Colonial Boy.

At the early age of sixteen he left his father's house;
Bushranging to the sunny south, Australia, he set out.
He robbed the wiry squatters, their stocks he did destroy;
A terror to Australia was this Wild Colonial Boy.

In sixty-one this daring youth commenced his wild career,
With a heart that knew no danger, no foeman did he fear.
He held the Beechworth mail-coach up, and robbed Judge MacEvoy,
Who trembled and gave up his gold to the Wild Colonial Boy.

He bade the Judge good morning, and told him to beware,
That he'd never rob a hearty chap who acted on the square;
"And never you rob a mother of her son and only joy
Or else he may turn outlaw like the Wild Colonial Boy."

One day along the mountainside Jack nimbly rode along,
Listening to the little birds, their merry little song.
Up rode three mounted troopers, Kelly, Davis and Fitzroy,
And cowardly tried to capture the Wild Colonial Boy.

Surrender now, Jack Dowling, you see it's three to one.
Surrender in the Queen's name, you daring highwayman.
Jack drew a pistol from his side, he aimed the lively toy;
"I'll shoot but not surrender," cried the Wild Colonial Boy.

He fired at trooper Kelly and he brought him to the ground
And on return from Davis received his mortal wound.
All tattered in his crimson gore was finished by Fitzroy;
How cowardly they did capture the Wild Colonial Boy.

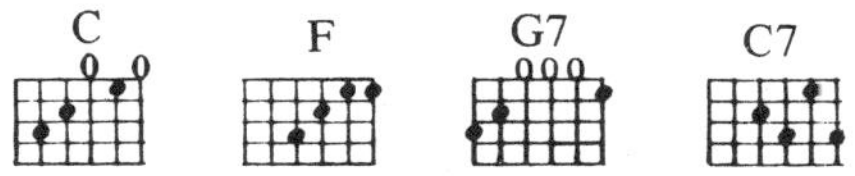

C F G7 C7

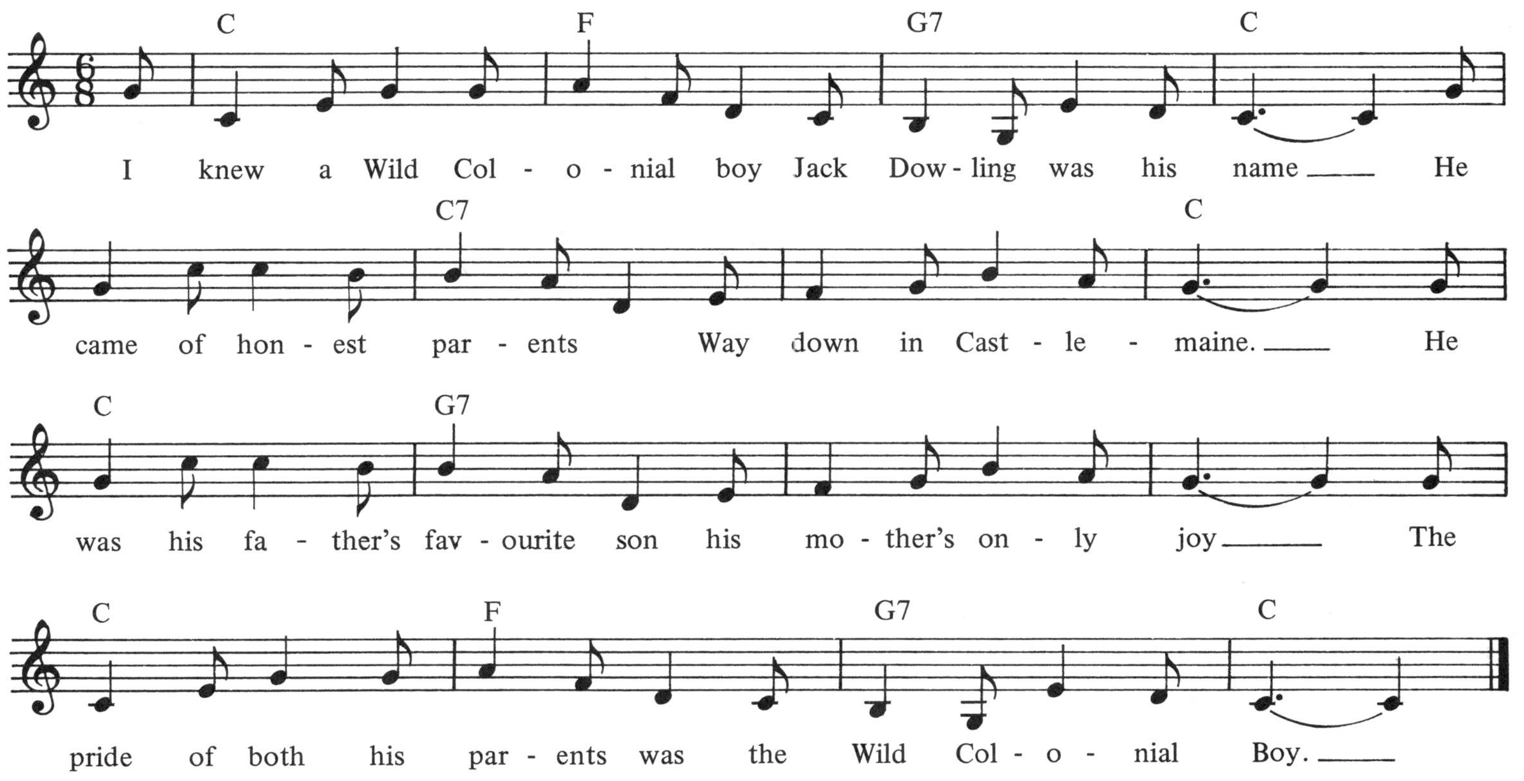

HA HA HA HA HA HA HA

The Wild Colonial Boy.

Bold Jack Donohue

The bushranger was, in general, looked upon as a sort of martyr to the convict system. It was he who had experienced the lash, the shame, the brutal taunt, from which convicts had suffered. It was he who rose against the dread consequences of their criminal law. He was the bold Robin Hood of their songs, and he was now the unfortunate victim of legal oppression, the captured of the chase.

It was commonly believed that any man capable of living in the Australian bush, by foul means or fair, was hero material. The story of Jack Donohue spread across the world – the king of all highwaymen!

From Joy Durst Memorial Australian Song Collection, *published by the Victorian Folk Music Club, Melbourne, 1980.*

There was a valiant highwayman of courage and renown,
Who scorned to live in slavery or humble to the Crown;
In Dublin city fair and free where first his breath he drew,
'Twas there they christened him the brave and bold Jack Donohue.

He scarce had been transported unto the Australian shore,
When he took to the highway as he had done before;
And every week in the newspapers was published something new
Concerning all the valiant deeds of bold Jack Donohue.

As Donohue was cruising one summer afternoon,
Little was his notion that his death would be so soon,
When to his surprise the horse-police appeared in his view,
And in quick time they did advance upon Jack Donohue.

The sergeant of the horse-police discharged his carbine
And called aloud on Donohue to fight or to resign;
"I'd rather range these hills around like wolf or kangaroo,
Than work one hour for the government," cried bold Jack Donohue.

Six rounds he fought the horse-police until the fatal ball,
Which pierced his heart with cruel smart caused Donohue to fall.
The sergeant and the corporal and all their cowardly crew,
It took them all their time to fell the bold Jack Donohue.

There were Freincy, Grant, bold Robin Hood and Brennan and O'Hare,
With Donohue the bushranger none of them could compare.
And how he's gone to heaven I hope with the saints and angels too,
May the Lord have mercy on the soul of bold Jack Donohue.

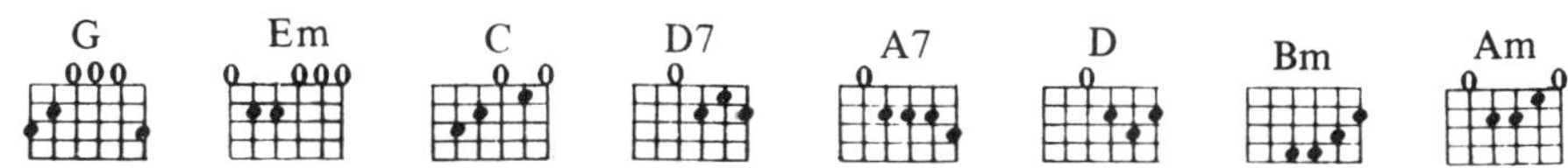
G Em C D7 A7 D Bm Am

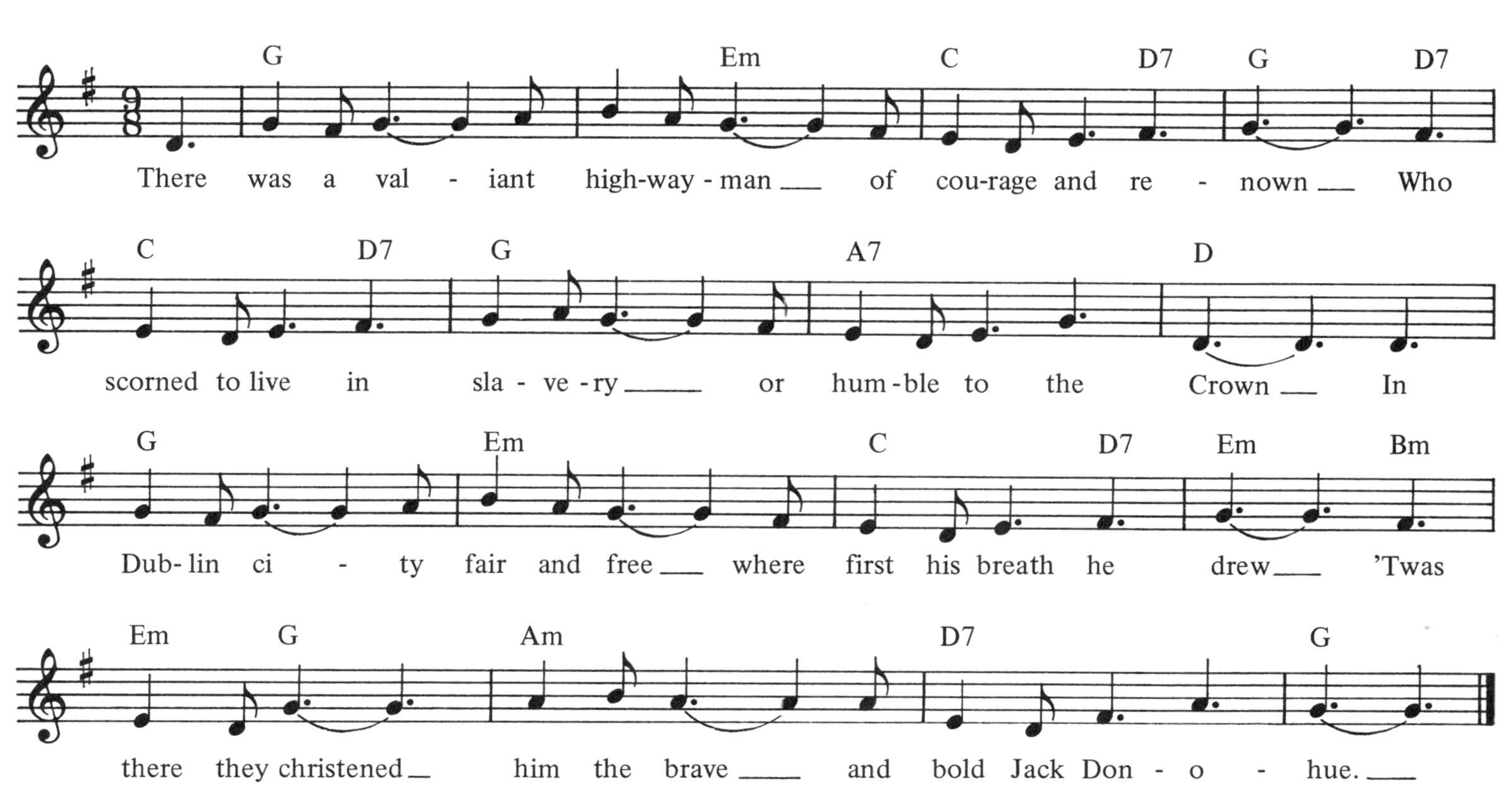
G Em C D7 G D7
There was a val - iant high-way - man of cou-rage and re - nown Who
C D7 G A7 D
scorned to live in sla - ve - ry or hum - ble to the Crown In
G Em C D7 Em Bm
Dub - lin ci - ty fair and free where first his breath he drew 'Twas
Em G Am D7 G
there they christened him the brave and bold Jack Don - o - hue.

The Morning of the Fray

Francis Christie was born at Boro Creek, near Goulburn, New South Wales, in 1830. A victim of circumstance, he turned bushranger and changed his name to Frank Gardiner, however, he was better known as "The Darkie" referring to his part-Aboriginal background. This song relates how his gang held up the gold-laden coach coming down from the Lachlan goldfields. The bounty of twelve thousand pounds was never found and legend has it that the gold is still buried out near Eugowra.

Original poem attributed to the bushranger, Frank Gardiner, from Old Pioneering Days in the Sunny South, *Charles MacAlister. This song version has been re-worked by British folklorist, A. L. Lloyd, who reckoned the poem too good not to be sung!*

It's all about bold Frank Gardiner, with the devil in his eye,
He said: "We've work before us, lads, we've got to do or die.
So blacken up your faces before the dead of night,
And it's over by Eugowra Rocks we'll either fall or fight."

CHORUS:
You can sing of Johnny Gilbert, Dan Morgan and Ben Hall,
But the bold and reckless Gardiner he's the boy to beat 'em all.

"**W**e'll stop the Orange escort with powder and with ball.
We'll shoot the coach to pieces and we'll down the peelers all.
We'll lift the diggers' money, we'll collar all their gold,
So mind your guns are killers now, my comrades true and bold."

So now off go the rifles, the battle has begun.
The escort started running, boys, all in the setting sun.
The robbers seized their plunder so saucy and so bold,
And they're riding from Eugowra Rocks encumbered with their gold.

And as with savage laughter they left that fatal place,
They cried: "We've struck bonanza, boys, we've won the steeplechase!"
And Gardiner their leader, he shouted aloud: "Hooray!
I think we've made our fortunes at Eugowra Rocks today!"

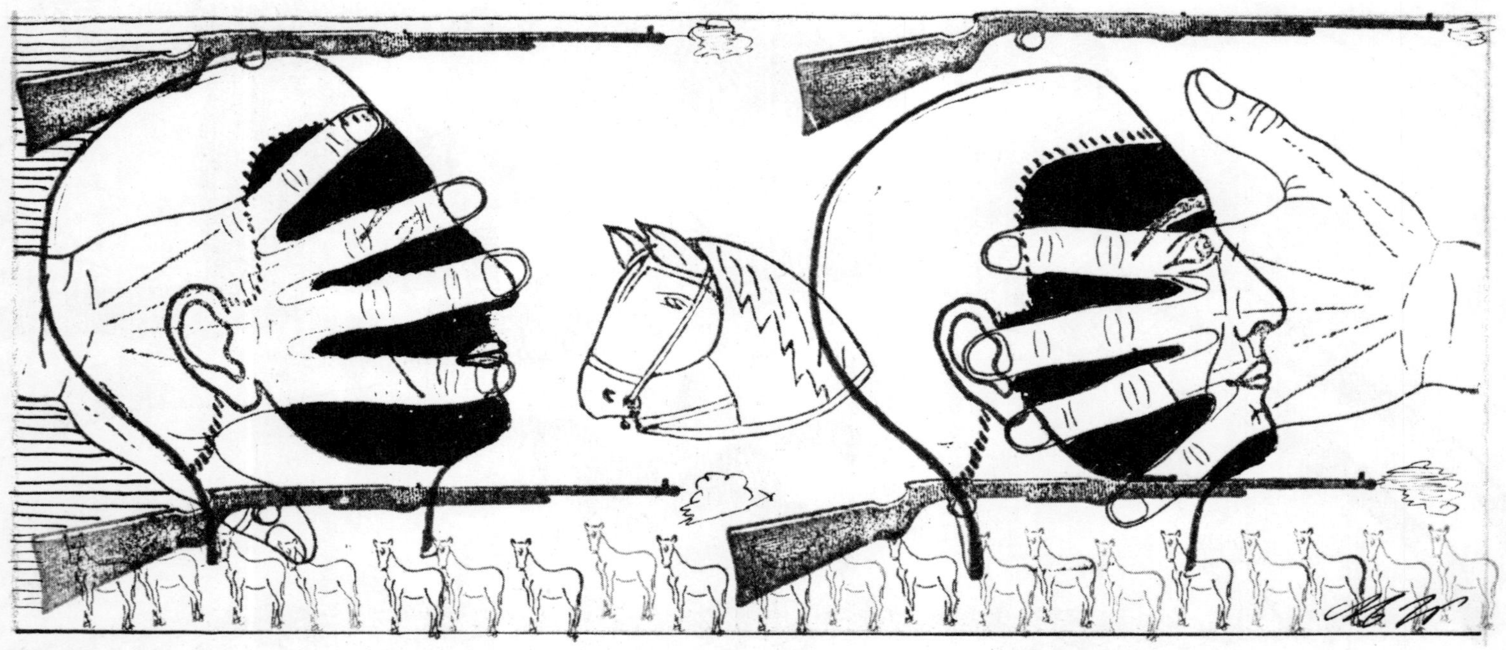

Dm B♭ Am
It's all about bold Frank Gard-ner__ with the De-vil in his eye___ he

Dm Am
said we've work be-fore us lads we've got to do or die.___ So

Dm B♭ F C
black-en up your fa-ces__ be-fore the dead of night and it's

Dm Am Dm
ov-er by Eu-gow-ra rocks we'll eith-er fall or fight. You can

Dm B♭ F C
sing of John-ny Gil-bert__ Dan Mor-gan or Ben Hall but the

C Am Dm
bold and reck-less Gard-ner he's the boy to beat them all.___

Frank Gardiner

To the Editor, Lachlan Miner Newspaper, 1862.

Dear Sir, ... It is said that I took the boots off a man's feet, and that I also took the last shillings that another man had, I wish it to be known that I did not do anything of the kind. The man that took the boots was in my company, and for doing so I discharged him ... silver, I never took from a man yet, and the shot that was fired at the sticking-up of Messrs. Horsington and Hewitt was by accident, and the man who did it I also discharged. As for a mean, low, petty, action – I never committed it in my life.

Fearing nothing, I remain, Prince of Tobymen,
Francis Gardiner, The Highwayman.

Frank Gardiner was captured and sentenced to thirty-two years gaol. After serving ten years he was remitted on the condition he left Australia. He travelled to America and opened a goldfields saloon where eventually he died of a bullet wound in a bar-room fight.

From Speewa No. 2 *published by Bush Music Club, Sydney. This version from Mrs Popplewell and collected by John Meredith and Nancy Keesing.*

Oh, Frank Gardiner he is caught at last he lies in Sydney jail,
For wounding Sergeant Middleton and robbing the Mudgee mail,
For plundering of the gold escort, the Carcoar Mail also:
And it was for gold he made so bold, and not so long ago.

His daring deeds surprised them all throughout the Sydney land,
And on his friends he gave a call, and quickly raised a band.
And fortune always favoured him, until the time of late,
Until Ben Hall and Gilbert met with their dreadful fate.

Young Vane, he has surrendered, Ben Hall's got his death wound,
And as for Johnny Gilbert, near Binalong was found,
He was all alone and lost his horse, three troopers came in sight,
And he fought the three most manfully, got slaughtered in the fight.

Farewell, adieu, to outlawed Frank, he was the poor man's friend.
The government has secured him, the laws he did offend.
He boldly stood his trial and answered in a breath,
"And do what you will, you can but kill; I have no fear of death!"

Day after day they remanded him, escorted from the bar,
Fresh charges brought against him from neighbours near and far,
And now it is all over; the sentence they have passed,
All sought to find a verdict, and "Guilty" 'twas at last.

When lives you take, a warning, boys, a woman never trust:
She will turn round, I will be bound, Queen's evidence, the first.
He's doing two-and-thirty years; he's doomed to serve the Crown,
And well may he say, he cursed the day he met with Mrs Brown.

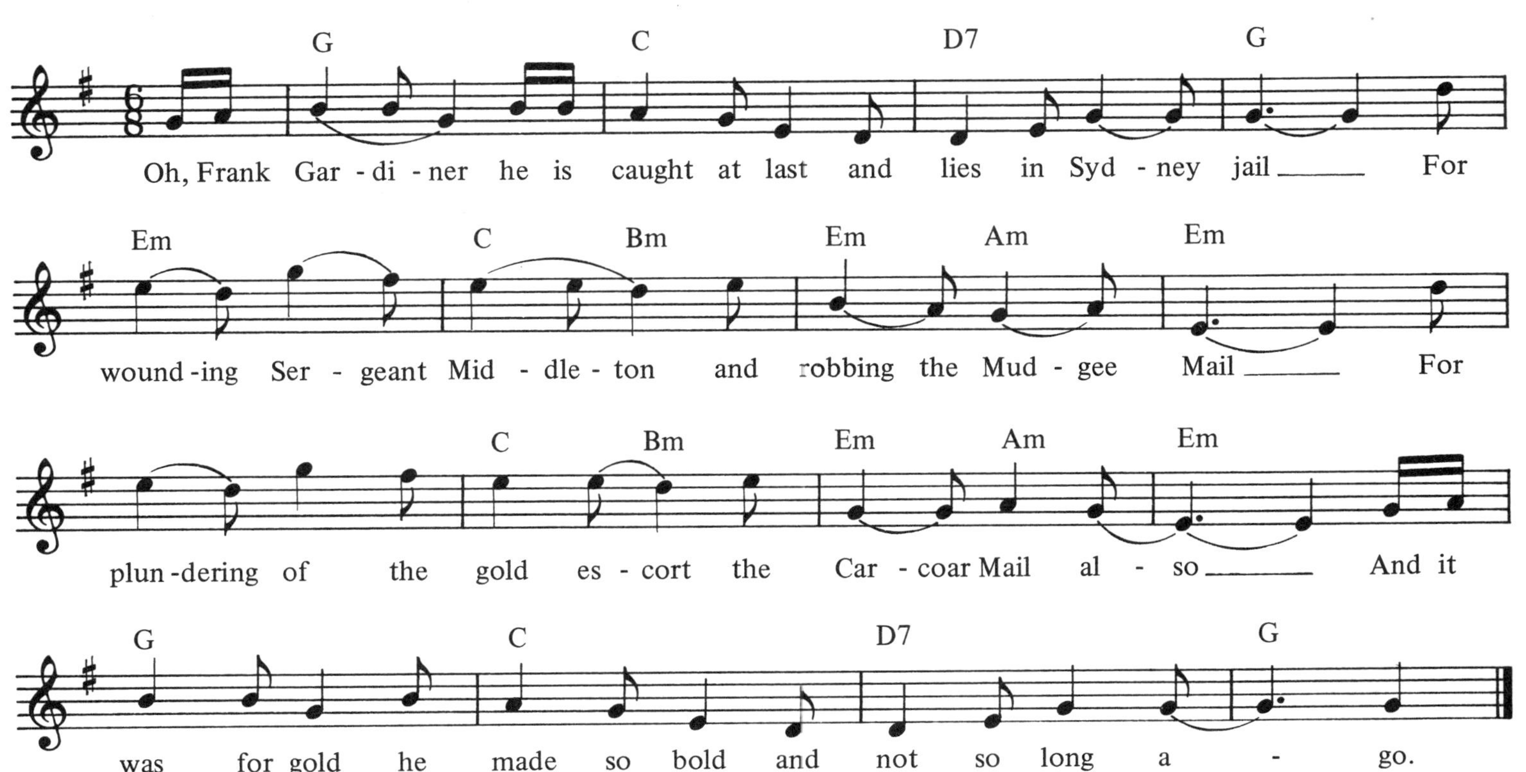

G C D7 Em Bm Am
G C D7 G
Oh, Frank Gar-di-ner he is caught at last and lies in Syd-ney jail ___ For
Em C Bm Em Am Em
wound-ing Ser-geant Mid-dle-ton and robbing the Mud-gee Mail ___ For
C Bm Em Am Em
plun-dering of the gold es-cort the Car-coar Mail al-so ___ And it
G C D7 G
was for gold he made so bold and not so long a-go.

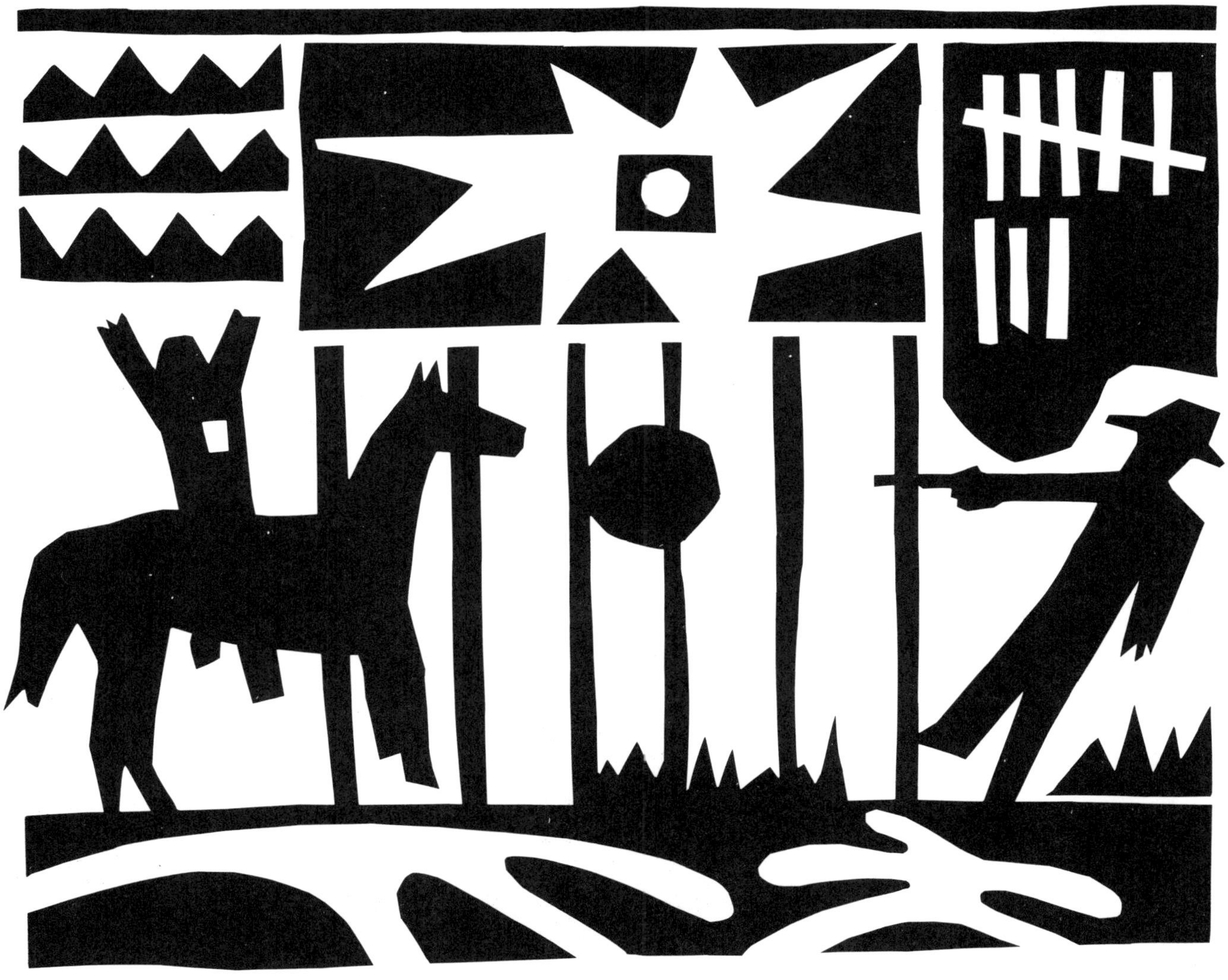

The Ballad of Ben Hall

In the 1860's the most successful and "noblest" bushranger was Ben Hall, native-born son of emancipated Irish and English parents. It was widely believed that the local constabulary forced Ben Hall off his property leaving him little option but to take to the open highways. As a bushranger Ben Hall established a reputation for robbing the wealthy and not the poor. He is celebrated in several traditional songs. Sir Fred refers to Sir Frederick Pottinger who was responsible for the "hunting" of Ben Hall. His inept handling of the case made him a public laughing stock, and led to his dishonourable discharge from the police force.

There are numerous versions of this ballad in print. Frank Clune included a very long and rather unsingable version in his Wild Colonial Boys. *Banjo Paterson printed another unsingable version in his collected works. I have decided to use the popular version as sung by members of the Bush Music Club, Sydney.*

Come all you sons of liberty and listen to my tale;
A story of bushranging days I will to you unveil.
It's of those valiant heroes, God bless them one and all!
So let us sit and sing: "God save the King, Dunn, Gilbert and Ben Hall."

Ben Hall he was a squatter, and he owned six hundred head;
A peaceful, quiet man was he until he met Sir Fred.
The troopers burnt his homestead down, his cattle perished all.
I've all my sentence yet to earn, was the word of brave Ben Hall.

John Gilbert was a flash cove, and young O'Meally too,
With Ben and Bourke and Dunn and Vane, they all were comrades true.
They bailed the Carcoar mailcoach up and made the troopers crawl.
There's a thousand pounds set on the heads of Dunn, Gilbert and Ben Hall.

From Bathurst down to Goulburn town they made the coaches stand,
While far behind, Sir Frederick's men went labouring thro' the land.
Then at Canowindra's best hotel they gave a public ball:
"We don't hurt them that don't hurt us," says Dunn, Gilbert and Ben Hall.

They held the gold-commissioner to ransom on the spot,
But young John Vane surrendered after Mickey Bourke was shot.
O'Meally at Goimbla did like a hero fall;
But "We'll take the country over yet," says Dunn, Gilbert and Ben Hall.

They never robbed a needy man, the records go to show,
But staunch and loyal to their mates, unflinching to the foe;
So we'll drink a toast tonight, my lads, their memories to recall.
Let us sit and sing: "God save the King, Dunn, Gilbert and Ben Hall!"

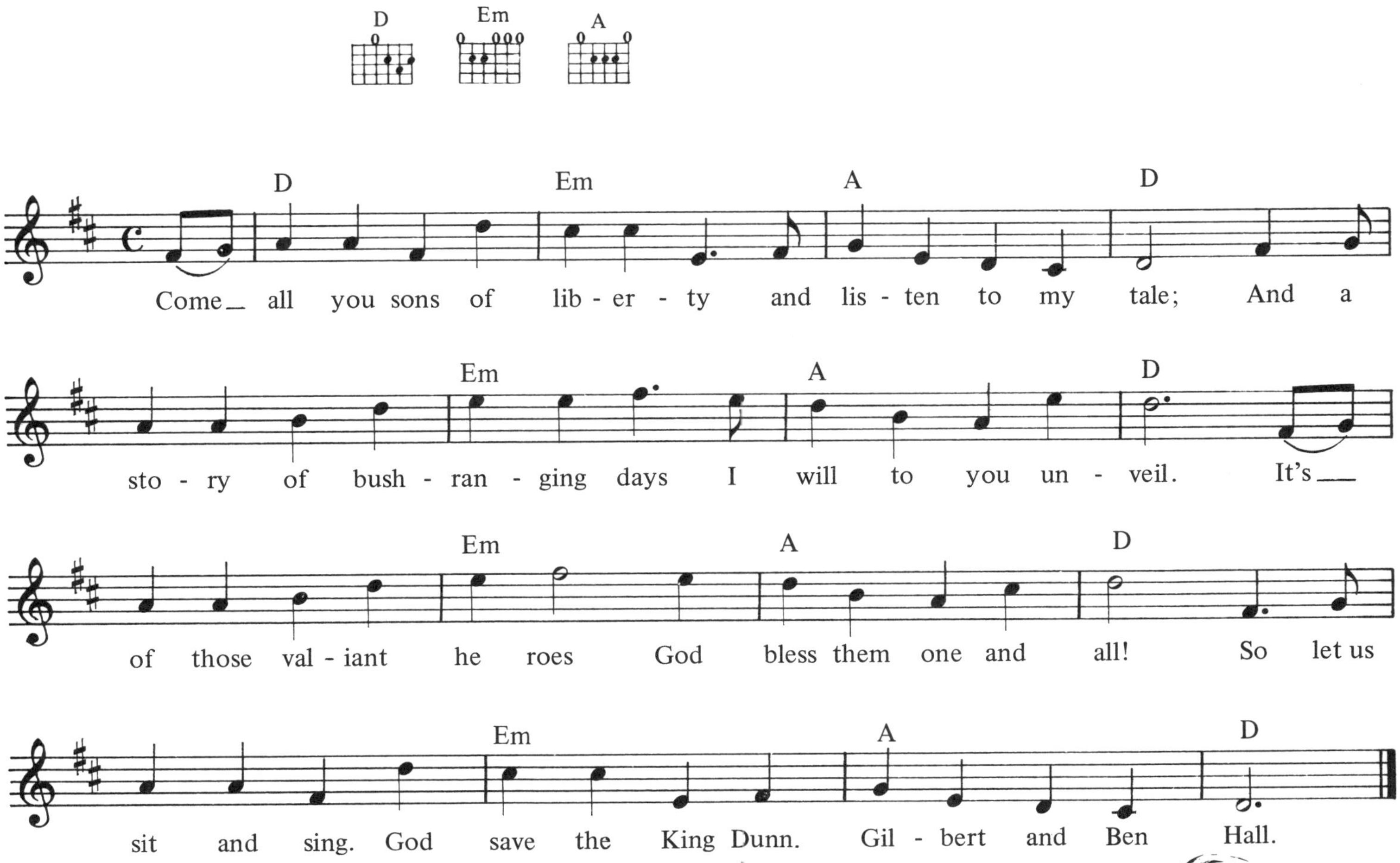

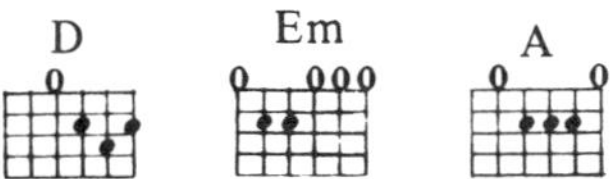

D Em A D
Come_ all you sons of lib - er - ty and lis - ten to my tale; And a
Em A D
sto - ry of bush - ran - ging days I will to you un - veil. It's_
Em A D
of those val - iant he roes God bless them one and all! So let us
Em A D
sit and sing. God save the King Dunn. Gil - bert and Ben Hall.

The Death of Ben Hall

"Poor Ben Hall, he had a property of his own near Forbes, and all the bad deeds that used to be done were pinned on poor Ben Hall. He was yarding his cattle this day and they came and took him away into the Forbes courthouse for trial for something he didn't do, and all his cattle were left in the stockyard to perish. The police could have pulled the sliprails down but they didn't.

And when he came out after doing a month in gaol the cattle were all carcasses. They burned his house down, his wife betrayed him and went off with another man ... Ben Hall, he took to the bush and turned out a highwayman. He had no choice but to become a bushranger." (From the reminiscences of Mrs Sally Sloane, Lithgow, 1978.)

On the morning of the fifth of May, 1865, Ben Hall was ambushed by ten troopers led by a black tracker, Bill Borgin. Hall's body, riddled with bullet holes, was paraded through the streets of Forbes by a triumphant police force.

From Speewa No. 3, *1955. Compare the Sally Sloane version from* Folk Songs of Australia, *Ure Smith.*

Come all Australia's sons to me,
A hero has been slain,
Cowardly butchered in his sleep,
Upon the Lachlan plain.

Ah, do not stay your seemly grief,
But let the teardrops fall,
Australian hearts will always mourn
The fate of bold Ben Hall.

He never robbed a needy man,
The records sure will show
How staunch and loyal to his mates,
How manly to the foe.

No brand of Cain e'er stamped his brow,
No widow's curse can fall;
Only the robber rich men feared
The coming of Ben Hall.

For ever since the good old days
Of Turpin and Duval,
The people's friends were outlaws,
And so was bold Ben Hall.

Yet savagely they murdered him,
Those coward bluecoat imps,
Who only found his hiding place
From sneaking peelers' pimps.

Yes, savagely they murdered him,
Oh, let your teardrops fall,
For all Australia mourns today
Her bravest son, Ben Hall.

No more he'll mount his gallant steed
To roam the ranges high;
Poor widow's friend in poverty,
Our bold Ben Hall, goodbye.

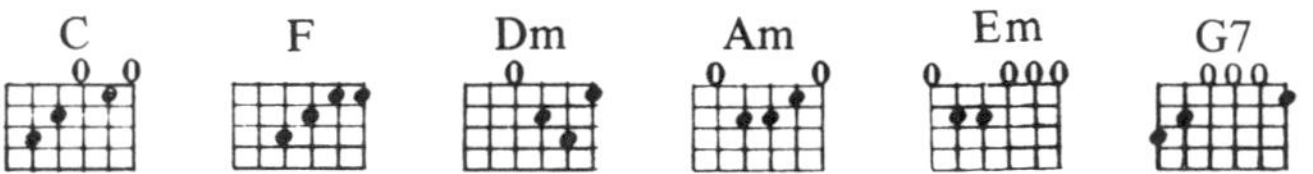
C F Dm Am Em G7

C F Dm C
Come all Aus-tra-lia's son's to me, A he-ro has been slain.
Am Dm F Em Dm G7 C
Cow-ard-ly butch-ered in his sleep up-on the Lach-lan Plain.

There were numerous "calls" on the goldfields. There was the call of "Joe" to warn unlicensed diggers that the police were approaching; there were the calls of the many travelling salesmen who hawked all manner of goods across the diggings. On the mine site the call of "look out below" refers to the ore-bucket being dropped on the windlass down the shaft. As most miners worked in pairs it was a standard warning to watch for the bucket.

From Charles Thatcher's Colonial Songster *C1857, Mitchell Library, Sydney. Thatcher gives the tune as "Smuggler King" but no one seems to be able to locate the original. The tune is from the singing of Sally Sloane and was collected by John Meredith.*

A young man left his native shores, for trade was bad at home;
To seek his fortune in this land, he crossed the briny foam;
And when he came to Ballarat, it put him in a glow
To hear the sound of the windlasses and the cry, "Look out below!"

Where'er he turned his wondering eyes great wealth he did behold,
And peace and plenty hand in hand, by the magic power of gold;
Quoth he, I am both young and strong, to the diggings I will go,
For I like the sound of the windlasses and the cry, "Look out below!"

Amongst the rest he took his chance, and his luck at first was vile,
But he still resolved to persevere, and at length he made his pile.
So says he, I'll take my passage, and home again I'll go,
And I'll say farewell to the windlasses and the cry "Look out below!"

Arrived in London once again, his gold he freely spent,
And into every gaiety and dissipation went;
But pleasure, if prolonged too much, oft causes pain, you know,
And he missed the sound of the windlasses and the cry, "Look out below!"

And thus he reasoned with himself: Oh, why did I return?
For the digger's independent life I now begin to yearn.
Here purse-proud lords the poor oppress, but there it is not so;
Give me the sound of the windlasses and the cry, "Look out below!"

So he started for this land again, with a charming little wife,
And he finds there's nothing quite comes up to a jolly digger's life.
Ask him if he'll go back again, he'll quickly answer, No,
For he loves the sound of the windlasses and the cry, "Look out below!"

F C Dm Am G7 Em Gm C7
F C F Dm Am
A young man left his na - tive shores for trade _ was bad at home _ To seek his for - tune
C Dm G7 C
in this land he crossed the bri - ny foam _ And when he came _ to Bal - la -rat it
C7 F Em Am Em
put him in _ a glow _ To hear the sound of the wind-las- ses and the cry Look out be -
Am F Gm F C7 F
low! _ to hear _ the sound of the wind - las - ses and the cry Look out be - low! _

B
O
N
K

During the goldrush days of the mid 1800's Australia saw several successful tours by Minstrel ensembles from both America and Britain. The "Hamfat Man" seems to fit comfortably into this characteristic song type. I presume the idea of the faithless Sara Ann "hooking" it off to Bathurst with a Chinese lover was an attempt to introduce racial humour.

From Chanson's Sydney Songster *with the tune the "Cuckoo's Nest", Mitchell Library, Sydney.*

White folks attention, and listen to my song,
I'll sing you a ditty, and I won't detain you long;
It's all about a pretty gal, whose name was Sara Ann,
And she fell deep in love with a ham fat man.

CHORUS:
Ham fat, soap fat, candle fat or lard,
Ham fat, cat fat, or any other man;
Jump into the kitchen as quick as you can,
With my roochee, coochee, coochee, the ham fat man.

The ham fat man, he fell deep in love,
All with Sara Ann, to be his turtle dove;
She dwelt in Sydney market, no. 13 was her stand,
And she sold polony sausages to the ham fat man.

Now the ham fat man, he couldn't stand the press,
For every day she wanted to buy a new dress;
His money it was gone and the faithless Sara Ann,
She hooked it off to Bathurst with a Chinaman.

Oh, all you young men take warning by my ditty,
Never trust a girl that lives in Sydney city;
For they're bound to play you falsely, and cheat you if they can,
Or serve you as they served out the ham fat man.

G D7 C
White folks attention and listen to my song I'll sing you a
ditty and I won't detain you long It's all about a pretty girl whose
name was Sara Ann And she fell deep in love with a Ham Fat
Man. Ham fat soap fat candle fat or lard. Ham fat
cat fat or any other man Jump into the kitchen As
quick as you can With my roo-chee coo-chee coo-chee the Ham Fat Man.

Coming Down the Flat

It would be hard to imagine life in the Australian bush without a hat. With sun that scorches into the land with a heat so intense that "you could fry an egg on the ground" – a hat is necessary. Of course, there are many types of bush hats and this gold-diggers' song mentions the ever-popular "cabbage tree" hat complete with streamers to scare off the flies, the digger wears a "wide-awake" as it is better suited for physical work, and finally, the troopers' leather cap gets a mention.

There was an old saying in the Victorian goldfields:
"On the goldfields of Ballarat,
You're scarce allowed to wear your hat;
Thrice lucky, he, who in its stead,
Will long get leave to wear his head!"

A Charles Thatcher song using a parody of "Coming Through The Rye", printed in The Barry O'Neil Songster.

If a body meet a body coming down the flat,
Should a body "Joe" a body, for having on a hat?
Some wear caps, some wide-awakes, but I prefer a hat,
Yet everybody cries out, "Joe!" coming down the flat.

The squatter loves his cabbage tree, with streamers hanging down,
He wears it always in the bush, and even when in town.
The cabbage tree may be his choice, but I prefer a hat,
Yet everybody calls out, "Joe!" coming down the flat.

The digger wears a wide-awake wherever he may go;
At the windlass, when washing up, and also down below.
The wide-awake may suit him well, but I prefer a hat,
Yet everybody cries out, "Joe!" coming down the flat.

The peeler has a leather cap about two pound in weight,
In pelting rain or broiling sun, to wear it is his fate.
The leather cap won't do for me, for I prefer a hat,
Yet everybody cries out, "Joe!" coming down the flat.

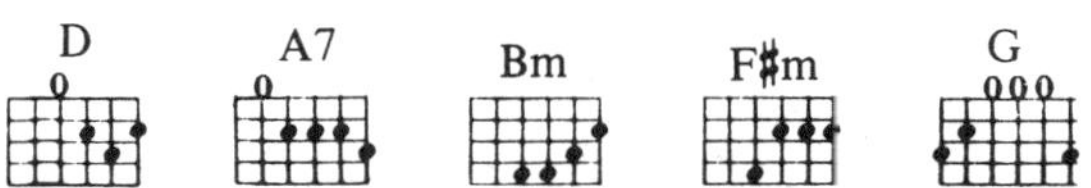
D
A7
Bm
F♯m
G

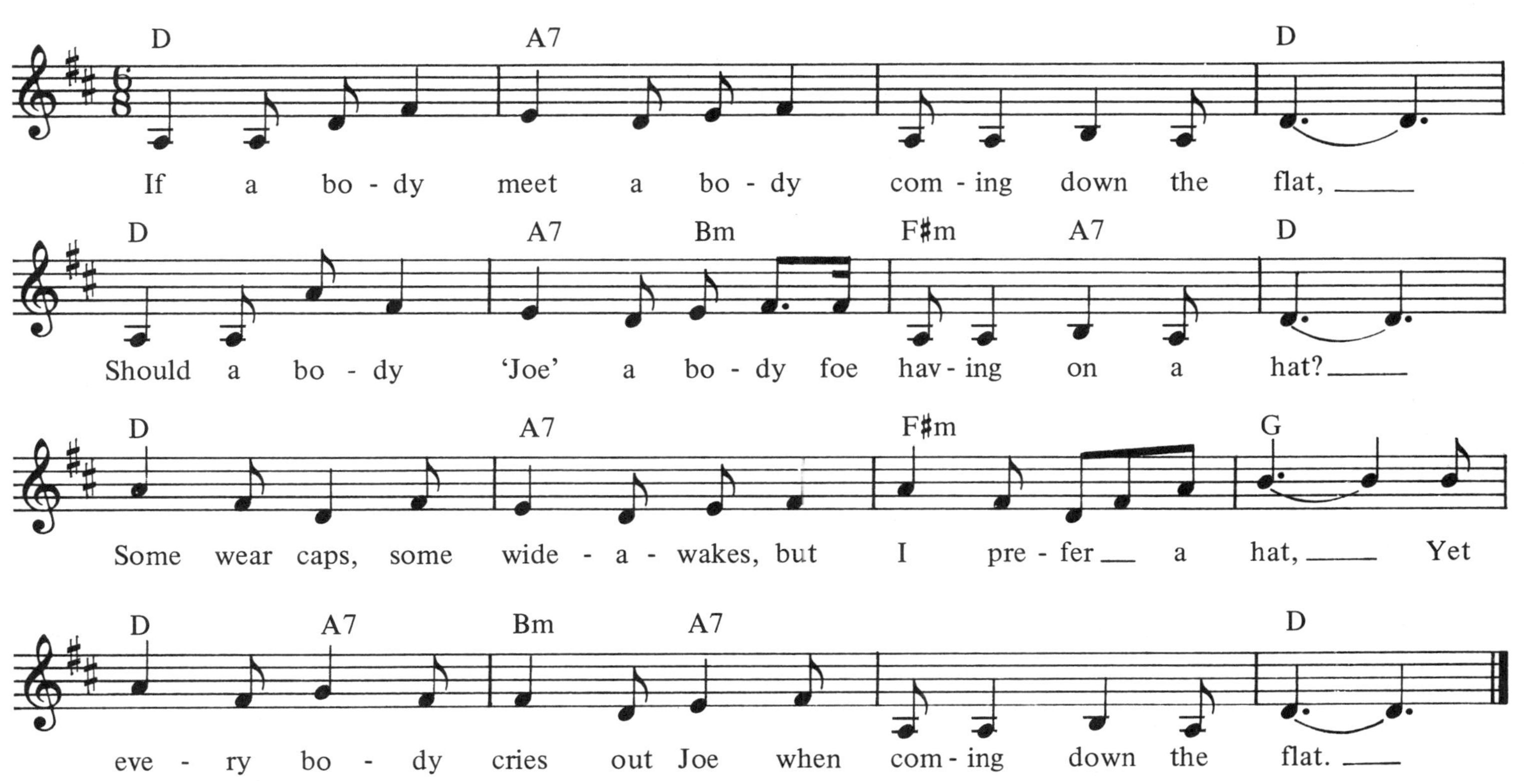
D A7 D
If a bo - dy meet a bo - dy com - ing down the flat,
D A7 Bm F♯m A7 D
Should a bo - dy 'Joe' a bo - dy foe hav - ing on a hat?
D A7 F♯m G
Some wear caps, some wide - a - wakes, but I pre - fer a hat, Yet
D A7 Bm A7 D
eve - ry bo - dy cries out Joe when com - ing down the flat.

Sam Holt

This popular song smacks of bush life – romance, gambling, bush work and mateship. Black Alice is described as "The old Mallee Gin with the straw through her nose, and teeth like a Moreton Bay shark". The song is in fact a parody on Ben Bolt which was written in 1848. In this case the parody is far better known than the original song.

A parody on Ben Bolt. Sung by swagman Jack Pobar, Toowoomba, Queensland, and collected by Warren Fahey, in 1973, Australian National Library.

Oh, don't you remember Black Alice, Sam Holt?
Black Alice, so dusky and dark.
Oh, the old Mallee Gin with the straw through her nose
And teeth like a Moreton Bay shark.

Or the terrible sheep-wash tobacco she smoked,
In a gunyah up there by the lake.
Or the grubs that she roasted, the lizards she stewed,
And the damper you taught her to bake.

Oh, don't you remember the moon's silvery sheen,
And the Warrego sandridges white?
And don't you remember the big bulldog ants
We caught in our blankets that night?

And don't you remember the creepers, Sam Holt,
That scattered their fragrance about?
And don't you remember the broken-down colt
You sold me and swore he was sound?

You were not the cleanest potato, Sam Holt,
You hadn't the cleanest of fins.
But you made your pile at the Tower, Sammy Holt,
And that covers the most of your sins.

And don't you remember the pasting you got
By the boys down in Callaghan's store,
When Tim Hooligan found a fifth ace in his hand
And you holding his pile upon four?

Oh, when's my time coming?
Perhaps never, I think,
And it's likely enough, your old mate
Will be humping his drum on the Hughenden Road,
To the end of the chapter of fate.

C F G G7

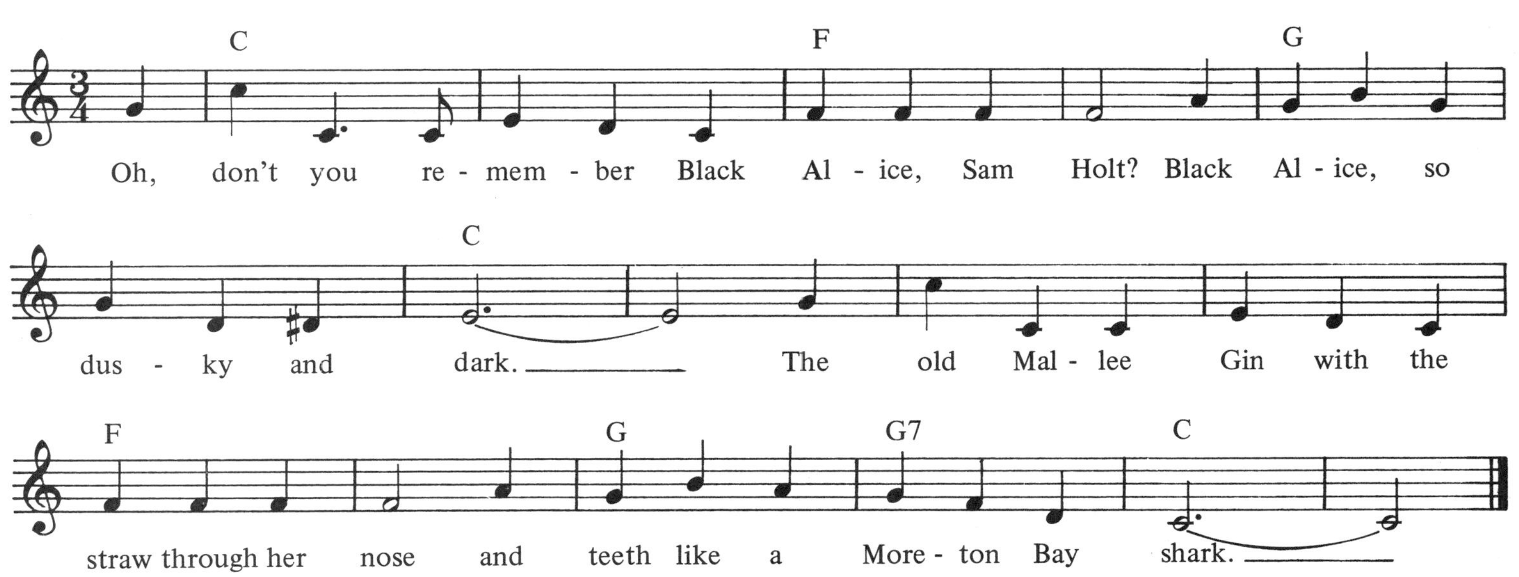

C F G
Oh, don't you re - mem - ber Black Al - ice, Sam Holt? Black Al - ice, so
C
dus - ky and dark. The old Mal - lee Gin with the
F G G7 C
straw through her nose and teeth like a More - ton Bay shark.

The Golden Gullies of the Palmer

Gold was discovered in Queensland's Palmer River in 1875. It was a re-enactment of the golden years of the 1860's with a whole new generation of fortune seekers arriving in well-laden boats from England, China and America. The track to the diggings was almost impenetrable. According to T. P. L. Weitmeyer in Missing Friends, *London, 1892, "a perfect famine was raging. Some men, after eating their horses and dogs, used to boil their blucher boots for twenty-four hours and eat them with weeds". Such was the lust for gold.*

Printed in Colonial Born *by G. Firth Scott. The Palmer River rushes date around the mid 1870's and the song would have been in circulation soon after. The tune is indicated as "Marching Through Georgia".*

Then roll the swag and blanket up, and let us haste away,
To the Golden Palmer, boys, where everyone they say,
Can get his ounce of gold or it may be more, a day,
In the Golden Gullies of the Palmer.

CHORUS:
Hurrah! Hurrah! We'll sound the jubilee,
Hurrah! Hurrah! And we will merry be,
When we reach the diggings, boys, there the nuggets see,
In the Golden Gullies of the Palmer.

Kick at troubles when they come boys, the motto be for all;
And if you've missed the ladder in climbing Fortune's wall,
Depend upon it boys, you'll recover from the fall,
In the Golden Gullies of the Palmer.

Then sound the chorus once again and give it with a roar,
And let its echoes ring boys, upon the sea and shore,
Until it reaches the mountains, where the gold is in galore,
In the Golden Gullies of the Palmer.

G C Em A7 D7

Then roll the swag and blan- ket up and let us haste a - way, To the Gol- den
Pal - mer boys, where eve - ry-one they say, Can get his ounce of gold or it
may be more a day, In the Gol- den Gul -lies of the Pal - mer. Hur -
- rah! Hur - rah! We'll sound the ju - bi - lee, Hur - rah! Hur -
- rah! and we will mer - ry be, When we reach the dig - gings boys,
there the nug - gets see, In the Gol- den Gul- lies of the Pal - mer.

The New Chum Chinaman

The Chinese were also struck with gold fever and despite much controversy they arrived in their thousands ready to wash, dig and shake the cradle. In a land where no-one could understand their strange language or customs they formed enclaves for their mutual protection. The Chinese immigration became a bitter question that finally led to the introduction of immigration control laws. In this rather lighthearted song the Irish digger feels the only way he is going to succeed is to turn himself into a Chinese digger. Pat McCann became Ah Pat!

From the singing of Mrs V. Leonard, Lappa Junction, North Queensland. Collected by Ron Edwards, in 1966. Informant indicated the song dated from the time of the Palmer River rushes when Cooktown had an eighty per cent Chinese population. Warren Fahey collected a similar version with a different chorus from Mr Joe Watson, Caringbah, New South Wales, in 1976.

Oh, what's the use of talking,
They won't let the white man live,
For if there's any work to do,
To the Chinaman they will give.
Come all you straight-haired natives,
Take my advice and plan,
Just turn your skin the right side in
And become a Chinaman.

CHORUS:
Oh, goodbye Mrs Doolin,
Oh, ta-ta Mrs Doyle,
No more I'll roam around Ireland,
Nor plague your emerald isle,
For I am bound for China,
It's there I will be found,
I'll go and join the Chinamen,
For Hong Kong I am bound.

As soon as I ever I put my foot
Upon the flowery shore,
I'll score the whiskers off my face,
They won't grow any more.
I'll turn my eyebrows upside down
My skin I'll yellow tan,
I'll eat my rice with chopsticks,
Like a new chum Chinaman.

I'll wear a pigtail six feet long,
And roll the lingo round,
I'll wear a pair of Chinese pants,
With bottoms neat and grand,
And I will call myself Ah Pat,
Though my name is Pat McCann,
And back to Queensland I will come,
As a new chum Chinaman.

I'll buy a pair of Chinese shoes
And I'll wear them on the land,
I'll meet some Chinese chaps some day,
And they'll grasp me by the hand,
They will say "Good day, good day,
Are you here to stay?
You are very welcome,
Welcome to our land."

I'll learn to carry baskets,
With a bamboo on my back,
I'll fill them up with yellow gold
That I find on the track.
So if I make my fortune
I'll be coming back
And marry the girl I left behind,
Her name is Magpie Black.

D G E7 A A7

D G
Oh what's the use of talk - ing, they won't let the white man give, for
D E7 A
if there's an - y work to do to the Chin-a - man they will give, come
D G
all you straight-haired na - tives take my ad - vice and plan, just
D A7 D
turn your skin to the right side in; be - come a Chin - a - man.
YELLOW TAN
Billington

The Carrier's Song

It is no secret that Australia has some of the most peculiar roadways in the world. In a continent where the roads seem never-ending and the climate ever-changing it is not uncommon to find roads thick with churned mud and next season the wet has been replaced by dry powdery dust. The old time carrier travelling by horse-drawn power would frequently curse the weather, be it wet or dry.

As printed in George Chanson's The Sydney Songster *published in the gold "heydays" of the 1860's. The tune is the much used "Bow Wow Wow".*

Dave Mathias

To sing you all a pleasant song, I now feel in the mind, sir.
For travelling on the road each day, there's something strange you'll find, sir.
It's strange to know the once good tracks no longer we can trust, sir,
For every road we travel now, there's nothing there but dust, sir.

CHORUS:
Dust! Dust! Dust! along the roads there's nothing there but dust, dust, dust.

I pity those poor carriers, who on the road oft travel,
With gibs of horses quite knocked up, by ruts and sand and gravel,
No water on the way they find, though they in vain may seek, sir,
For dust has filled each waterhole, each gully and dry creek, sir.

If to New England e'er they go, and take much heavy loading,
I fear they'll find their horses then will need some extra goading.
As stuck upon the Moonbi Range, in them they cannot trust, sir.
Do all they can, they will not pull the high load through the dust, sir.

Now, too much rain's a different thing to what we do require,
In rainy weather well we know, you can't keep in the fire,
As stuck upon some little creek, you ask to get a pull out,
From some bull puncher, who has just got his own team with wool out.

CHORUS: (for last two verses)
Rain! Rain! Rain! along the roads there's nothing there but rain, rain, rain.

So now I've sung in humble rhyme the trials of the road, sir,
Of what a driver must endure, who takes a heavy load, sir.
How he may be stuck fast enough for many, many weeks, sir,
Though 'twould be nought if government would only bridge the creeks, sir.

F C7 B♭

F C7 F
To sing you all a plea - sant song, I now feel in the mind, — sir, For
C7 F C7
travel - ling on the road each day, there's some- thing strange you'll find, — sir It's
F B♭ C7 F
strange to know that once good tracks no lon - ger we can trust, — sir, For
B♭ F C7
eve - ry road we tra - vel now there's noth - ing there but dust, — sir.
F B♭ F
Dust! Dust! Dust! a - long the roads there's noth - ing there but dust, dust, dust. —

I've Been to Australia, Oh!

Life in the colonies saw the creation of many songs relating the woes of peculiar society. This classic and epic song whines its way through just about every misfortune a new arrival could expect. It's got the lot!

From a broadside in the Mitchell Library, Sydney. The music has been set to the Irish song "The Old Alarm Clock" by Declan Affley, 1981.

One time I wasn't pleased at home, so I away did go,
With all my goods and chattels unto Australia-oh!
As big as Old Dan Lambert, I weigh'd thirteen stone all right,
And when I returned they took me for a yard of tripe.

CHORUS:
So now my friends take my advice, and never think to go,
Or you will rue the day you went unto Australia-oh.

I had two and twenty hundred pounds, I had, upon my life,
I had bonnets, hats, two dogs and cats, for me and my dear wife;
When landing on Australia's shore, I knew not what to do,
They robbed me of my hat and shirt, my stockings, coat, and shoes.

A black man took away my wife, that was a treat for me,
They stole my wig just like a pig, and tied me to a tree,
A woman let me loose, and made me dig the ground,
Potatoes there, I do declare, are eighteenpence a pound.

A pound of steak is seven bob, twelve shillings for a mop,
And two and twopence-halfpenny for a pound of mutton chops;
Ten and sixpence for an ounce of tea, oh, dear! such nobby stuff,
And three and sevenpence-farthing for half an ounce of snuff.

Two shillings for a glass of gin, and ninepence for a leek,
And if old ladies want to buy a bit of pussy's meat
The rogues will charge them half a crown, how cruel is not that,
And scarcely give them half enough to satisfy a cat.

There, table beer I do declare, is thirteen bob a pot,
And they'll charge you half a guinea for a bottle of ginger pop;
Two and ninepence for a baked sheep's head, a shilling for a pipe,
And six and threepence-farthing for half a pound of tripe.

Sixpence-halfpenny for a lollipop, and ninepence for a lemon,
One and twopence-halfpenny for a little pickled herring;
Tenpence for a cabbage small, from an Australian garden;
For a bit of soap to wash your shirt, thirteen and threepence-farthing.

Fifty-seven pounds a year for a house that's got no windows,
Two and tenpence-halfpenny for a nightcap full of cinders,
Sixpence for a needle, made of Australian lead,
And one and eightpence-halfpenny for a dirty skein of thread.

They'll charge you seven shillings for a pint of mouldy peas,
Six and ninepence-farthing for a pound of rotten cheese.
Of going a-gold-digging, friends, I think I've had my full,
May the devil take Australia, I'll live with Old John Bull.

All them that like to emigrate, across the seas may go,
They'll never catch me again going to Australia-oh.

D
Bm
Em
A
G
E7
A7

D Bm Em A D G
One time I was-n't pleased at home, so I a-way did go, With all my goods and chat-tles un-
E7 A7 G D Em
-to Aust-ra-lia-o, As big as old Dan Lam-bert I weighed thir-teen stone all right, And when
D Em A7 D G D
I re-turned they took me for a yard of tripe. So now my friends take my ad-vice, and
Em A D Em A7 D
ne-ver think to go, Or you will rue the day you went un-to Aust-ra-lia-o.

A very complete text detailing the exploits of the famous Kelly Gang. Ned Kelly was born in Victoria in 1855. He was the son of a Tipperary Irishman sentenced at the age of twenty-one to seven years transportation for stealing two pigs. The Kelly gang were not highway robbers but concentrated on the banks at Euroa, where they took two thousand pounds, and Jerilderie, where they took two thousand, one hundred and forty-one pounds. There have been countless ballads, poems, plays, stories, paintings and films about the Kellys but Ned is best remembered for two sentences: when he was hanged in Melbourne in 1880 his last words were "such is life", and the statement: "Game as Ned Kelly" is now an accepted part of the Australian language. (Continued next spread.)

The Ballad Of The Kelly Gang

This very complete text from the repertoire of the late Joe Watson of Caringbah, New South Wales, was collected in 1974 by Warren Fahey. Australian Traditional Singer – Joe Watson, published in Folklore Occasional Paper No.8, *Banksiaman Press.*

Oh Paddy dear and did you hear the news that's going round?
On the head of bold Ned Kelly they have placed five thousand pound;
For Byrne, Steve Hart and Dan a thousand each they'll give,
But if the sum was doubled, sure, the Kelly boys would live.

It was in November '78 when the Kelly gang came down,
Just after shooting Kennedy at famed Euroa town,
Blood horses they were all upon, revolvers in their hands;
They took the township by surprise, and gold was their demand.

Into the bank Ned Kelly walked to bail up, oh he did say:
"Unlock your safes, hand out your cash, be quick, do not delay."
Without a murmur they obeyed the robber's bold command,
Ten thousand pounds in silver and gold they gave into his hand.

"**O**ut with all the firearms you have," the audacious robber said,
"Hand out all your cartridges, or – a bullet through your head.
Your wives and children must come, and make them look alive.
Get into this conveyance and we'll take 'em for a drive."

Oh they drove them to a station about five miles away,
Where twenty men already had been bailed up all that day;
A hawker shared their fate as everybody knows,
He came in handy to the gang, supplying them with clothes.

They destroyed communication by cutting down the wire,
And of their left-off clothing they made a small bonfire.
Throughout the whole affair, my boys, they never fired a shot,
And the way they worked was splendid and they'll never be forgot.

It's hard to think such plucky hearts in crime should be employed,
But for police and prosecution they've all been much annoyed.
Revenge is sweet and in the bush they can defy the law;
Such sticking-up and plundering, colonials never saw!

Oh Paddy dear do shed a tear, I can't but sympathise!
Those Kelly's are the devil, and they've made another rise:
This time to cross the Billabong Creek, near Morgan's ancient beat,
They've robbed the banks of thousands and in safety did retreat.

They rode into Jerilderie at twelve o'clock one night.
They roused the police out from their beds, who were in a hell of a fright.
They took them in their nightshirts, though I'm afraid to tell;
And covered them with revolvers and locked them in a cell.

They then acquainted the womenfolk, that they intended to stay,
To take possession of the camp, until the following day.
They fed their horses in the stalls, without the slightest fear,
And went to rest their weary limbs till daylight did appear.

So next morning it was Sunday, of course they must be good;
They dressed themselves in trooper's clothes and Ned he chopped some wood.
No one was expecting them; for troopers all they passed —
And Dan, the most religious one, took the trooper's wife to mass.

Oh they spent the day most pleasantly with plenty of good cheer,
With beef steaks and onions, tomato sauce and beer.
The ladies in attention indulged in pleasant talk,
And just to ease the troopers' minds – they took their wives for a walk!

On Monday morning early, still masters of the ground,
They took their horses to the forge and had them all shod all round.
Their packs were brought and mounted there, plans laid out all so well,
In company with the bobbies they stuck up the Royal Hotel.

Sure they bailed up all the servants and locked them in a room,
Saying, "Do as we do bid you, or death will be your doom."
A Chinese cook "No savvy," cried, not knowing what to fear,
But they brought him to his senses with a lifting under the ear.

So they shouted for all hands and they paid for all they drank,
Then two of them remained in charge and two went to the bank.
The manager could not be found, so Kelly in great wrath,
Searched high and low and found him in his bath!

But now where they've gone is a mystery, the bobbies cannot tell,
And until I hear from them – I'll bid you all farewell!

NED KELLY, THE BUSHRANGER.

My Name is Edward Kelly

This rare Kelly ballad captures the hatred the Kelly gang felt for the police force. This feeling of anger and frustration also spread throughout the population, many siding with the Kelly gang. In the eyes of the bush-workers, and of a great many other colonists, bushrangers derived added prestige merely from being, so to speak, the traditional opponents of the police.

Outstanding ballad from the singing of Cyril Duncan, Hawthorne, Queensland. Collected by Warren Fahey, in 1973, and appears in Australian Folklore Unit Index, Australian National Library, Canberra. Note variations from earlier collected version (Bob Michell and Stan Arthur) that appears in Penguin Book of Australian Folksongs.

My name is Edward Kelly, I'm honoured vastly well.
I rule supreme, my word is law, wherever I may dwell.
My friends are all united, my mates and army near;
We sleep beneath some shady tree, no danger do we fear.

Now the first of my adventures was through my sister dear,
Who was grossly insulted and put in bodily fear;
And when I came to hear of this it made my heart ache;
I took to the hills to have revenge, all for my sister's sake.

I am young and in my youthful days, I'm twenty-four years old.
I spent some time in vanity among young girls so bold;
But now I am a-robbing, and loudly my guns do roar.
'Twas there I shot poor Kennedy, which grieved my heart full sore.

In Mansfield that fair township where I was bred and born,
Oft times have I roamed those hills from dark till early morn,
But now I am a-robbing upon the Queen's Highway;
We fight the traps and rob the banks, and never run away.

Now the troopers they are all sent out to search the country round,
To bring in this notorious gang, but the Kelly's can't be found.
The Kelly's are in the ridges, the police drew up in ranks,
I think it's time, and off we go, and rob another bank.

I never would surrender to any coat of blue,
Or any man that wears a crown belonged to the crew.
They're game, there is no doubt of it, when they are on the beat,
But it took ten traps to take Ben Hall when he was fast asleep.

I'd rather die like Donahue, that bushranger so brave,
Than be taken by the Government to be treated like a slave.
I'd rather fight with all my might as long as I'd eyes to see;
I'd rather die ten thousand deaths than die on the gallow's tree.

Now all young men take my advice, that's bent on a roving life;
Pray do not roam but stay at home, settle down and take a wife.
For if you go a-robbing upon the Queen's Highway
You'll have to fight with all your might, or else lay down and die.

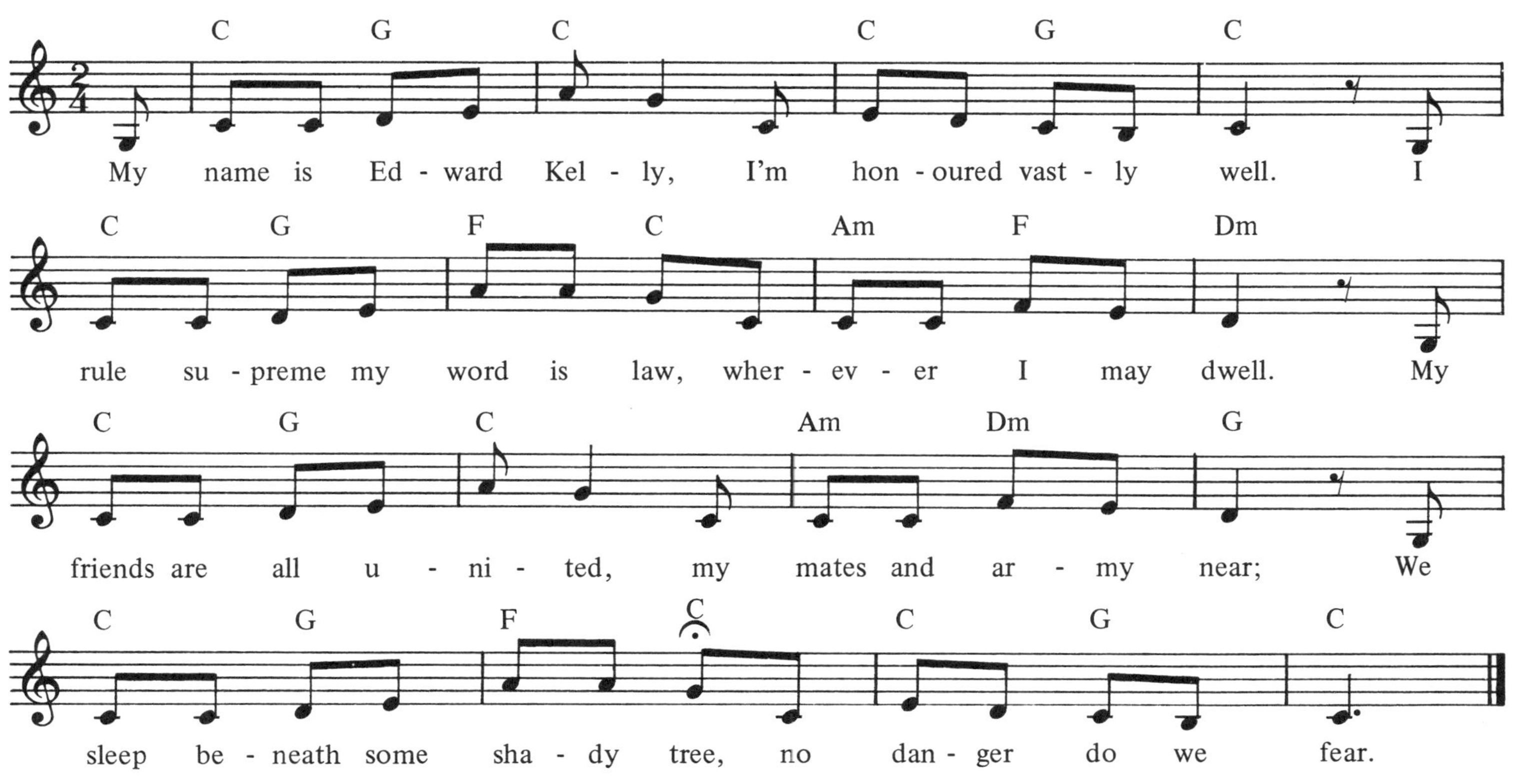
C G F Am Dm
C G C C G C
My name is Ed - ward Kel - ly, I'm hon - oured vast - ly well. I
C G F C Am F Dm
rule su - preme my word is law, wher - ev - er I may dwell. My
C G C Am Dm G
friends are all u - ni - ted, my mates and ar - my near; We
C G F C C G C
sleep be - neath some sha - dy tree, no dan - ger do we fear.

Farewell to Greta

A strange but somewhat dramatic song telling of the Kelly brothers separation from their sister. The first two verses see Ned Kelly addressing his sister Kate and verses three, four and five have Kate farewelling her brothers and warning them to stick together.

> *"And so they took Ned Kelly and hanged him in the jail,*
> *For he fought singlehanded although in iron mail.*
> *And no man singlehanded can hope to break the bars;*
> *It's a thousand like Ned Kelly who'll hoist the Flag of Stars".*
> *— John Manifold.*

A composite of two collected versions. Verses one and two from Jack Pobar, Toowoomba, Queensland, collected in 1973, by Warren Fahey, and verses three, four and five from Mrs Peatey, collected in 1959 by members of the Folk Lore Society of Victoria.

Farewell, my home in Greta, my sister Kate farewell,
It grieves my heart to leave you, but here I cannot dwell;
They placed a price upon my head, my hands are stained with gore,
And I must roam the forest wild, within the Australian shore.

But if they cross my chequered path, by all I hold on earth,
I'll give them cause to rue the day their mothers gave them birth.
I'll shoot them down like carrion crows that roam our country wide,
And leave their bodies bleaching along some woodland side.

Oh, Edward, darling brother, surely you would not go
So rashly to encounter with such a mighty foe;
Now don't you know that Sydney and Melbourne are combined,
And for your apprehension, Ned, there are warrants duly signed?

To eastward lies great Bogong, towering to the sky,
From east to west and then you'll find that's Gippsland lying by.
You know the country well, Ned, so take your comrades there,
And profit by your knowledge of the wombat and the bear.

And let no childish quarrelling cause trouble in the gang,
But stick with one another and guard my brother Dan;
See, yonder ride four troopers, one kiss before we part;
Now haste and join your comrades: Dan, Joe Byrne and Stevey Hart.

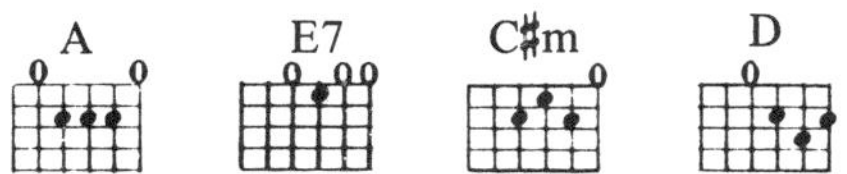
A
E7
C♯m
D

A E7 C♯m D A E7
Fare - well my home in Gre - ta ___ my ___ sis - ter Kate fare - well It
A E7 A
grieves my heart to leave you ___ But here I can not dwell.

Pint Pot and Billy

An odd song from the goldfields that hints at gold fever. "Once you get the taste of gold", so claim the old-time prospectors, "you can't ever rid yourself of the dream because dreams sometimes come true". Mention is made of two bushrangers – the infamous "Mad Dan" Morgan and Ben Hall. Scroggins is a general term applied to squatters. I remember talking to an old prospector who worked the mullock heaps of Bendigo: "Every now and then you'll come across a pipe or a leader. Trouble is, there's an awful lot of Victoria with it, too!"

As sung by Cyril Duncan of Hawthorne, Queensland. Collected by Warren Fahey, in 1973. A recorded version appears on "Man Of The Earth" Larrikin Records LRF001.

I dined with the swells in famed Piccadilly,
Took tea with my cousins in Horsemonger Lane,
And now I am stranded on my own native shore,
I'll go back to Australia to the goldfields again.

When I asked for a nobbler they asked what I meant sir,
I called them all "new chums" and that served them right.
Oh dear, don't I sigh for my famous stock horses,
I had when droving on One Man Plain.

A mountain flash rider, a son of old Scroggins,
Oh dear, don't I wish I was back there again.
Oh don't you remember Ben Hall and his troupe sir,
Who stuck up the escort and well-guarded mail?

And about that wretch Morgan I could yet relate sir,
But history would serve me to tell a sad tale.
Then give me Australia with my pint pot and billy,
Making tea in the shade of the gum-tree again.

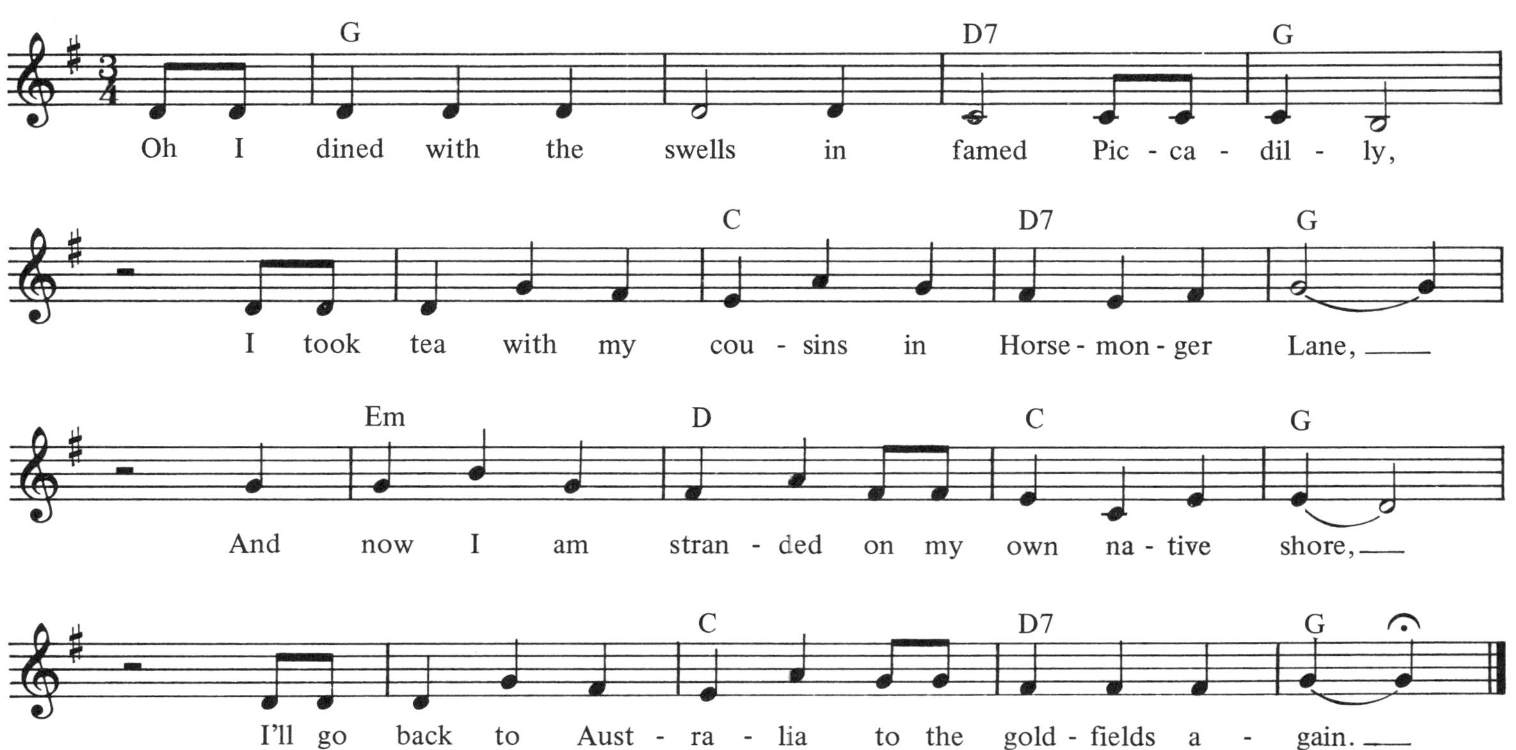
G D7 C Em D
G D7 G
Oh I dined with the swells in famed Pic - ca - dil - ly,
C D7 G
I took tea with my cou - sins in Horse - mon - ger Lane, ___
Em D C G
And now I am stran - ded on my own na - tive shore, ___
C D7 G
I'll go back to Aust - ra - lia to the gold - fields a - gain. ___

Oh, Give Me a Hut

This song appears as an anthem to bush life. Where many songs talk about the misfortunes and struggles of setting up a new life in the outback this song unfolds the many pleasures:

"I cast my eyes on the plain before me, and saw my flock of sheep studding the plain, with my working bullocks at a little distance ... As we sat at breakfast that morning in my rude cottage, with the bare walls of logs of trees and the shingle roof above us, all rough enough, but spacious, and a little too airy, I began to have a foretaste of that feeling of independence and security of home and subsistence which I have so many years enjoyed." (Reminiscences of a pioneer.)

Words from the Hurd Collection, Brisbane Library. The music is given as "The Gum Tree Canoe" and "Kitty Cray". I have used the more popular music as sung in the folk revival.

Sydney flute player
Ken Grenhalgh

Oh give me a hut in my own native land,
Or a tent in Australia where the tall gum trees stand,
I don't care how far in the bush it may be,
If there's one faithful heart that will share it with me.

Australia's the land of my childhood and birth,
Oft-times I think of its beauty and mirth,
With the scenes of my childhood contented I'd be,
If a dear faithful heart would just share it with me.

'Tis pleasant to rise at the break of the day,
And chase the wild horse in the hills far away,
For he dances and prances and snorts in his glee,
And is yarded at night by a native like me.

How I long to be where the emu does stray,
And the wild native dog calls aloud for his prey,
Where the kangaroo and the wallaroo and the wombat so rare,
Are found with the bandicoot and the wild native bear.

So give me a hut in my own native land,
Or a tent in Australia where the tall gum trees stand,
I don't care how far in the bush it may be,
If there's one faithful heart that will share it with me.

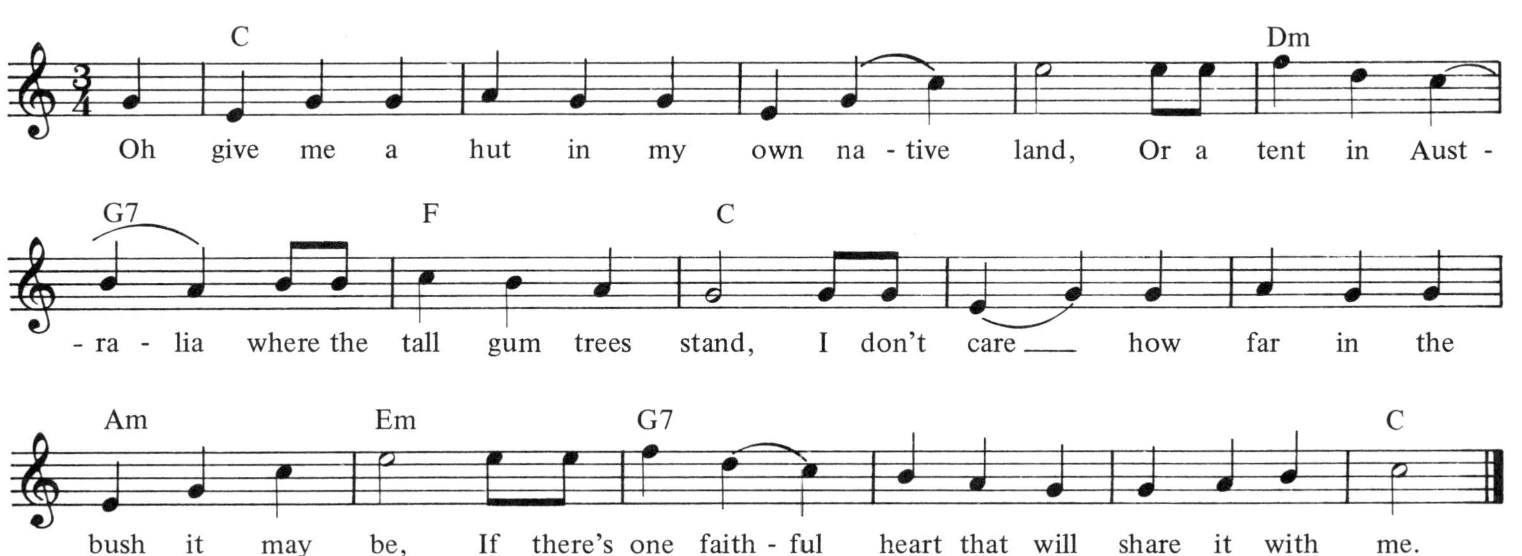

C Dm G7 F Am Em
C Dm
Oh give me a hut in my own na - tive land, Or a tent in Aust -
G7 F C
- ra - lia where the tall gum trees stand, I don't care how far in the
Am Em G7 C
bush it may be, If there's one faith - ful heart that will share it with me.

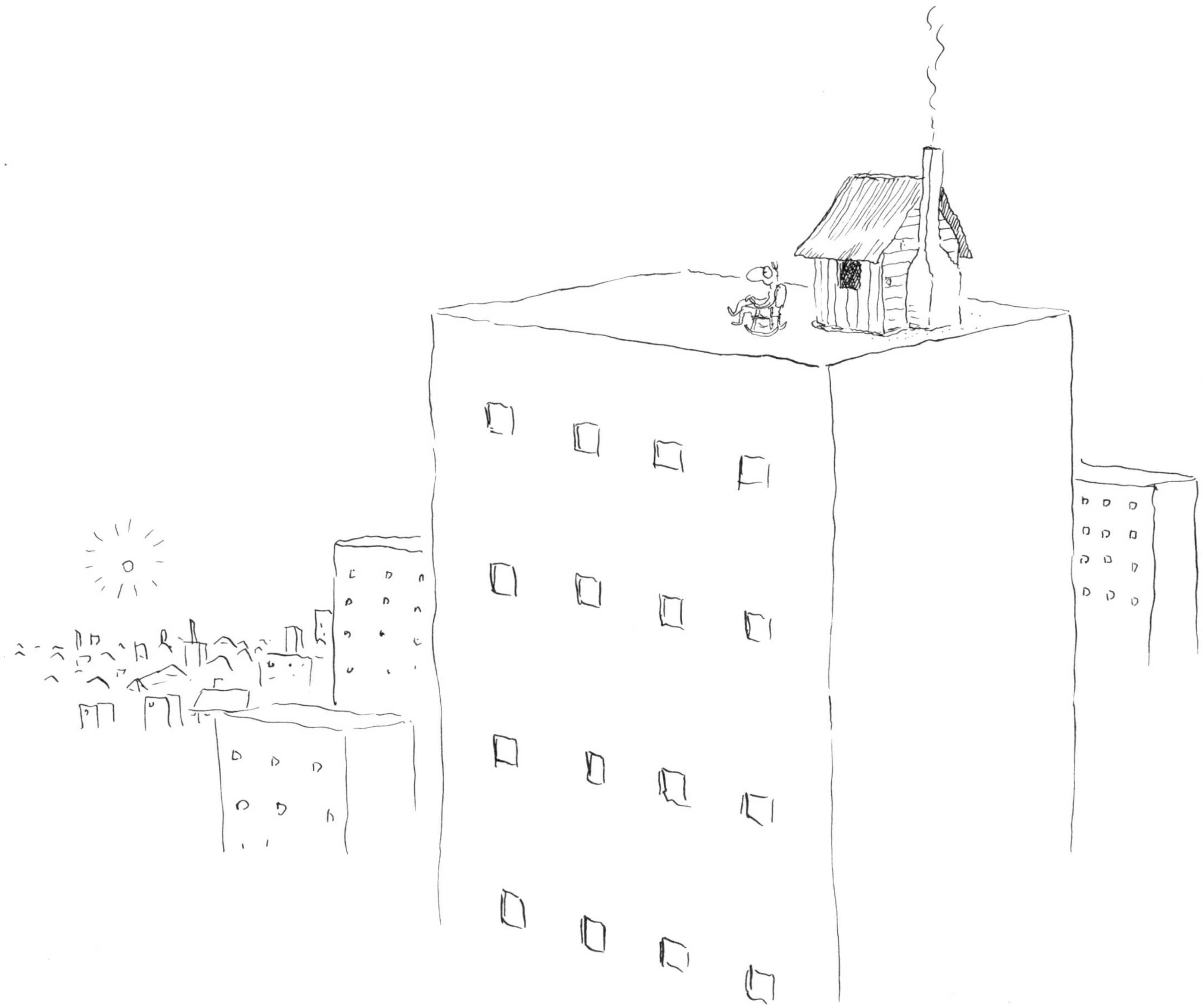

中国紅茶
SHANGHAI.

SHEARERS, DROVERS AND BUSH LIFE

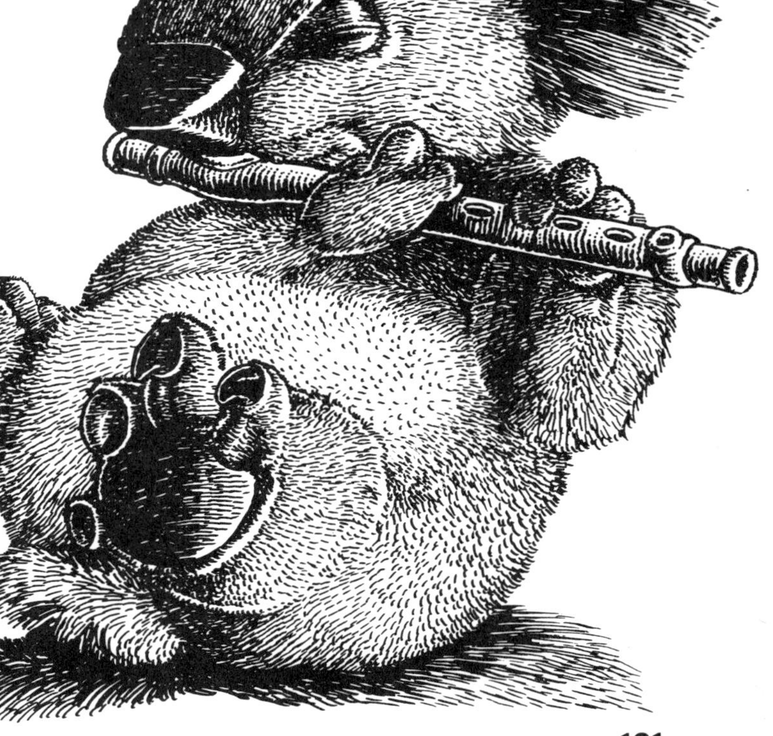

Introduction 3

As the "Rush Away!" days of the goldrush era subsided the Australian saw the opportunity to take stock of himself and his country. The gold rushes of the 1850's and 1860's had certainly changed the face of the country and it was now possible to move freely from town to town. Tracks were now roads, shacks now cottages, life "up the country" was a reality.

For many of our pioneering ancestors life "up the country" was the real Australia. Here was an endless plain where the very air smacked of freedom. The memories of prison hulks, chain-gangs and hostile natives were long forgotten – replaced by memories of gold fortunes, cattle and sheep.

The wool industry, long established as the nation's most important asset, was still booming. By the 1880's the station-owners and shearers had a real sense of national pride – that the workmen had achieved much more than professional skills! The station-owner was still "king" and conditions for the shearer and his workmates were not good. Wages were low and the shearers were paid piecemeal, a practice that allowed the station-owner to refuse payment if he felt a sheep was badly shorn. Conditions in the shearers' quarters were also bad with lice-ridden bedding and dubious rations. The wool-baron was king and he knew it!

Kings have been known to topple and it wasn't long before the shearers realised they had the winning hand for it was they who peeled the fleece from the fat, greasy sheep and it was they who washed, crutched and lambed the flocks. Times change and many a bitter battle was fought between the station-owner and the shearer. In the 1890's the shearers took to unprecedented strike action that revolutionised the entire industry and set a standard for the entire Union movement in Australia.

At the same time another group of "kings" was quickly moving into the economy – the cattle "kings". Great herds of cattle now grazed the plains and with them came horse-mounted drovers who had developed skills unequalled in the world. The sight of the lonely drover and his escort of two or three yapping cattle dogs is still a familiar sight in the Australian outback. It was, and in many cases still is, a peculiar life with endless weeks in the saddle with evenings spent hunched around burning campfires. It was a life of "salt-beef, damper and billy tea" mixed with the ever-shifting sound of cattle hooves. It was a life suited to men who desired to be alone with the peace of the earth.

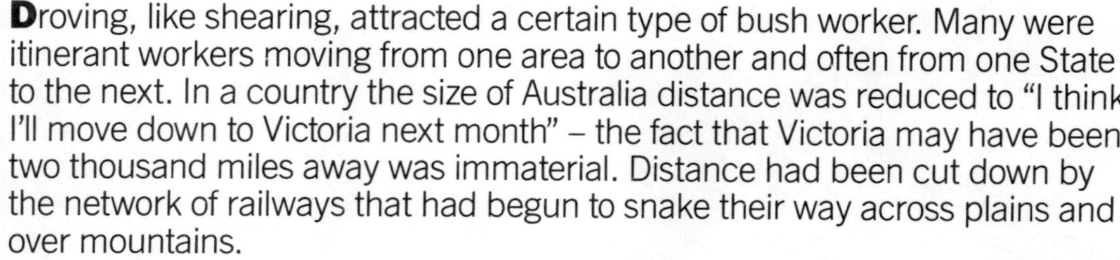

Droving, like shearing, attracted a certain type of bush worker. Many were itinerant workers moving from one area to another and often from one State to the next. In a country the size of Australia distance was reduced to "I think I'll move down to Victoria next month" – the fact that Victoria may have been two thousand miles away was immaterial. Distance had been cut down by the network of railways that had begun to snake their way across plains and over mountains.

These bushmen were bred of Australia. They were "rough and tumble" men always ready for a fight, a drink or a season of sweat-hard work. It was their life and theirs alone. They were Australian sons.

The songs they composed and sang reflected their lifestyles. The days of the English armchair historian and observer were over, now there were

Australians the calibre of Henry Lawson and Banjo Paterson, who not only wrote about Australia but in an Australian style. Both these gifted writers became household names and through the pages of *The Bulletin* magazine and the *Ben Bowyang Reciters* the poems and songs of Australia found eager audiences right across the country. These were the "golden days" of our folk song repertoire when the myths and yarns of our pioneering heritage became such an important part of our "feeling Australian".

Ted Simpson, bush poet

The songs in this collection are songs about the average Australian. The shearer who works hard and plays hard by letting off steam in the pub or of the man from Tumba-bloody-Rumba who reckons he's tried his hand at just about every bush job. They are the songs of our heroes, be they ryebuck shearers, champion boxers, Lachlan Tigers or the never-tiring Flash Stockman who is "just too bloody good to be in one". These songs are the spirit of Australia.

The Limejuice Tub

As the sea passage from England to Australia became financially viable many young men travelled to begin a new life working in the Australian bush. The new arrivals were nicknamed "new chums" and they were said to have arrived on "Limejuice Tubs", so called because of the regular ration of limejuice and vinegar given to prevent outbreaks of scurvy.

Collected in 1973 by Warren Fahey from the singing of Mr Gilmer, Maryborough, Queensland. This seems to be the only collected version of this song. A. L. Lloyd admitted re-working the version that has become popular within the folk revival. Lloyd sings a version on the Topic record "The Australian Legend".

Now the shearing comes throw down your drums
Step onto the board you spanking chums
When once you've crossed the briny deep
You gammon you can shear a sheep.

You never saw a sheep before
Until you reached the Australian shore
When into the bush, by the lord it's true,
You'd swear the sheep were kangaroos.

CHORUS:
Oh a rowdem a rowdem a rub a dub dub
We'll drive 'em back to the limejuice tub.

Oh, there's lots of learners, suckers of gums,
Cockatoo's sons and big new chums,
All they want is to clip the wool
They try the shears with a tug and a pull.

They make a mull and lots of scars
Such a bawling out for tar
By the Lord Harry the poor jumbucks
Are tommy-hawked by the great humbugs.

Now you at home won't be warn-ed
But come humping swag to this country
Sixteen thousand miles you've come
To hump about a blanket drum.

And when you meet upon the road
To kill the time throw down your load,
It's at the sun you give a look
It will soon be time to see the cook.

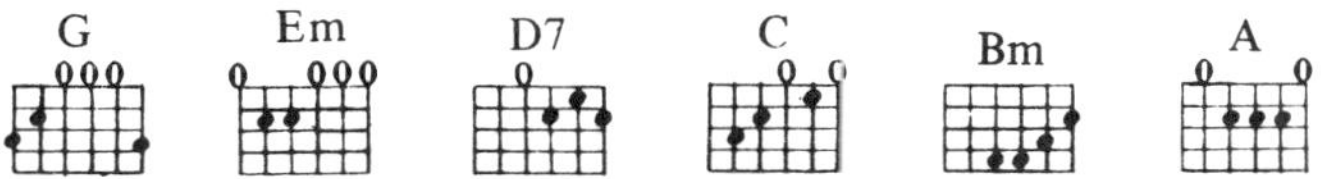

G Em G

Now the shear - ing comes throw down your drums step on to the board you

C D7 G Em

spank - ing chums ______ When once you've crossed the bri - ny deep you

Bm G D7 G

gam - mon you can shear a sheep You nev - er saw a

D7 G A D7

sheep be - fore un - til you reached the Aus - tra - lian shore ______ When

G D7 Em G C D7

in - to the bush by the Lord it's true, you'd swear the sheep were Kan - ga - roos. Oh

G Em G C D7

a rowdem a rowdem to my rub a dub dub we'll drive 'em back to the lime-juice tub.

The Old Bark Hut

"Necessity is the mother of invention" and, by all accounts, necessity led to all types of make-shift dwellings for the average bushman. Newspaper became wallpaper, empty jam tins became saucepans and memories became firm friends. Although there is a fair degree of nonsense in this verse there is also the message that "if you're not mighty careful, you'll go with a hungry gut" – just one of the misfortunes of life in an old bark hut!

From the singing of Mr Jacob Lollbach, MBE, Grafton, New South Wales, in 1973, collected by Warren Fahey. When I recorded this song Mr Lollbach was 103 years of age! He told me he had learnt the song from an old bullock driver, Jack Horner, who sang it to the tune of "The Wearing of The Green".

Mr Lollbach Jnr., 1973

Oh, my name is Bob the Swagman, and before you all I stand,
And I've had many ups and downs while travelling through the land,
I once was well-to-do, my boys, but now I'm all stumped up,
And I'm forced to go on rations in an old bark hut.

CHORUS:
In an old bark hut, in an old bark hut,
I'm forced to go on rations in an old bark hut.

Ten pounds of flour, ten pounds of beef, some sugar and some tea,
That's all they'll give a hungry man until the seventh day,
If you don't be mighty sparing, you'll go with a hungry gut,
For that's one of the great misfortunes in an old bark hut.

The bucket you wash your feet in is to boil your beef in too,
They'd say you're getting mighty flash if you should ask for two,
I've a billy and a pint-pot and a broken-handled cup,
And they all adorn the table in the old bark hut.

The table is not made of wood, as many you have seen,
For if I had one half so good, I'd think myself serene;
No, it's only an old dry sheet of bark – God knows when it was cut,
It was blown down off the rafters of the old bark hut.

Now, furniture, there's no such thing, 'twas never in the place,
Except the stool I sit upon, and that's an old gin case,
It does me for a safe as well, but you must keep it shut
Or the flies would make it canter round the old bark hut.

If you should leave it open and the flies should find your meat,
They'll scarcely leave a single piece that's fit for man to eat,
But you musn't curse or grumble – what won't fatten will fill up,
And what's out of sight is out of mind in the old bark hut.

In summer when the weather's warm, this hut is nice and cool,
And you'll find the gentle breezes blowing in through every hole.
You can leave the old door open, or you can leave it shut,
There's no fear of suffocation in the old bark hut.

In the winter time, preserve us all – to live in it's a treat,
Especially when it's raining hard, and blowing wind and sleet,
The rain comes down the chimney, and your meat is black with soot,
That's a substitute for pepper in the old bark hut.

I've seen the rain come in this hut just like a perfect flood,
Especially through that great big hole where once the table stood,
There's not a blessed spot, my boys, where you can lay your nut,
But the rain is sure to find you in the old bark hut.

So beside the fire I make my bed, and there I lay me down,
And think myself as happy as a king that wears a crown,
But just as you're dozing off to sleep a flea will wake you up,
Which makes you curse the vermin in the old bark hut.

Such flocks of fleas you never saw, they are so plump and fat,
And if you make a grab at one he'll spit just like a cat,
Last night they got my pack of cards and were fighting for the cut,
And I thought the devil had me in the old bark hut.

So now my friends, I've sung my song, and that as well as I could,
I hope the ladies present will not think my language rude,
And all you younger people, in the days when you grow up,
Remember Bob the Swagman, and the Old Bark Hut.

The Cockies of Bungaree

Bungaree is located in Victoria and it is well known as a potato growing community. This is the sort of song one can imagine the weary, back-sore potato digger would readily relate to. Potato "chipping" is considered to be "one of the worst jobs in the world". Today the work is done by machines.

A. L. Lloyd collected this version in the 1930's and it appeared on his Wattle Recording in 1957, "On the Banks of The Condamine". Simon McDonald had a good version as collected by Norm O'Connor and Maryjean Officer

Simon McDonald

Now, all you blokes, take my advice and do your daily toil,
But don't go out to Bungaree to work on the chocolate soil.
For the days they are so long, my boys, they'll break your heart in two
And if ever you work for cocky Bourke you very soon will know.

CHORUS:
Oh we used to go to bed, you know, a little bit after dark.
The room we used to sleep in, it was just like Noah's Ark:
There were dogs and rats and mice and cats and pigs and poulteree.
I'll never forget the time we had while down in Bungaree!

On the thirsty Monday morning, sure, to work I had to go.
My noble cocky says to me, "Get up! You're rather slow."
The moon was shining gloriously, and the stars were out, you see,
And I thought before the sun would rise I'd die in Bungaree.

Oh, he called me to my supper at half past eight or nine,
He called me to my breakfast before the sun could shine,
And after tea was over, all with a merry laugh,
The bloody old cocky says to me, "We'll cut a bit of chaff."

"**N**ow when you are chaff-cutting, boys, isn't it a spell?"
"Yes, be Jove," says I, "it is, and it's me that knows it well!"
For many of those fellows with me they disagree,
For I hate the jolly nightwork that they do in Bungaree.

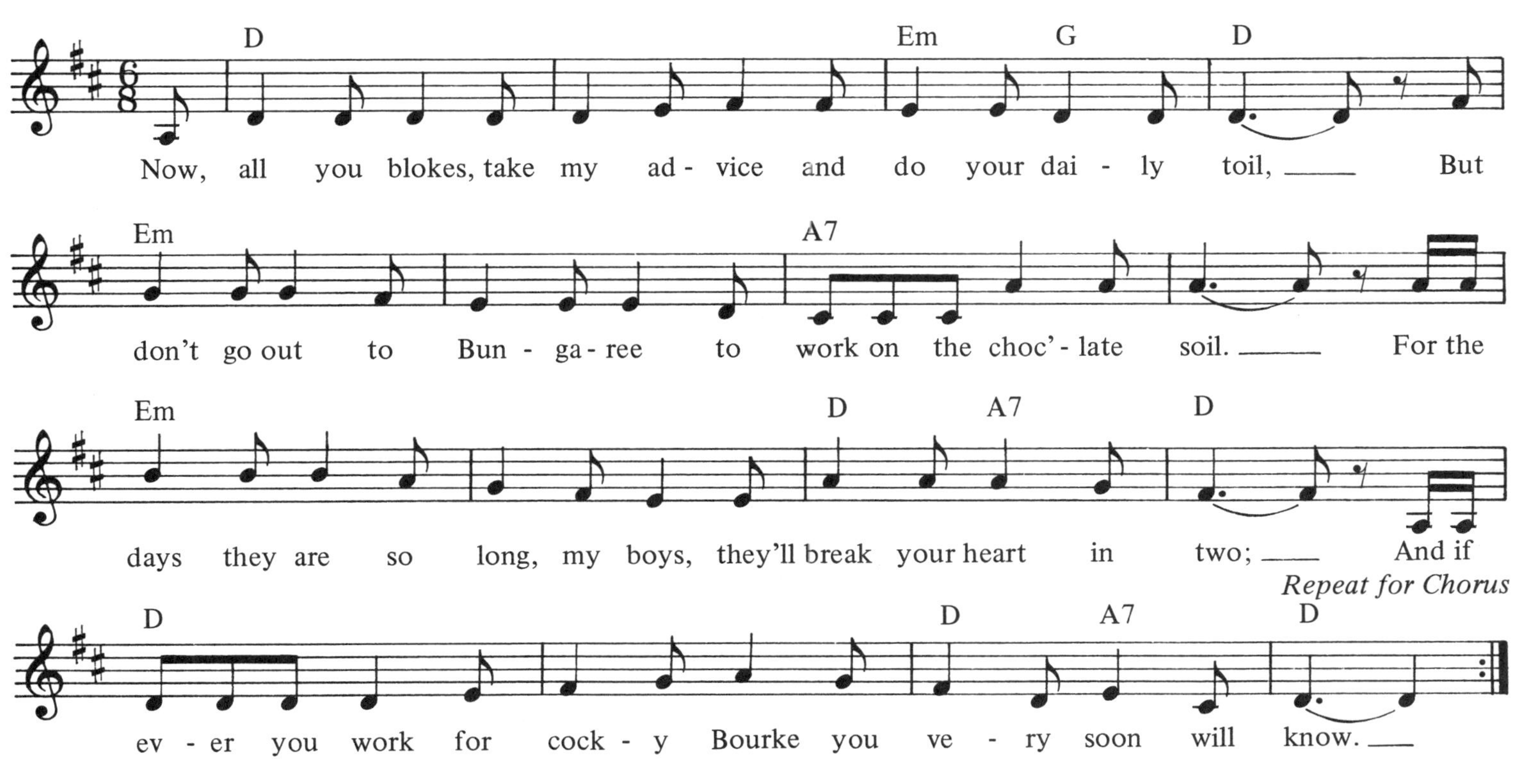
D Em G A7
Now, all you blokes, take my ad - vice and do your dai - ly toil, But
don't go out to Bun - ga - ree to work on the choc' - late soil. For the
days they are so long, my boys, they'll break your heart in two; And if
Repeat for Chorus
ev - er you work for cock - y Bourke you ve - ry soon will know.

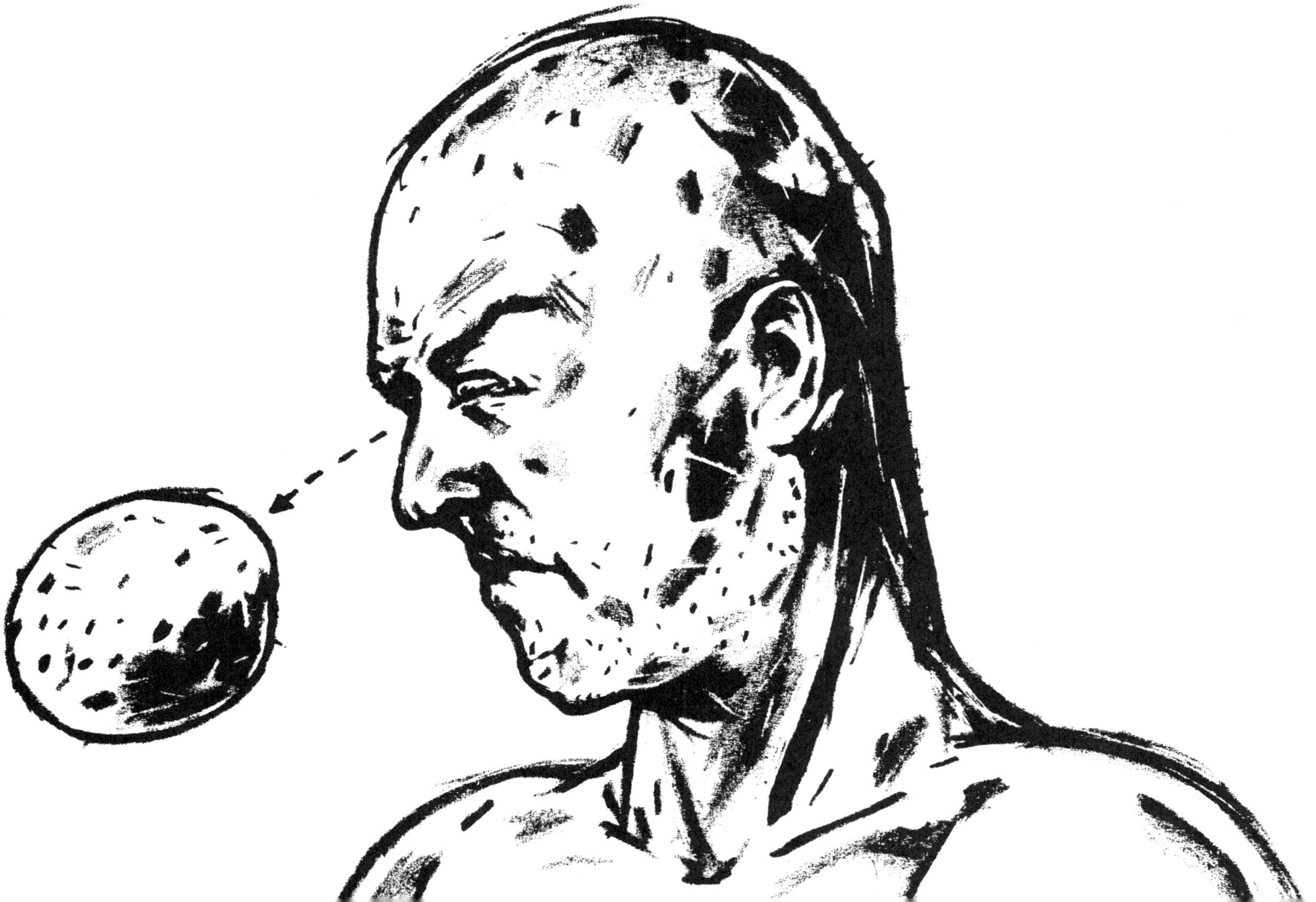

The Springtime it Brings on the Shearing

Life for the operator of a sheep station is very seasonal. The peak of the year is obviously the shearing season when the giant fleeces are classed, bailed and stamped for auction. Shearing brings the itinerant workers, be they rouseabouts, station cook, tar-boys, contractors or shearers. In they come and for solid weeks they sweat, swear, grumble and sweat some more. When the season is complete off they move until next year.

Collected by Dr Percy Jones from an adaptation of the poem "On the Wallaby Track" by E. J. Overbury. This is the popularised version.

Shearer, Forbes, NSW

Oh, the springtime it brings on the shearing,
And it's then you will see them in droves,
To the west country stations all steering,
A-seeking a job off the coves.

CHORUS:
With a ragged old swag on my shoulder,
And a billy quart-pot in my hand,
I tell you we'll 'stonish the new chum,
To see how we travel the land.

You may talk of your mighty exploring,
Of Landsborough, McKinley and King;
But I feel I should only be boring,
On such frivolous subjects to sing.

For discovering mountains and rivers
There's one for a gallon I'd back,
Who'll beat all your Stuarts to shivers:
It's the man on the Wallaby Track.

From Billabone, Murray and Loddon,
To the far Tatiara and back,
The hills and the plains are well trodden,
By the men on the Wallaby Track.

Oh, and after the shearing is over,
And the wool season's all at an end,
It is then you will see those flash shearers
Making johnny-cakes round in the bend.

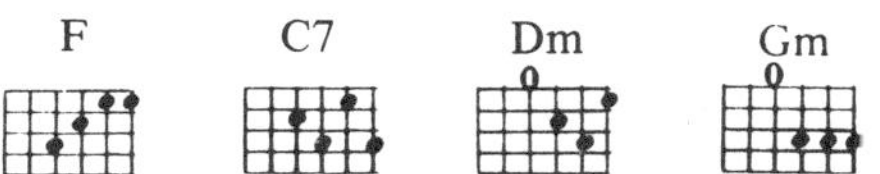
F C7 Dm Gm

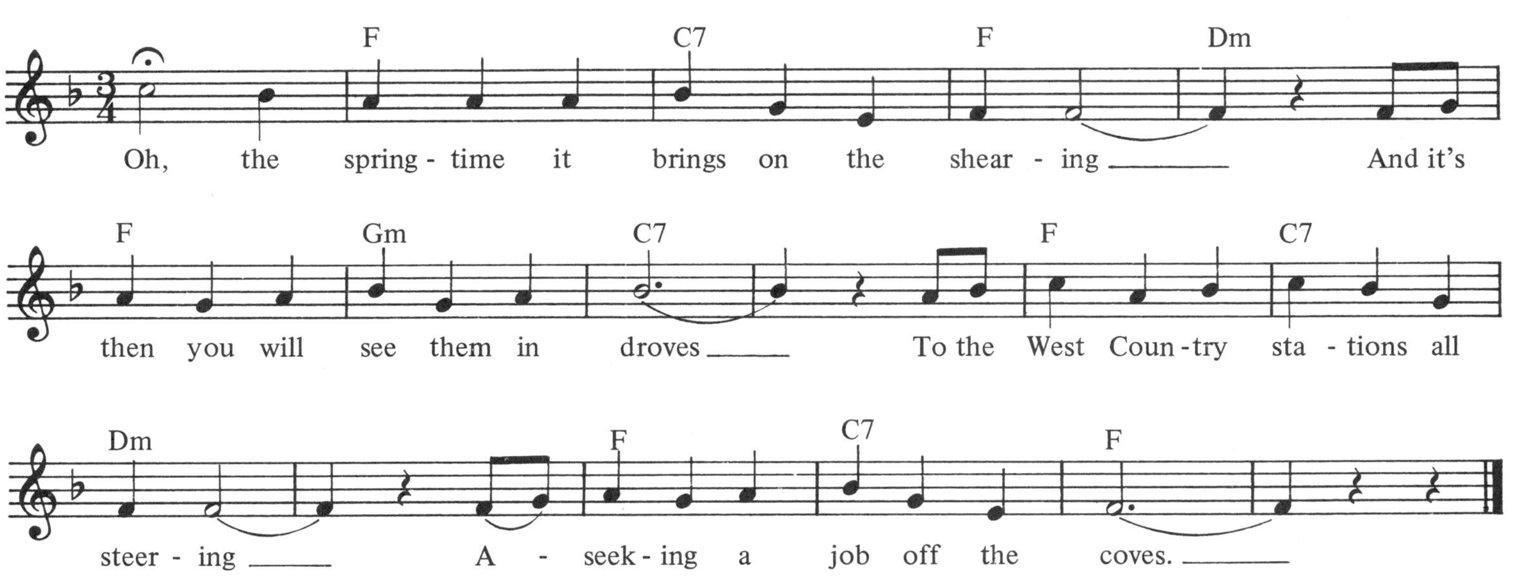
F C7 F Dm
Oh, the spring-time it brings on the shear-ing And it's
F Gm C7 F C7
then you will see them in droves To the West Coun-try sta-tions all
Dm F C7 F
steer-ing A-seek-ing a job off the coves.

Travelling Down the Castlereagh

A good song that takes the singer on a tour of outback shearing stations. Notice the pointed reference to "scab-labour" in the sheds and "there were eight or ten Chinamen shearing in a row". The Shearers' Union was a mighty force in the bush and a real thorn in the side of the usually greedy station-owner. In the days when the merino was king the shearers were still getting appalling conditions. With the Shearers' Union came solidarity and by the 1890's the face of the sheep industry had completely changed.

Also known as "A Bushman's Song". It seems as if it is a Banjo Paterson composition, however it has certainly found its way into the tradition. This version recorded from Joe Watson, Caringbah, New South Wales, by Warren Fahey, in 1973.

I was travelling down the Castlereagh, and I'm a station-hand,
I'm handy with a rope and pole, I'm handy with a brand,
And I can ride a rowdy colt, or swing an axe all day,
But there's no demand for a station-hand along the Castlereagh.

So it's shift boys, shift, for there isn't the slightest doubt
That we'll have to make a shift for the stations further out,
With the pack-horse runnin' after, for he follows like a dog,
And we trot across the country at the old jig-jog.

This old black horse I'm riding – If you notice what's his brand,
He wears the crooked R, you see – none better in the land.
He takes a lot of beatin', and the other day we tried,
For a bit of a joke, with a racing bloke, for twenty pounds a side.

It was shift, boys, shift, for there wasn't the slightest doubt
That I had to make him shift, for the money was nearly out;
But he cantered home a winner, with the other one at the flog –
He's a red-hot sort to pick up with his old jig-jog.

I asked a cove for shearing once along the Marthaguy:
"We shear non-union here," says he. "I call it scab," says I.
I looked along the shearin' floor before I turned to go –
There were eight or ten dashed Chinamen a-shearin' in a row.

It was shift, boys, shift, for there wasn't the slightest doubt
It was time to make a shift with the leprosy about,
So I saddled up my horses, and I whistled up my dog,
And I left his scabby station at the old jig-jog.

I went to Illawarra, where my brother's got a farm;
He's got to ask the landlord's leave before he lifts an arm;
The landlord owns the countryside – man, woman, dog and cat,
You mustn't dare to speak to him, before you lift your hat.

It was shift, boys, shift, for there wasn't the slightest doubt
That little landlord god and I would soon have fallen out;
Was I to touch my hat to him? Was I his bloody dog?
So I makes for up the country at the old jig-jog.

But it's time that I was movin', I've a mighty way to go
Till I drink artesian water from a thousand feet below;
Till I meet the overlanders with the cattle comin' down –
And I'll work a while till I make a pile, then have a spree in town.

So it's shift, boys, shift, for there isn't the slightest doubt
We've got to make a shift for the stations further out:
The pack-horse runs behind us, for he follows like a dog,
And we cross a lot of country at the old jig-jog.

C F G7 D7

C F G7 C
I'was trav - 'ling down the Cas - tle - reagh and I'm a sta - tion hand I'm

G7 F C D7 G C
han - dy with a rope and pole I'm han - dy with a brand And I can ride a row - dy colt or

F G7 C G7 F C
swing an axe all day But there's no de - mand for a sta - tion hand a -

G7 C *Chorus:* F C
- long the Cas - tle - reagh So it's shift, boys, shift for there isn't the sligh - test doubt that we've

G7 Am D7 G7 C
got to make a shift for the sta - tions fur - ther out With the pack-horse run - ning af - ter for he

F G7 C G7 F C G7 C
fol-lows me like a dog, We must strike a - cross the coun - try at the old jig - jog.

Another Fall of Rain

One of the victories of the Shearers' Union was to force the squatter "to pay the shearers off" during a rainy period. As the shearers were paid piecemeal it was only fair that they be paid for time – time meant money! In this song we find the shearers eagerly scanning the clouded skies for the first sign of rain. When the rain comes it's off to the huts to play "ante-up", cards, dice and to yarn.

This version is from Paterson's Old Bush Songs *and it is based on a poem by John Shaw-Neilson called "Waiting For The Rain". Paterson gave the tune as "The Little Log Cabin in the Lane".*

The weather had been sultry for a fortnight's time or more,
And the shearers had been driving might and main,
And some had got the century who'd ne'er got it before,
And now all hands were wishing for the rain.

CHORUS:
For the boss is getting rusty and the ringer's caving in,
For his bandaged wrist is aching with the pain,
And the second man, I fear, will make it hard for him,
Unless we have another fall of rain.

A few had taken quarters and were coiling in their bunks,
When we shore the six-tooth wethers from the plain,
And if the sheep get harder, then a few more men will funk,
Unless we have another fall of rain.

Some cockies come here shearing; they would fill a little book
About this sad, dry weather for the grain.
But here is lunch a-coming, make way for Dick the cook,
Old Dick is nigh as welcome as the rain.

But the sky is clouding over, and the thunder's muttering loud,
And the clouds are driving eastward o'er the plain,
And I see the lightning flashing from the edge of yon dark cloud,
And I hear the gentle patter of the rain.

So lads, put on your stoppers, and let us to the hut,
Where we'll gather round and have a friendly game,
While some are playing music and some play ante-up,
And some are gazing outward at the rain.

But now the rain is over, let the pressers spin the screw,
Let the teamsters back the wagon in again,
And we'll block the classer's table by the way we put them through,
For everything is merry since the rain.

LAST CHORUS:
And the boss, he won't be rusty when his sheep they all are shorn,
And the ringer's wrist won't ache much with the pain
Of pocketing his season's cheque of fifty pounds or more,
And the second man will press him hard again.

Let the boss bring out the bottle, let him wet the final flock,
For the shearers here may ne'er meet all again;
Some may meet next season, but perhaps not even then,
For soon we will all vanish like the rain.

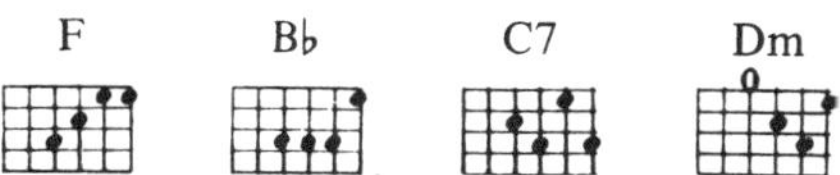

F B♭ F
The__ wea-ther had been sul-try for a fort-night's time or more and the

C7 F
shea-rers had been driv-ing might and main____ And__ some had got the

B♭ F C7 F
cen-tu-ry who ne're got it be-fore And_ now all hands were wish-ing for the rain.___

Chorus:

B♭ F
__ For the boss is get-ting rus-ty and the ring-er's ca-ving in For his

Dm B♭ F C7 F
ban-dag'd wrist is ach-ing with the pain____ And the se-cond man I fear_ will_

B♭ F C7 F
make it hard for him Un - less we have an-oth-er fall of rain.____

The Lachlan Tigers

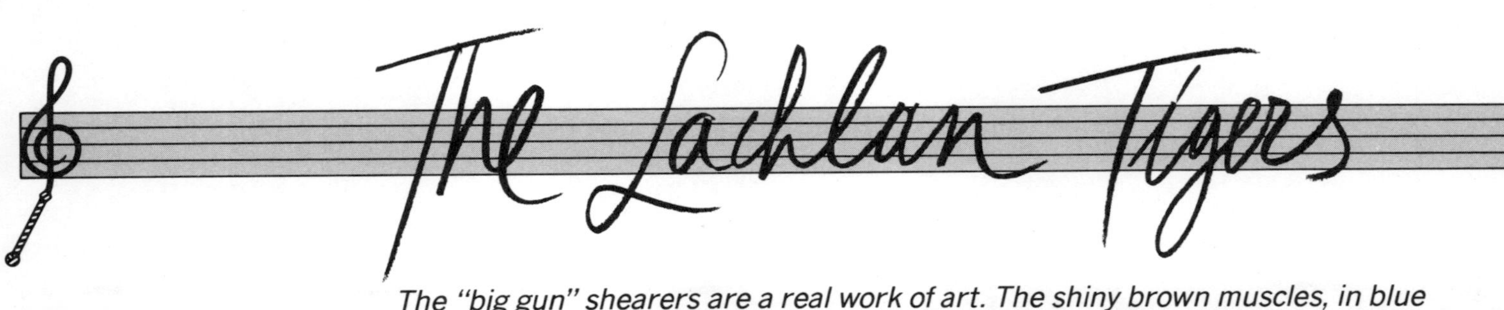

The "big gun" shearers are a real work of art. The shiny brown muscles, in blue singlets, peeling off the fleece from each fat, impotent, struggling sheep – much as a housewife peels a potato! One old shearer commented to me that "a shed full of big-gun shearers is like a cage full of tigers". The Lachlan region is a prime sheep raising area and is situated in the west of New South Wales. Many of our shearing songs have been collected in this area.

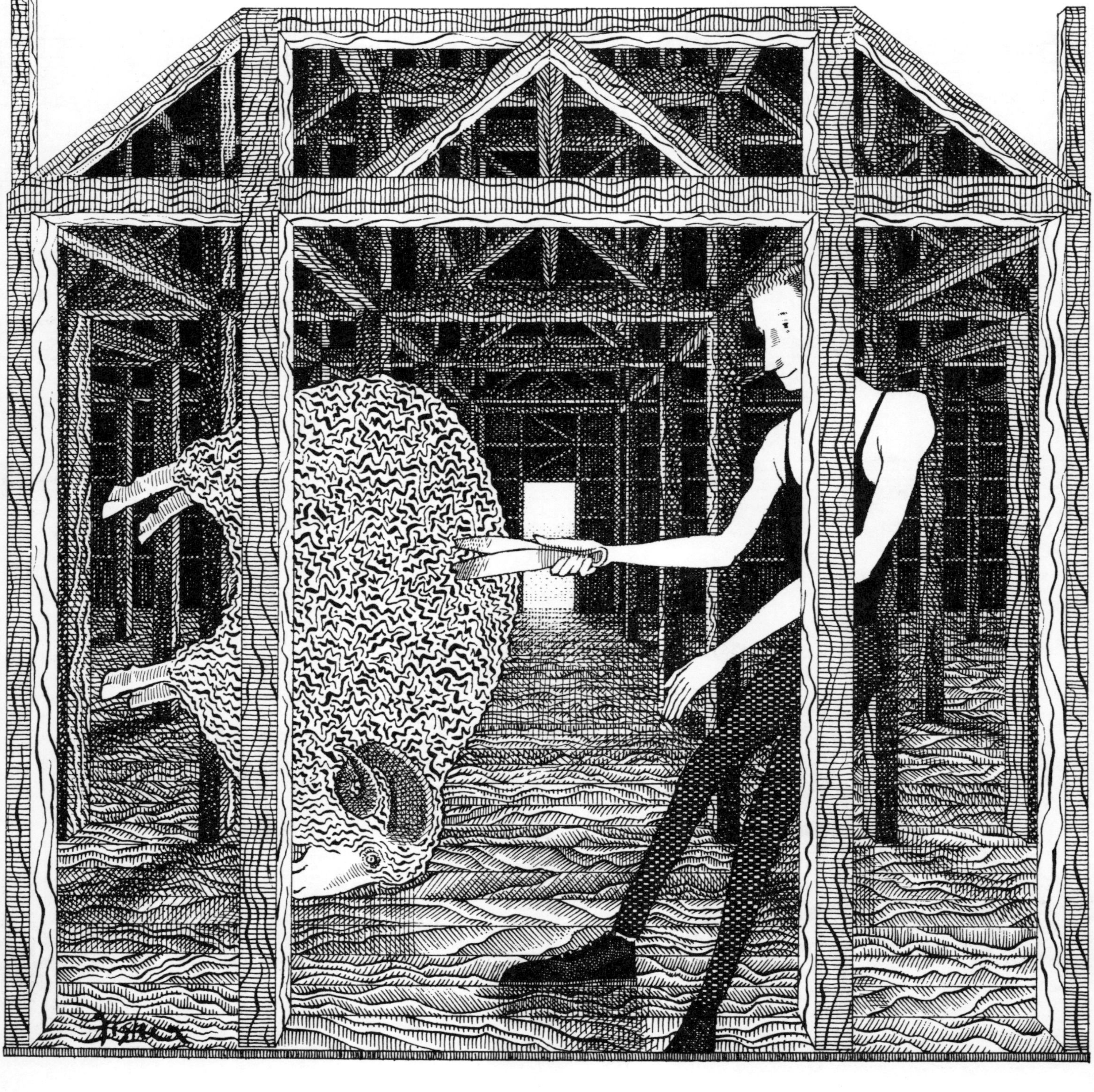

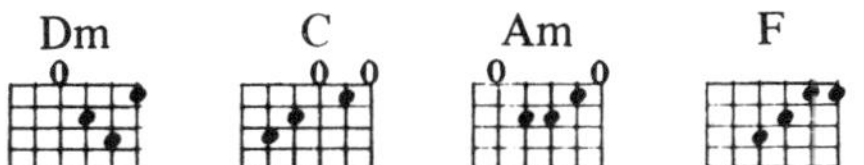

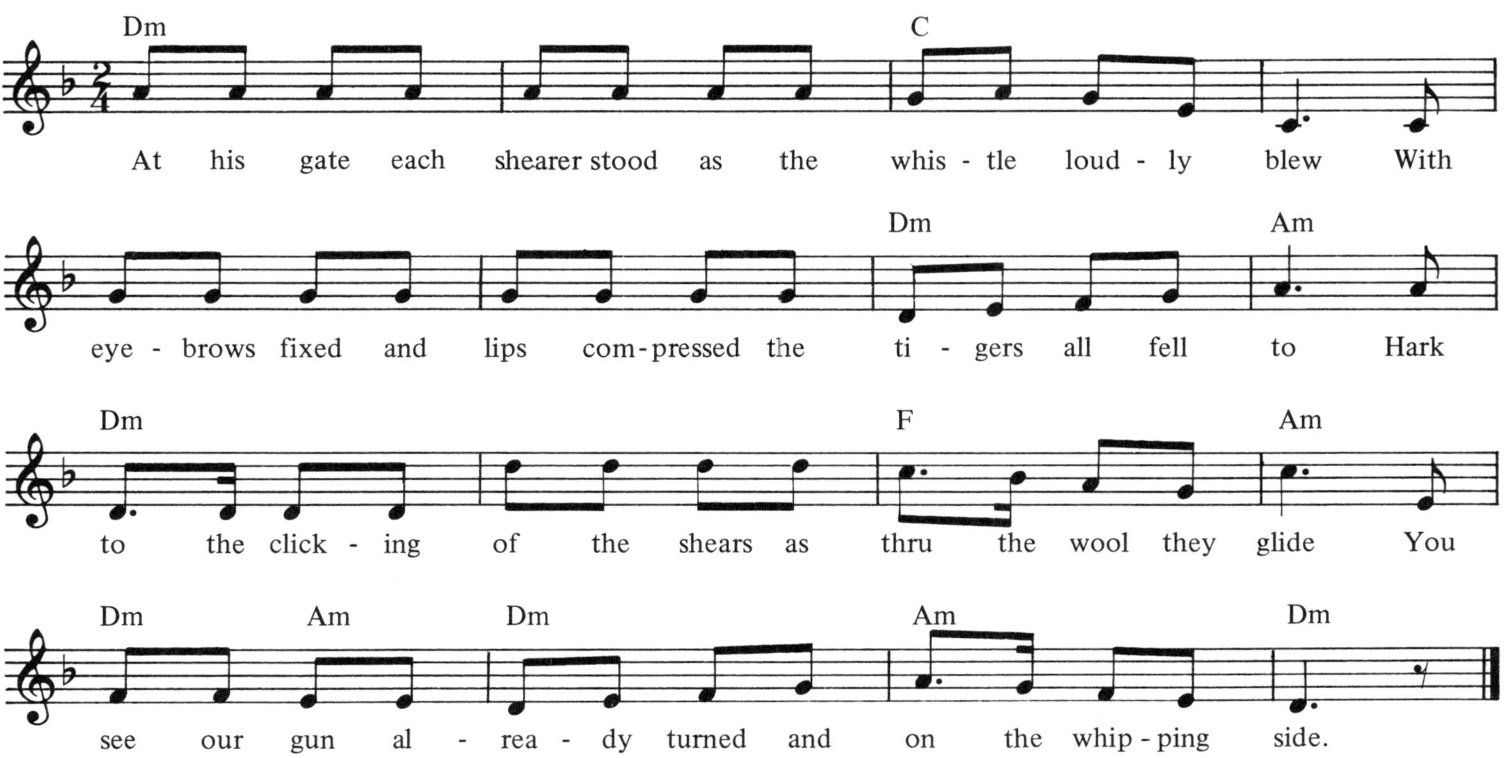

From the singing of Mrs S Colley, Bathurst, New South Wales, in 1973. Collected by Warren Fahey. Mrs Colley knew the song as "At Each Gate the Shearer Stood".

At his gate each shearer stood as the whistle loudly blew,
With eyebrows fixed and lips compressed the tigers all fell to.
Hark to the clicking of the shears as through the wool they glide,
You see our gun already turned and on the whipping side.

CHORUS:
A lot of Lachlan tigers, it's plain to see we are,
Hark to our burley ringer as he loudly calls for tar;
"Tar here", calls one, and quick the tar-boy flies;
"Sweep those locks away!" another loudly cries.

The scene it is a lively one and ought to be admired,
There's never been a better board since Jackie Howe expired.
Along the board the gaffer walks with his face all in a frown,
And passing by the ringer, says, "You watch, my lad, keep down.

"I must have those bellies off and topknots too, likewise,
My eye is quick, so none of your tricks, or off you'll go like flies."
Oh, curses on our gaffer, he's never on our side,
To shear a decent tally in vain I've often tried.

I have a pair of Ward and Pain's that are both bright and new,
I'll rig them up and let you see what I can really do,
For I've shore on the Bogan, where they shear them by the score,
But such a mob as this to clip I never saw before.

The singer of this shearing song recalled a tale where he was staying at a weatherbeaten old pub near Mudgee. "The pub had paper thin walls and in the next room this joker had the cook bailed up. They were hugging and kissing and making a real noise. As the bloke become more and more amorous the well proportioned cook began to giggle. She was a real howler. It was well after midnight and I heard this tired voice from the bedroom on the other side of the 'hot spot' – 'Look Madge,' it said, 'For heaven's sake either give in or go home!'"

From Mr Joe Watson, Caringbah, New South Wales, in 1974. Collected by Warren Fahey. Compare with "Tomahawking Fred" as printed in Paterson's Old Bush Songs.

Some shearing I have done and some prizes I have won
Through my knuckling down so close to the skin,
But I'd rather tomahawk any day than shear a flock
For that's the only way I'll make some tin.

CHORUS:
And I am just about to cut for the Lachlan
To turn a hundred out, I know the plan,
Give me sufficient cash, and you'll see me make a splash,
For I'm Tambaroora Ted, the ladies' man.

Put me on the shearing floor and it's there I'll bet for sure
That I'll give to any ringer ten sheep start,
For it's on the whipping side it's away from them I'll glide
Just like a bullet or a dart.

Of me you may have read for I'm Tambaroora Ted
My shearing laurels are known both near and far,
I'm the don of the Riverine, 'midst the shearers cut a shine,
And the tar boys say I never call for tar.

Hove in and go ahead for I'm Tambaroora Ted
On the shearing floor, my boys, I cut a shine;
There is Ricketts, and Jack Gunn shearing prizes they have won,
But my tally's never under ninety-nine.

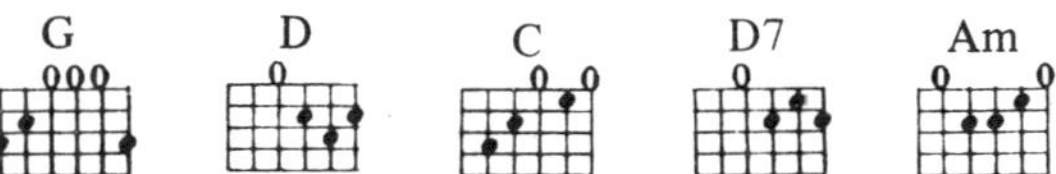

G G G D C
Now some shear-ing I have done and some pri - zes I have won, Through my

D7 G G
knuck-ling down so close on the skin ____ But I'd ra - ther tom - a -

G D C D7
hawk an - y - day than shear a flock, For that's the on - ly way I make some

G G G Am D7
tin, I am just a - bout to cut out for the Lach - lan, To turn a hun - dred

G G G
out I know the plan, Give me suf - fi - cient cash and you'll

D C D7 G
see me make a splash, For I'm Tam - ba - roo - ra Ted, the la - dies man.

The Big-gun Shearer

There are endless stories about shearers closing off the season and heading for the "big smoke" of the city to spend their well-earned cheque. Many of them only got as far as the first shanty pub. Whenever they did make it to the city it was nearly always a case of acute culture shock with the shearer heading back to the bush with a powerful hangover, no money and a headful of stories of how the city "smart alecs" had taken him down. A "big gun" was the name given to top shearers.

From Bill Bowyang's Bush Recitations No. 5, *Mitchell Library, Sydney. The final verse is from Bill Scott of Queensland who also suggests the tune "The Winnipeg Whore".*

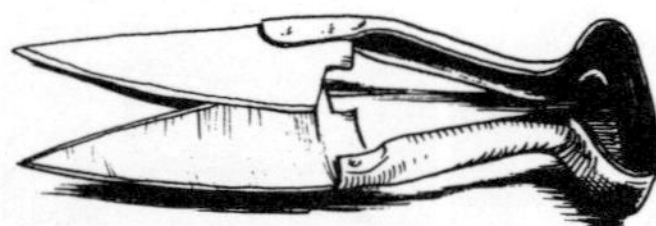

The "Big Gun" toiled, with his heart and soul,
Shearing sheep to make a roll
Out in the backblocks, far away,
Then off to Sydney for a holiday.

Down in the city he's a terrible swell,
Takes a taxi to the Kent Hotel,
The barmaid says, "You do look ill,
It must have been rough tucker, Bill."

In the city he looks a goat
With his Oxford bags and see-more coat,
He spends his money like a fool, of course,
That he worked for like a bloomin' horse.

He shouts for everyone round the place
And goes to Randwick for the big horse race,
He dopes himself with backache pills
And talks of high tallies and tucker bills.

And when it's spent he's sick and sore,
The barmaid's looks are kind no more,
His erstwhile friends don't care a hoot,
He goes back to the bush per what? – Per boot.

Back in Bourke where the flies are bad
He tells of the wonderful times he's had,
He tells of the winners he shouldn't have missed,
And skites of the dozens of girls he's kissed.

He stands on the corner cadging fags,
His shirt tail showing through his Oxford bags,
He's pawned his beautiful see-more coat,
He's got no money – oh, what a goat!

He's got no tucker and he can't get a booze,
The soles have gone from his snakeskin shoes,
He camps on the bend in the wind and rain
And waits for shearing to start again.

All you blokes with a cheque to spend
Don't go to the city where you've got no friends.
Head for the nearest wayside shack,
It's not so far when you've got to walk back.

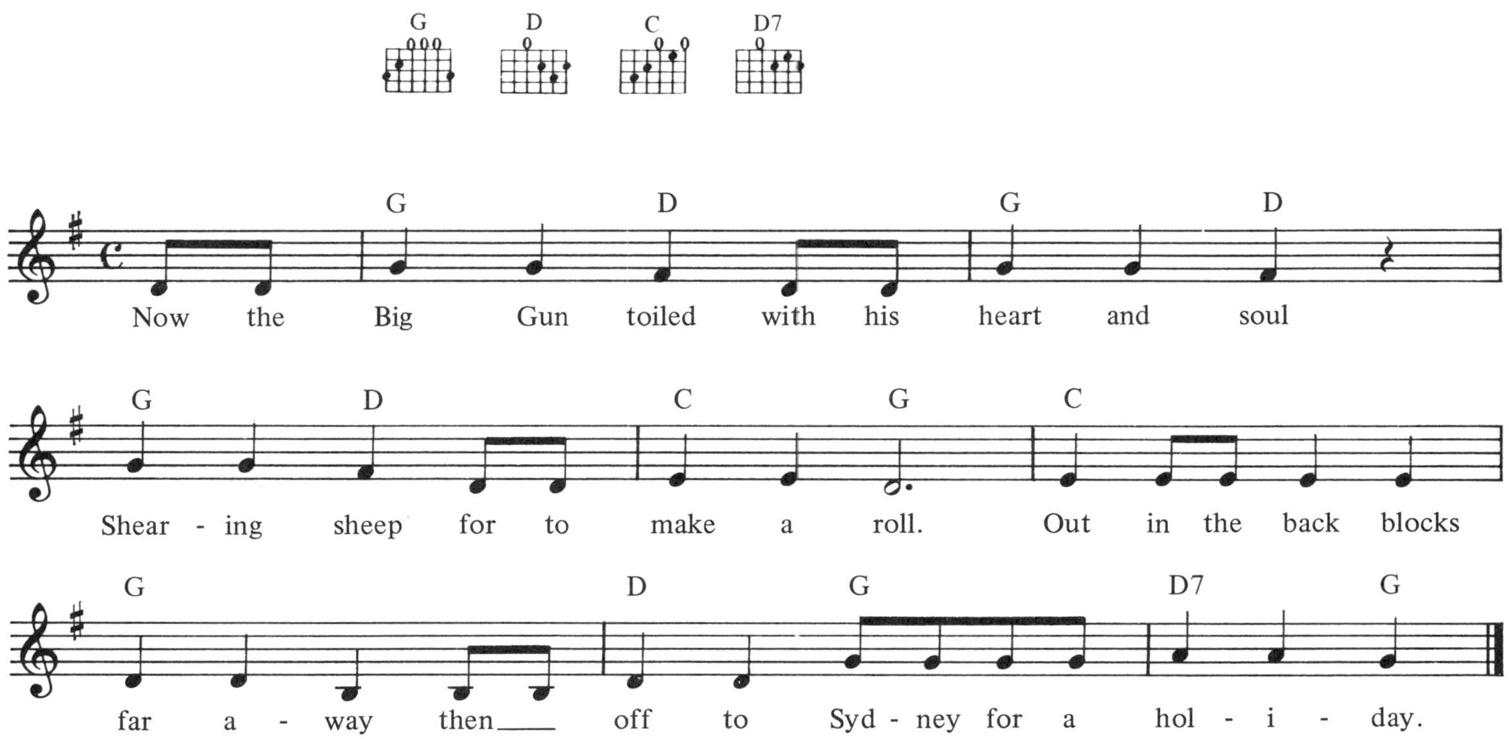

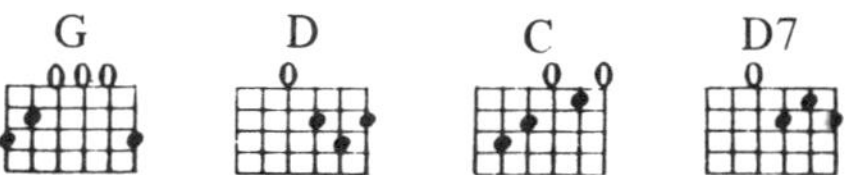

G D C D7
G D G D
Now the Big Gun toiled with his heart and soul
G D C G C
Shear - ing sheep for to make a roll. Out in the back blocks
G D G D7 G
far a - way then___ off to Syd - ney for a hol - i - day.

SYDNEY 70
BOURK
Billington

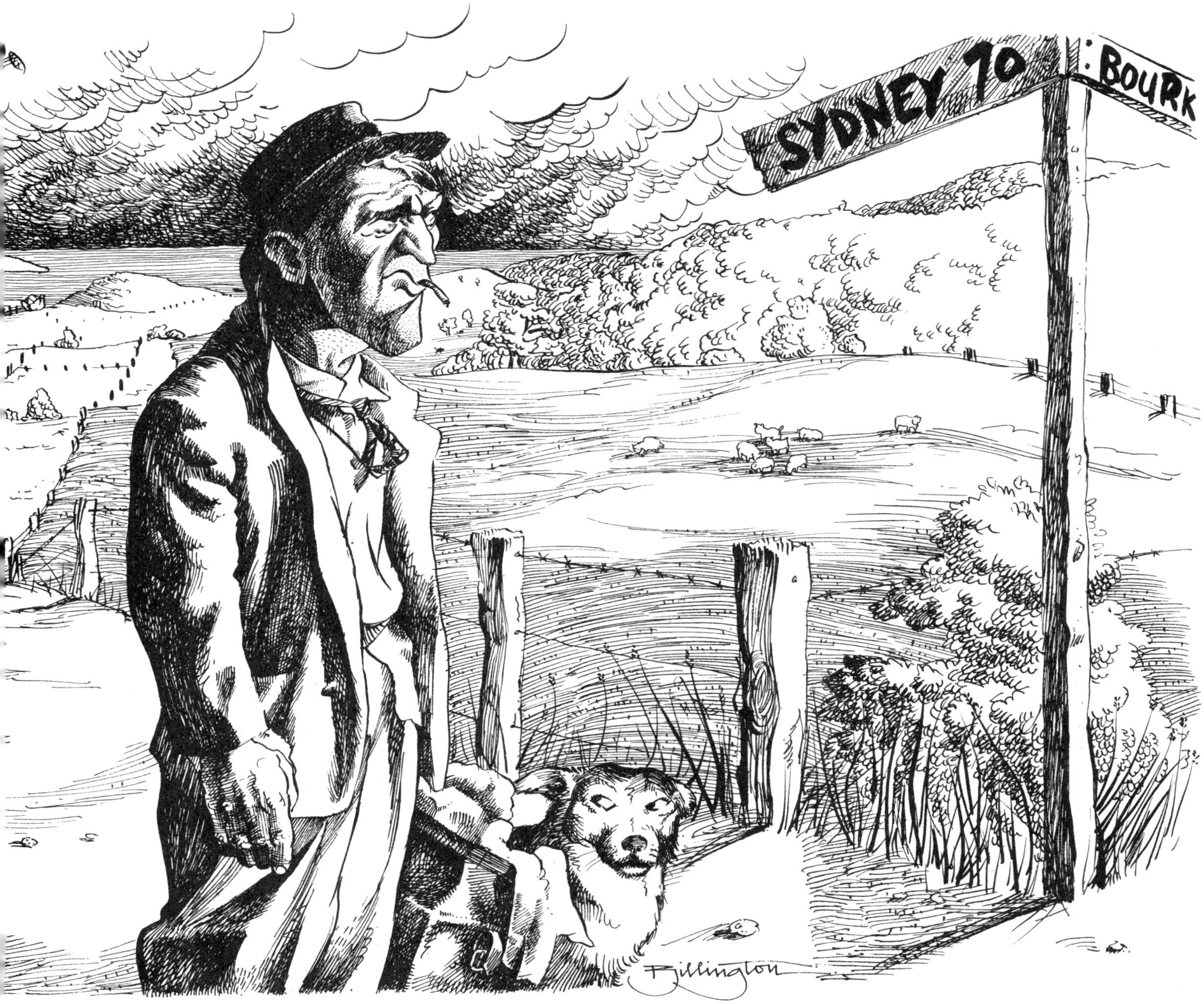

Jog Along 'til Shearing

"Bush workers either talked a lot or said very little", according to one old timer I questioned. "When they did talk it was usually of dreams – a big win at the horse races, girls they should have married, jobs they should have taken." There was always talk but somehow the shearers nearly always "jogged back" for the next season. It was usually "Good to see you again Jack", "Goodaye Jake", "Not you again, Bill" – the shearing season was like a magnet!

From the singing of Mr Joe Cashmere, Sylvania, New South Wales, in 1953. Collected by Russell Ward. It appears in Steward and Keesing's Old Bush Songs *as "The Truth Is In My Song So Clear". The tune is "Bow, Wow, Wow".*

The truth, it's in my song so clear, without a word of gammon:
The swagmen travel all the year waiting for the lambin'.
Now when this dirty work is done, to the nearest shanty steering,
They meet a friend, their money spend, then jog along till shearing.

CHORUS:
Home sweet home, that is what they left it for, their home sweet home.

Now when the shearing season comes, they hear the price that's going;
New arrivals meet old chums, then they start their blowing.
They say that they can shear each day their hundred pretty handy,
But eighty sheep is no child's play if the wool is close and sandy.

When the sheds are all cut out, they get their bit of paper,
To the nearest pub they run, they cut a dashing caper.
They call for liquor plenty and they're happy while they're drinking,
But where to go when the money's done, it's little they are thinking.

Sick and sore next morning, they are when they awaken,
To have a drink, of course they must, to keep their nerves from shakin',
They call for one, and then for two, in a way that's rather funny,
Till the landlord says, "Now this won't do; you blokes have got no money!"

They're sleeping on verandahs and they're lounging on the sofas,
Then to finish up their spree, they're ordered off as loafers,
They've got no friends, their money's gone, and at their disappearing,
They give three cheers for the river bend and jog along till shearing.

G D7 A7 C

G D7 G
The truth it's in my song so clear with - out a word of gam-mon The

D7 A7 D7 G
swag-men tra - vel all the year wait-ing for the lam-bin' Now when this dir- ty

C G D7 G
work is done to the near - est shan - ty steer - ing They meet a friend their

C D7 G C
mo - ney spend then jog a - long till shear - ing ___ Home sweet

G C D7 G
home that is what they left it for their home sweet home. ___

Back in the 1890's there were many blade shearers who could manage to shear their 300 a day "just like the legendary Jackie Howe". This was the same time when Allen Cameron made his still undisputed record of shearing a staggering two hundred lambs in two hours! The "Ryebuck" shearer was the "boss of the board" – the best shearer in the shed.

This version was collected by John Meredith and appeared in Singabout Vol. 2, No. 1, *1957. John Manifold points to another variant that has the following two lines:*
"Of a squatter outback on the gulf I've heard
With a face like a dried-up buffalo turd".
These lines have found their way into the folk revival version which adds:
"If you think he's ugly then you should see his bird".

I come from the south and my name it's Field,
And when my shears are properly steeled,
A hundred and more I have very often peeled,
And of course I'm a ryebuck shearer.

CHORUS:
If I don't shear a tally before I go,
My shears and stone in the river I'll throw,
I'll never open Sawbees to take another blow,
And prove I'm a ryebuck shearer.

There's a bloke on the board and he's got a yellow skin,
A very long nose and he shaves on the chin,
And a voice like a billy-goat dancing on a tin,
And of course he's a ryebuck shearer.

There's a bloke on the board and I heard him say
That I couldn't shear a hundred sheep in a day,
But some fine day I'll show him the way,
And prove I'm a ryebuck shearer.

Oh, I'll make a splash, but I won't say when,
I'll hop off me tail and I'll into the pen,
While the ringer's shearing five, I'll shear ten,
And prove I'm a ryebuck shearer.

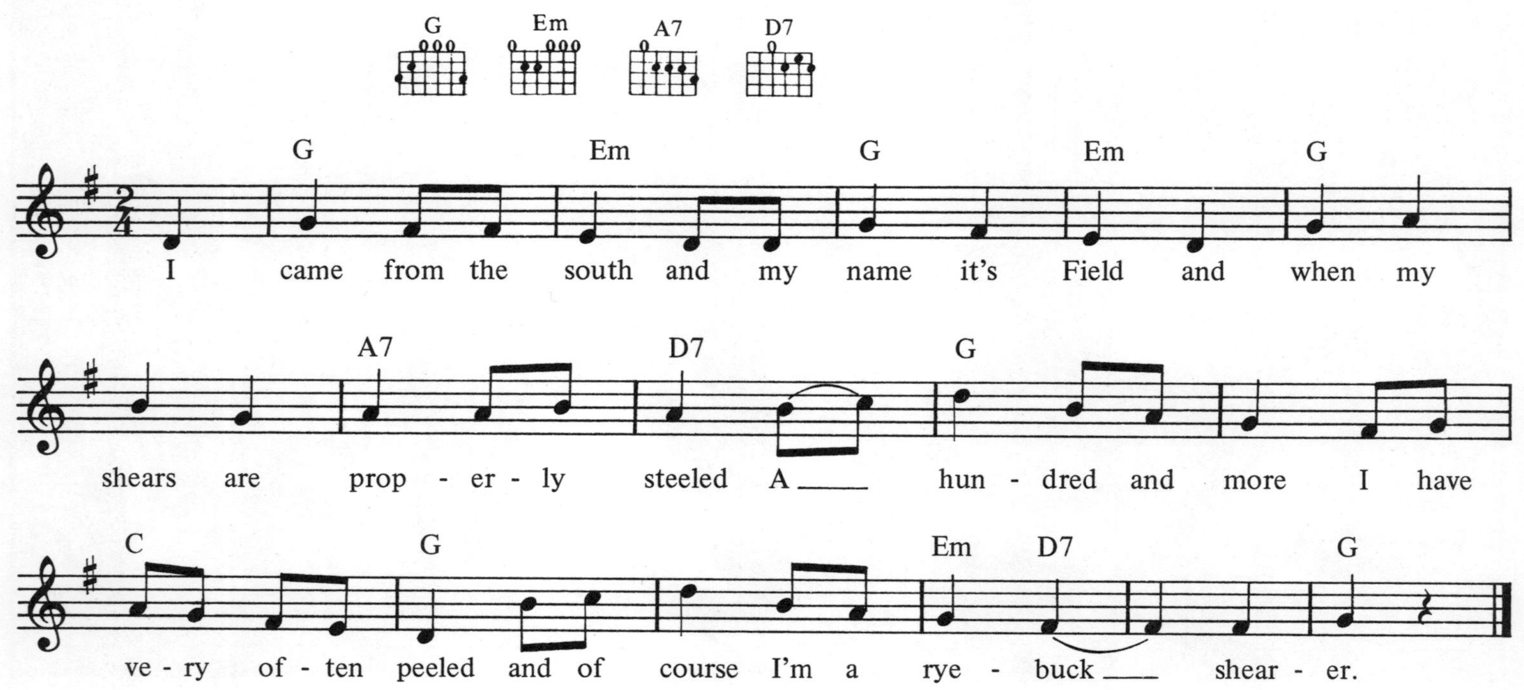

ONE

Flash Jack from Gundagai

Australia can boast some rather peculiar place names that seem to be the combined result of Aboriginal dialect, bushman's spelling and inventive guesswork. It is not unusual to find songs that rattle off an assortment of names – Barcoo, Cudjingie, Moulamein, Coleraine and One Tree Plain. "Wolseleys" and "B-Bows" are brands of hand shears.

"There's joy to be had in the life of a drover. It can be a bugger of a life sometimes – hot sun then rain, insects and loneliness – but the pleasures are there and, besides, it's in me blood." (Australian drover, 1973.)

This song seems to have been collected by A. L. Lloyd during the 1920's. Vance Palmer printed a version in his Old Australian Bush Ballads *(to a different tune). The Lloyd tune is the popular tune.*

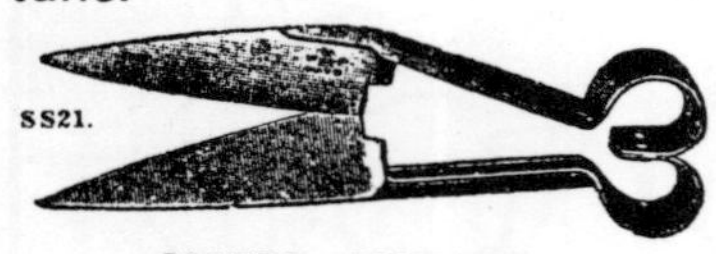

SHEEP SHEARS
B.B.A. & T.U.S. 8/6 DAGGING SHEARS 7/-
Cooper E-B HANDPIECE £5/17/6
Known by all for long Service
The original No - Rock Shear that works so easily and that costs so little to maintain! Cuts sweetly with light tension, thus lessening wear on its parts and lengthening the "life" of combs and cutters. The handpiece with the new type capped bearings.

I've shore at Burrabogie and I've shore at Toganmain,
I've shore at Big Willandra and on the old Coleraine,
But before the shearing was over I longed to get back again,
Shearing for old Tom Patterson, on the One Tree Plain.

CHORUS:
All among the wool, boys, all among the wool,
Keep your blades full, boys, keep your blades full,
I can do a respectable tally myself whenever I like to try,
And they know me round the backblocks as Flash Jack from Gundagai.

I've shore at Big Willandra and I've shore at Tilberoo,
And once I drew my blades, boys, upon the famed Barcoo,
At Cowan Downs and Trida, as far as Moulamein,
But I always was glad to get back again to the One Tree Plain.

I've pinked 'em with the Wolseleys and I've rushed with B-Bows, too,
And shaved 'em in the grease, boys, with the grass-seeds showing through.
But I never slummed a pen, my lads, whatever it might contain,
When shearing for old Tom Patterson, on the One Tree Plain.

I've been whaling up the Lachlan, and I've dossed on Cooper's Creek,
And once I rung Cudjingie shed, and blued it in a week;
But when Gabriel blows his trumpet, lads, I'll catch the morning train,
And push for old Tom Patterson's, on the One Tree Plain.

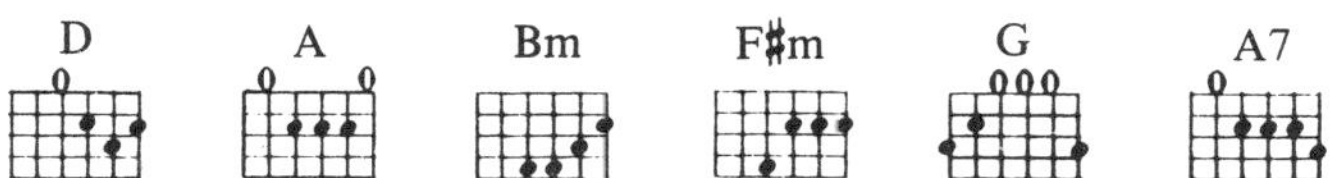
D
A
Bm
F♯m
G
A7

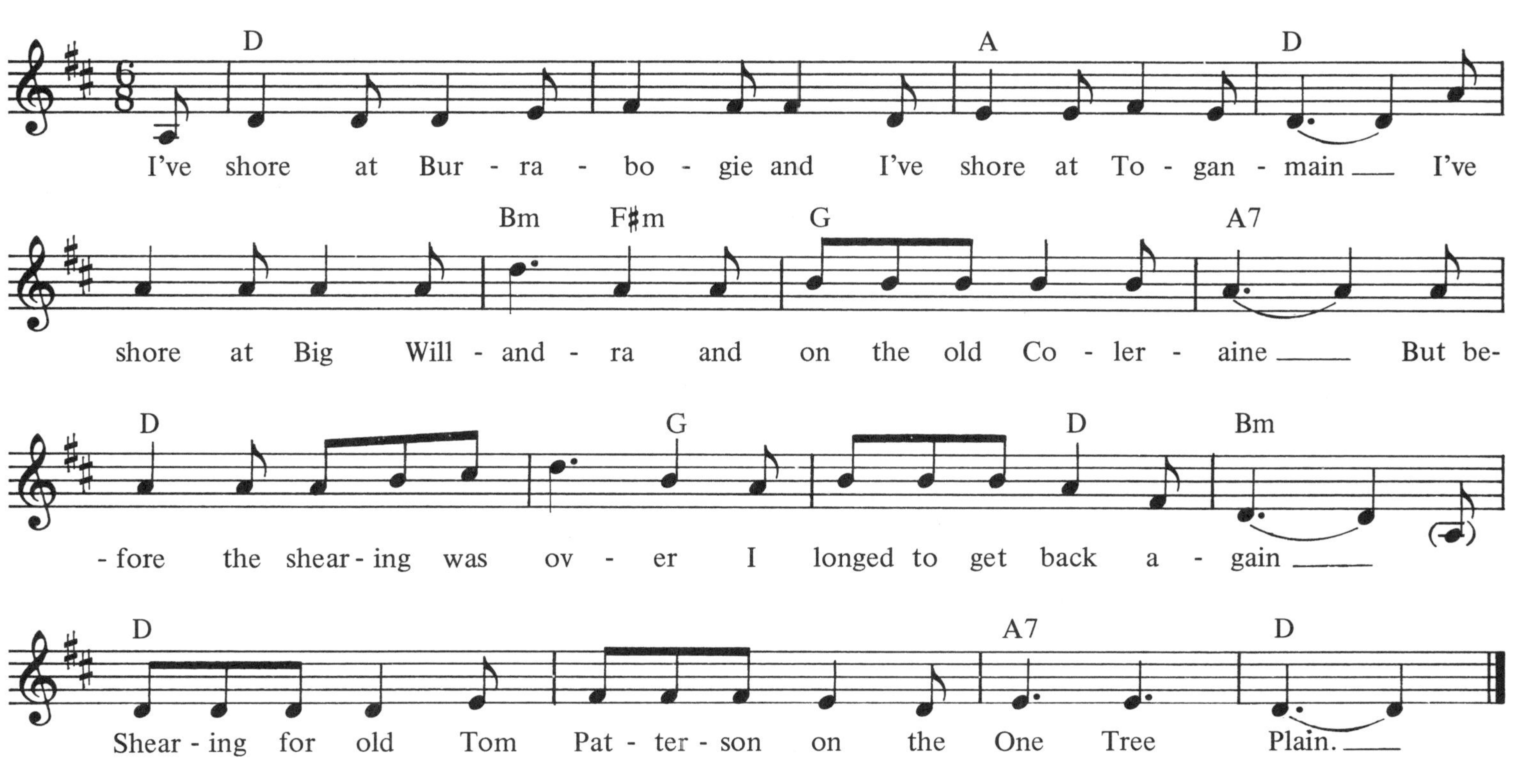
D A D
I've shore at Bur - ra - bo - gie and I've shore at To - gan - main ___ I've
Bm F♯m G A7
shore at Big Will - and - ra and on the old Co - ler - aine ___ But be-
D G D Bm
- fore the shear - ing was ov - er I longed to get back a - gain ___
D A7 D
Shear - ing for old Tom Pat - ter - son on the One Tree Plain. ___

Bluey Brink

The story of the thirsty shearer who barged into the bar and swallowed the first liquid he spotted. It was sulphuric acid!

"The German likes his beer,
The Pommy likes his half-and-half –
Because it brings good cheer.
The Scotsman likes his whiskey,
The Irishman likes his hot.
The Aussie has no national drink –
So he drinks the bloody lot!"

(Traditional toast)

This song seems to be the work of British folklorist and singer A. L. Lloyd. After spending several years in Australia Lloyd collected and re-worked many good songs. He acknowledges this one came to him from "old man Adams" of Cowra, New South Wales.

There once was a shearer by name Bluey Brink,
A devil for work and a devil for drink,
He could shear his two hundred a day without fear
And drink without winking, four gallons of beer.

Now Jimmy the barman, who served out the drink,
He hated the sight of this here Bluey Brink,
Who stayed much too late and who came much too soon,
At morning, at evening, at night, and at noon.

One morning as Jimmy was cleaning the bar
With sulphuric acid he kept in a jar,
Old Bluey came yelling and bawling with thirst,
"Whatever you've got, Jim, just hand me the first!"

Now, it ain't put in history, it ain't down in print,
But Bluey drank acid with never a wink,
Saying, "That's the stuff, Jimmy, why, strike me stone dead,
This'll make me the ringer of Stephenson's shed."

Now all that day long, as he served out the beer,
Poor Jimmy was sick with his trouble and fear,
Too worried to argue, too anxious to fight,
Seeing the shearer a corpse by the night.

But early next morning, as he opened the door,
Along came old Bluey, howling for more,
With his eyebrows all singed and his whiskers deranged,
And holes in his hide like a dog with the mange.

Says Jimmy, "And how did you like the new stuff?"
Says Bluey, "It's fine, but I ain't had enough;
It gives me great courage to shear and to fight,
But why does that stuff set me whiskers alight?

"**I** thought I knew drink, but I must have been wrong,
For what you just gave me was proper and strong,
It set me to coughing, and you know I'm no liar,
And every damn cough set me whiskers on fire!"

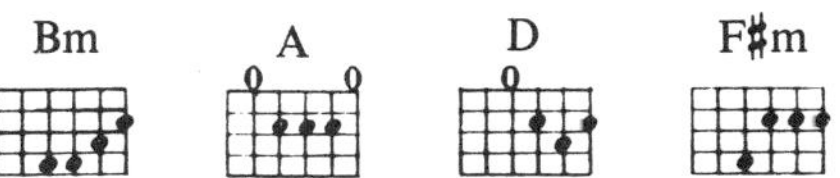
Bm
A
D
F♯m

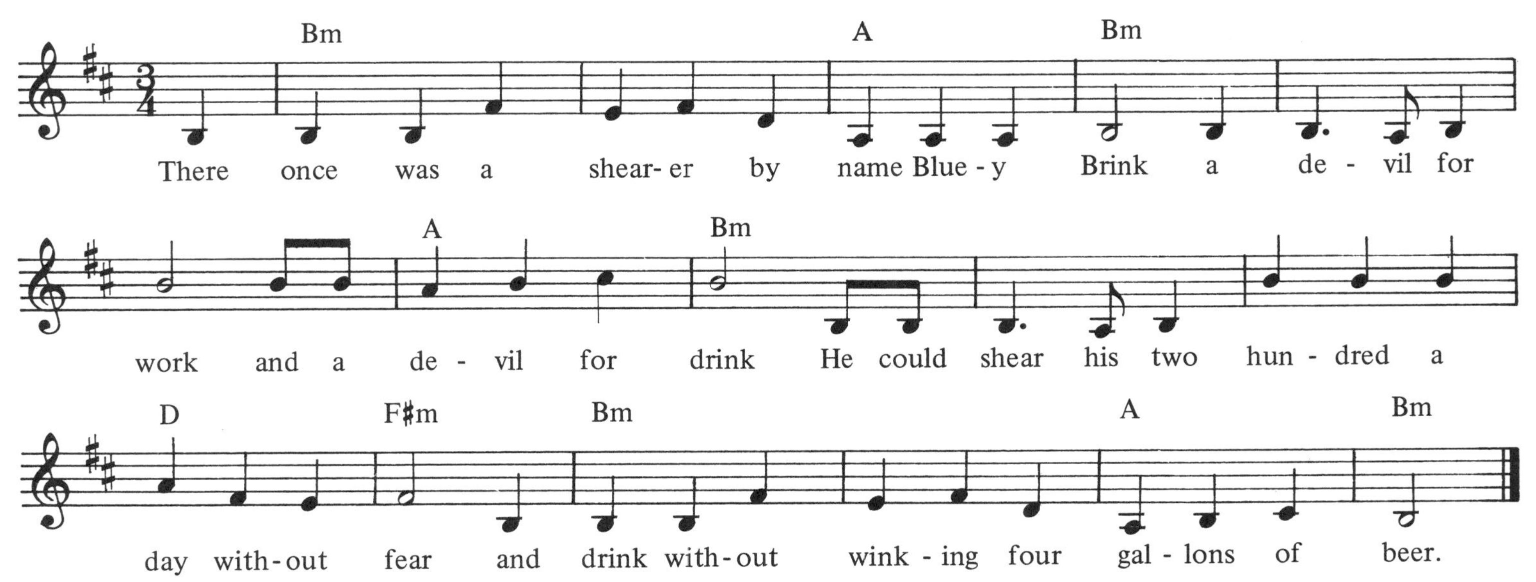
Bm A Bm
There once was a shear-er by name Blue-y Brink a de-vil for
A Bm
work and a de-vil for drink He could shear his two hun-dred a
D F♯m Bm A Bm
day with-out fear and drink with-out wink-ing four gal-lons of beer.

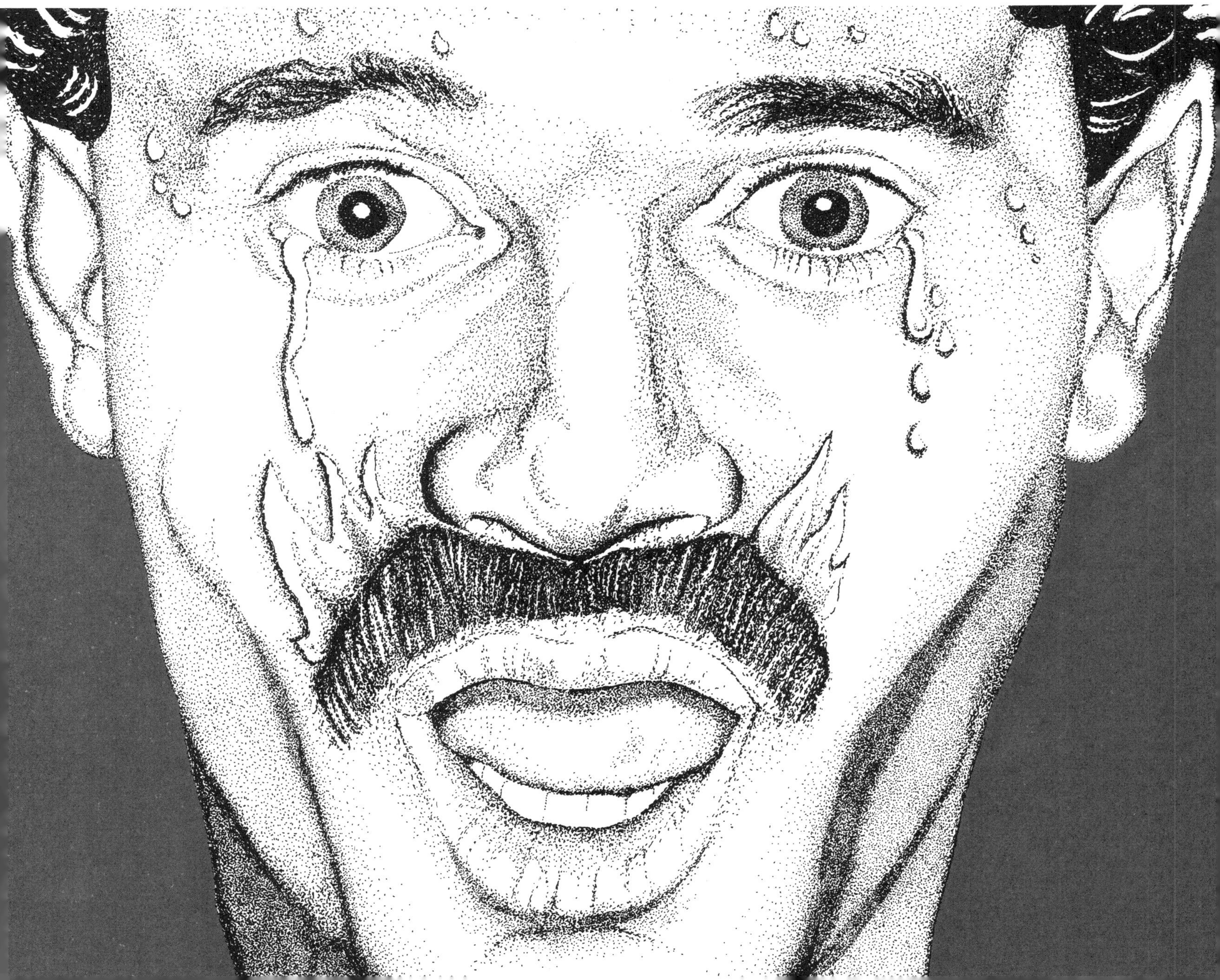

Here's a toast to the man who invented beer!

"See that big white cloud up there –
All white and frothy at the top –
Just like a jug of beer?
It's time to have a drink, boys,
For if that cloud should burst,
The drink would all run out . . .
. . . For it's just a cloud of thirst."

(Traditional toast)

"I have no pain, dear Mother, now,
But Oh, I am so dry.
Connect me to a Brewery
And leave me there to die."

(Traditional toast)

From the singing of Cyril Duncan. Collected by Warren Fahey, in 1973, Hawthorne, Queensland. Cyril learnt the song from his uncle.

A long time ago way back in history
When all they had to drink was nothing but cups of tea
Along came a man by the name of Charlie Mopps,
And he invented a wonderful drink and he gave it the name of hops.

CHORUS:
Oh, he should have been an Emperor, a Sultan or a King
And all his praises ever shall we sing
Oh, look at what he's done for us, he's filled our hearts with cheer
Lord bless Charlie Mopps – the man who invented beer!

When beer was first invented it was very very dear
Fancy paying a "chaser" for a glorious glass of beer!
People of the day were foolish, so they say,
They used to chew the hops and throw the beer away.

You can talk about inventors of today being up to date,
Our animated pictures and our photographs so great
But the greatest inventor of them all, to me is plain and clear
– it's Charlie Mopps – the man who invented beer.

The day that Charlie died, he came to Heaven's gate,
He said to Saint Peter, "Now, tell me how I rate?"
Saint Peter looked at him and said: "Now, who the hell are you?"
He said: "I'm Charlie Mopps!" and Peter said: "Straight through!"

At the Central, Imperial, the Rose and Crown as well,
One thing you can be sure, it's Charlie's beer they sell,
So come on, all you lucky lads, at ten o'clock she stops
For five short seconds remember Charlie Mopps.

(count one . . . two . . . three . . . four . . . five . . . then into chorus)

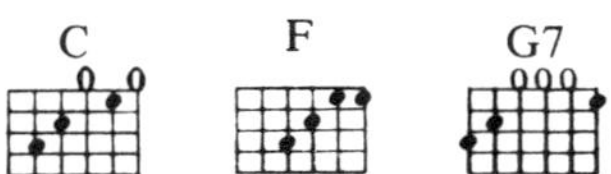
C
F
G7

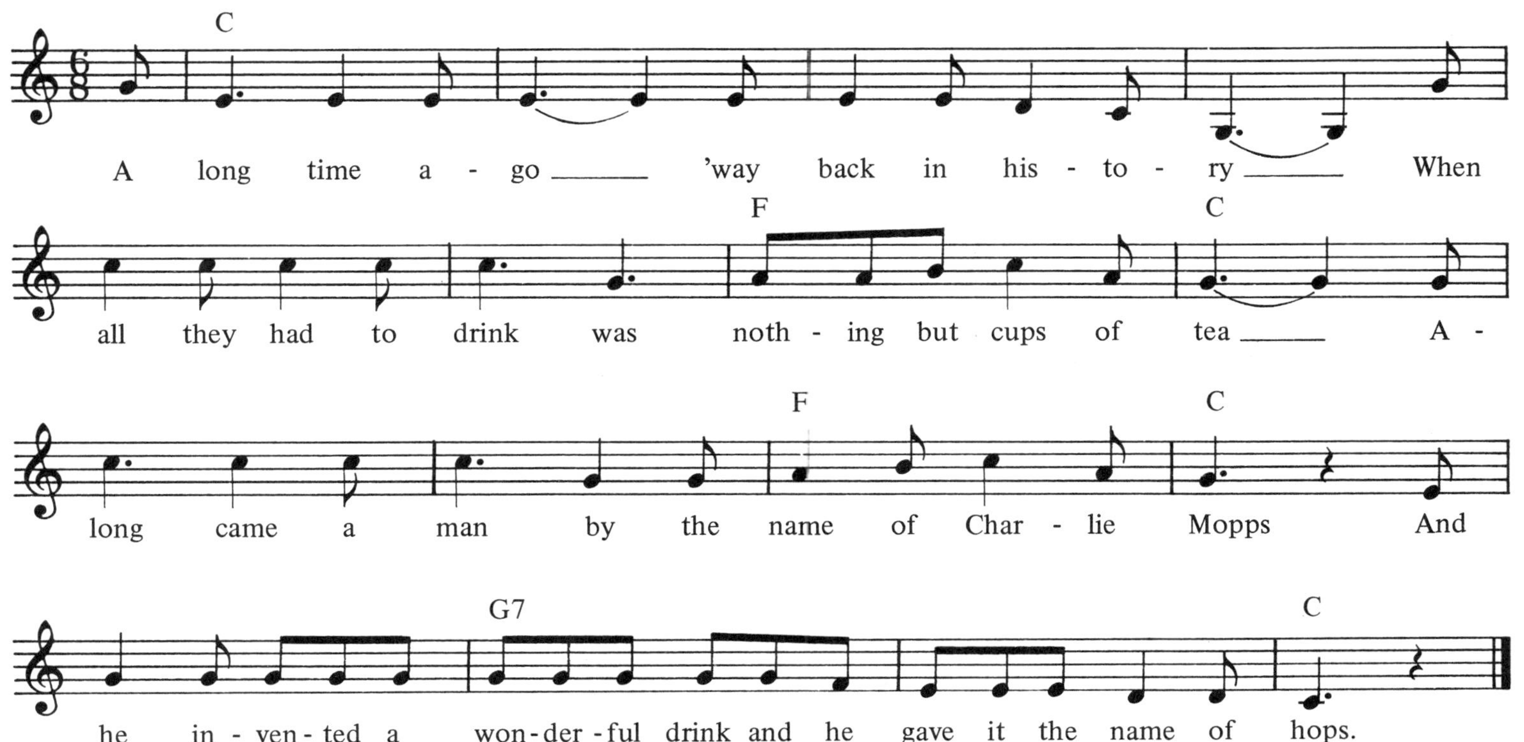
C
A long time a - go ___ 'way back in his - to - ry ___ When
all they had to drink was noth - ing but cups of tea ___ A -
F C
long came a man by the name of Char - lie Mopps And
F C
he in - ven - ted a won - der - ful drink and he gave it the name of hops.
G7 C

Undoubtedly the best known of all the shearing songs. Chock full of all the excitement and noise of the sheds, this classic song is widely known throughout Australia. The days of the "clicking" hand shears have been replaced by the whine of the electric shears. Progress!

This is the best known version of the song. It is available from several printed sources, however. This version is from the singing of swagman Jack Pobar of Toowoomba, Queensland, and was collected by Warren Fahey in 1973. Jack Pobar commented: "Here it is and it's all *Australian!"*

Out on the board the old shearer stands,
Grasping his shears in his thin bony hand,
Fixed is his gaze on a bare-bellied yeo –
Glory if he gets her won't he make the ringer go.

CHORUS:
Click go the shears, boys, click, click, click,
Wide is his blow and his hands move quick,
The ringer looks around and is beaten by a blow,
And curses the old snagger with the bare-bellied yeo.

In the middle of the floor in his cane-bottomed chair,
Sits the boss of the board with his eyes everywhere;
Notes well each fleece as it comes to the screen,
Paying strict attention that it's taken off clean.

The tar boy is there and awaiting in demand,
With his blackened tar pot in his tarry hand,
Sees one old sheep with a cut upon its back;
Here is what he's waiting for – it's "Tar here Jack!"

The Colonial Experience man, he is there of course,
With his shiny leggings on, just off his horse.
He gazes all around like a real connoisseur,
Scented soap and brilliantine, smelling like a whore.

Shearing is all over and we've all got our cheques,
Roll up your swags, boys, we're off on the tracks,
The first pub we come to it's there we'll have a spree,
And everyone that comes along, it's "Come and drink with me!"

Down by the bar the old shearer stands,
Grasping his glass in his thin bony hand,
Fixed is his gaze on a green painted keg,
Glory he'll get down on it ere he stirs a leg.

There we leave him standing, shouting for all hands,
While all around him every shouter stands,
His eyes are on the keg which now is lowering fast,
He works hard, he drinks hard, and goes to hell at last.

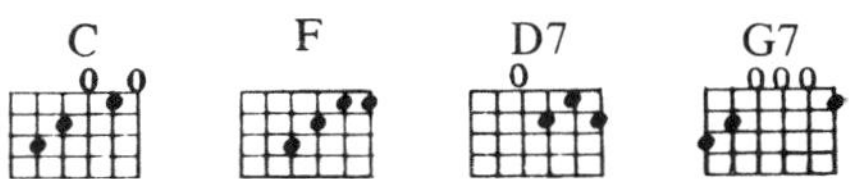

C F C D7 G7
Out on the board the— old shear-er stands Grasp-ing his shears in his thin bo-ny hand

C F G7 C
Fixed is his gaze on a bare-bel-lied yeo Glo-ry if he gets her won't he make the ring-er go.

Chorus:

G7 C F C G7
Click go the shears boys click click click Wide is his blow and his hands move— quick— The

C F G7 C F C
ringer looks a-round and is beaten by a blow And cur-ses the old snag-ger with the bare-bel-lied yeo.

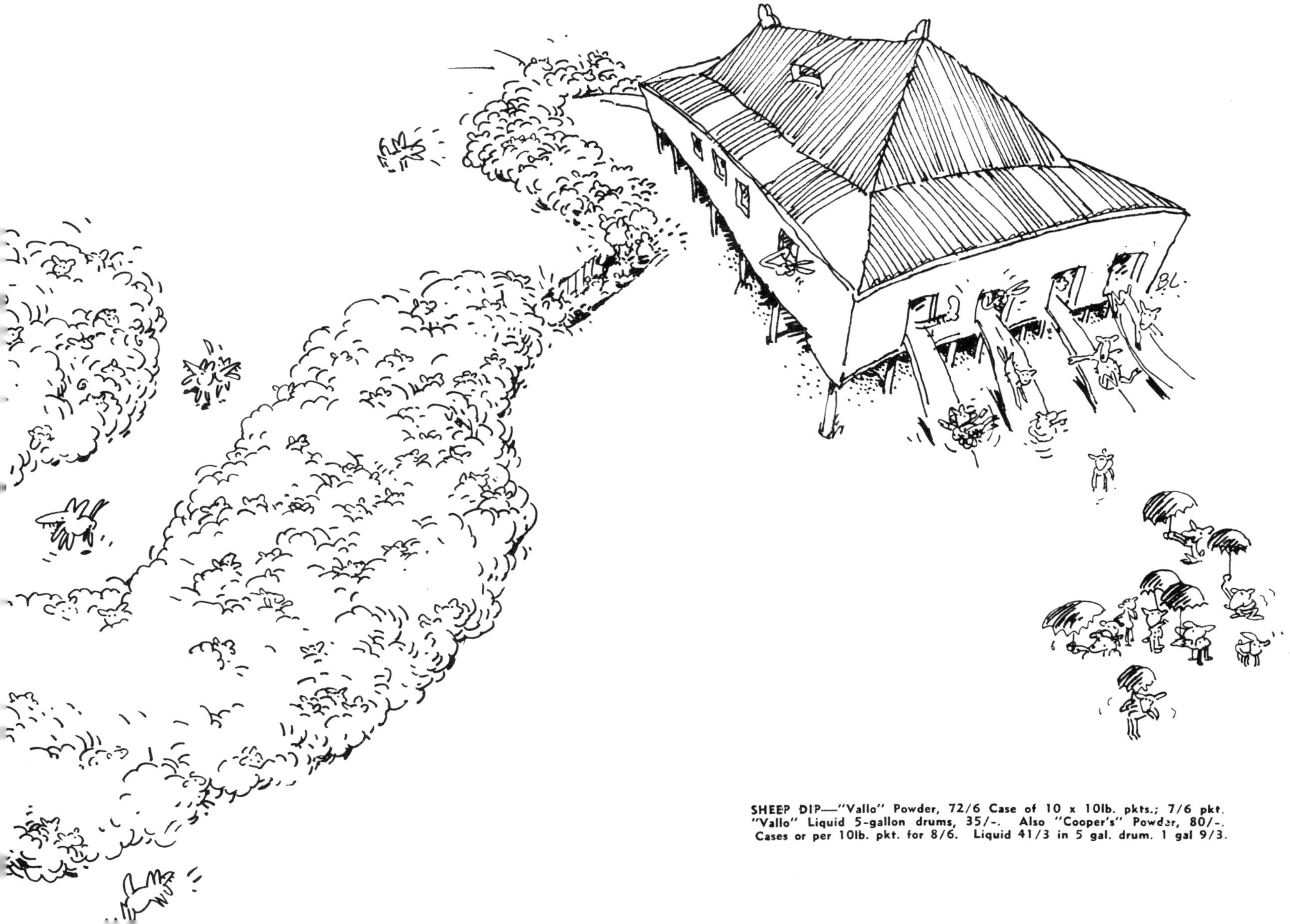

BL.

SHEEP DIP—"Vallo" Powder, 72/6 Case of 10 x 10lb. pkts.; 7/6 pkt. "Vallo" Liquid 5-gallon drums, 35/-. Also "Cooper's" Powder, 80/-. Cases or per 10lb. pkt. for 8/6. Liquid 41/3 in 5 gal. drum. 1 gal 9/3.

The Banks of the Condamine

This song is based on a very old British ballad known as "The Banks of the Nile". Both songs share the theme of the young girl offering to dress up as an associate of her lover. In this case she offers to dress as a shearer in typical bush attire of moleskin trousers and to travel with him on his shearing rounds. The shearer of today is sometimes seen with his wife, both travelling and living in a modern caravan – mobile home. Times change!

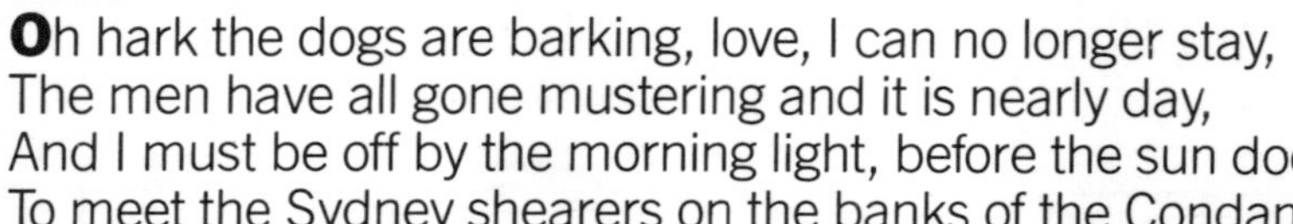

This version was printed in Bandicoot Ballads, *1951. Compare with the horse-breaking version that is in the Hurd Collection, Brisbane Library.*

MAN
Oh hark the dogs are barking, love, I can no longer stay,
The men have all gone mustering and it is nearly day,
And I must be off by the morning light, before the sun does shine,
To meet the Sydney shearers on the banks of the Condamine.

WOMAN
Oh Willy, dearest Willy, I'll go along with you,
I'll cut off all my auburn fringe and be a shearer too,
I'll cook and count your tally, love, while ringer-o you shine,
And I'll wash your greasy moleskins on the banks of the Condamine.

MAN
Oh Nancy, dearest Nancy, with me you cannot go,
The squatters have given orders, love, no woman should do so;
Your delicate constitution is not equal unto mine,
To stand the constant tigering on the banks of the Condamine.

WOMAN
Oh Willy, dearest Willy, then stay at home with me,
We'll take up a selection and a farmer's wife I'll be,
I'll help you husk the corn, love, and cook your meals so fine,
You'll forget the ram-stag mutton on the banks of the Condamine.

MAN
Oh, Nancy, dearest Nancy, pray do not hold me back!
Down there the boys are waiting, and I must be on the track.
So here's a goodbye kiss, love, back home I will incline
When we've shore the last of the jumbucks on the banks of the Condamine.

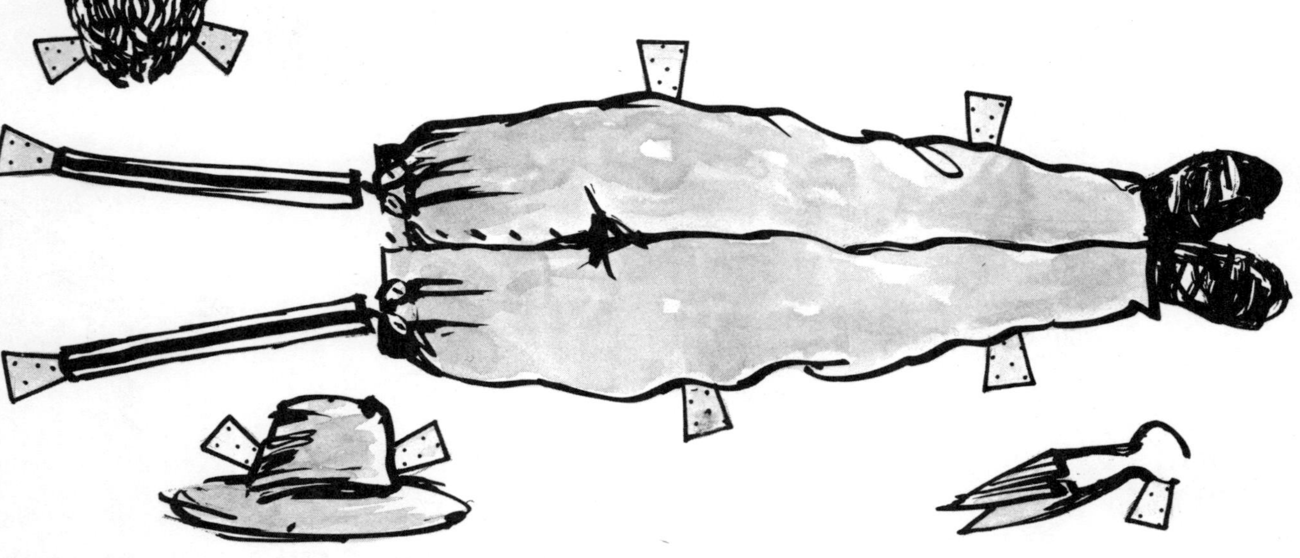

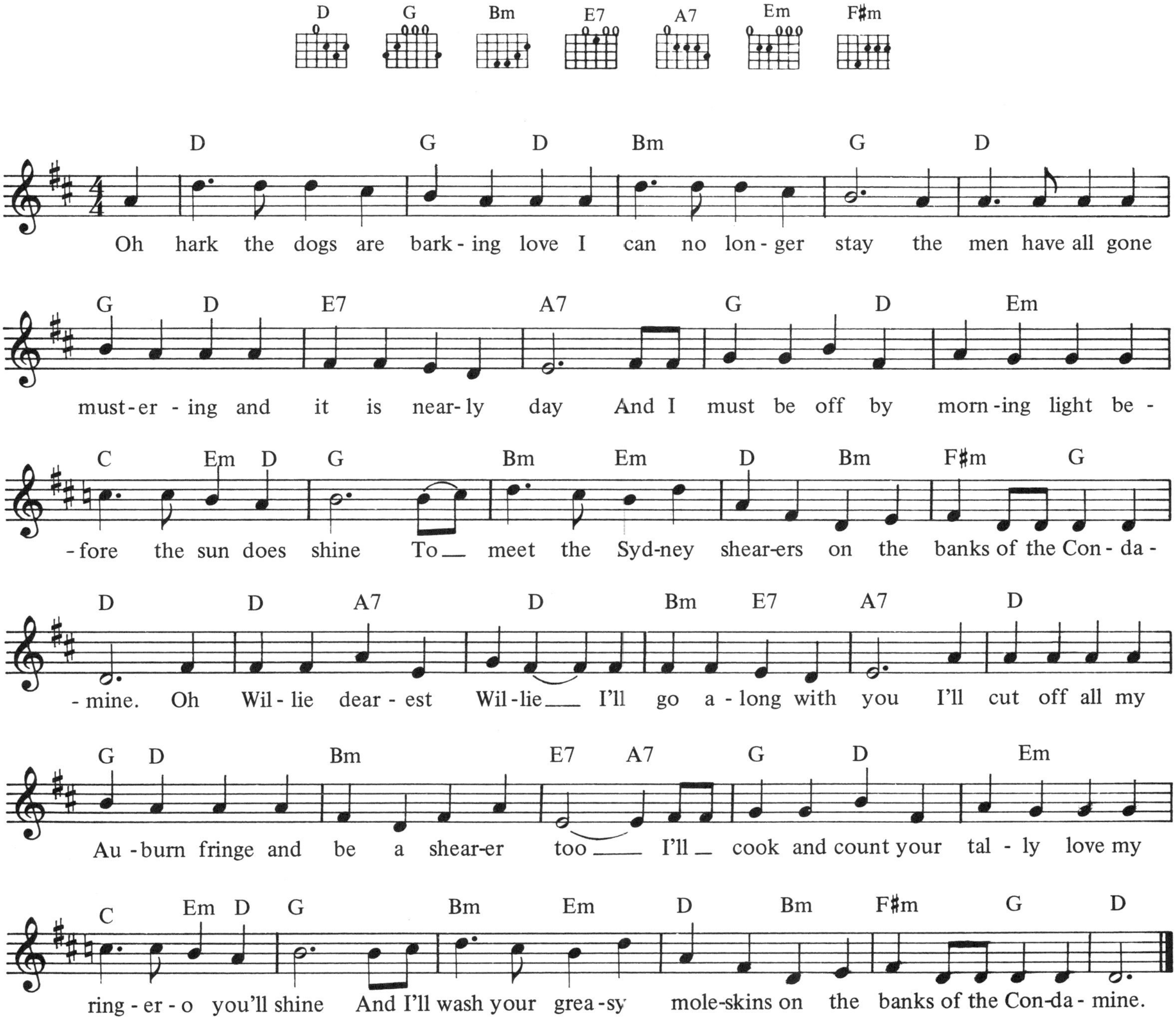

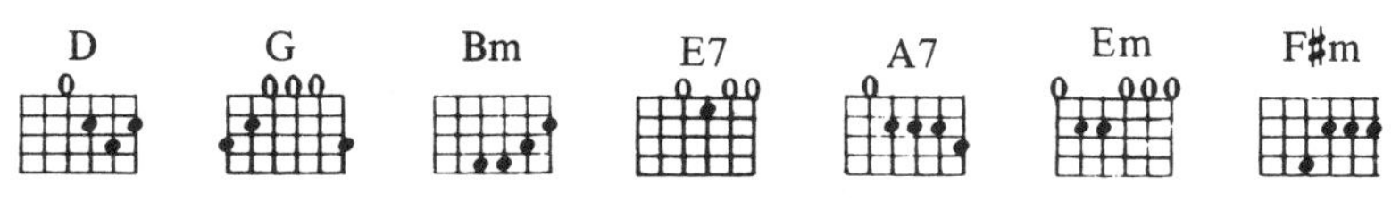

D G Bm E7 A7 Em F♯m
D G D Bm G D
Oh hark the dogs are bark - ing love I can no lon - ger stay the men have all gone
G D E7 A7 G D Em
must - er - ing and it is near - ly day And I must be off by morn - ing light be -
C Em D G Bm Em D Bm F♯m G
- fore the sun does shine To meet the Syd - ney shear - ers on the banks of the Con - da -
D D A7 D Bm E7 A7 D
- mine. Oh Wil - lie dear - est Wil - lie I'll go a - long with you I'll cut off all my
G D Bm E7 A7 G D Em
Au - burn fringe and be a shear - er too I'll cook and count your tal - ly love my
C Em D G Bm Em D Bm F♯m G D
ring - er - o you'll shine And I'll wash your grea - sy mole - skins on the banks of the Con - da - mine.

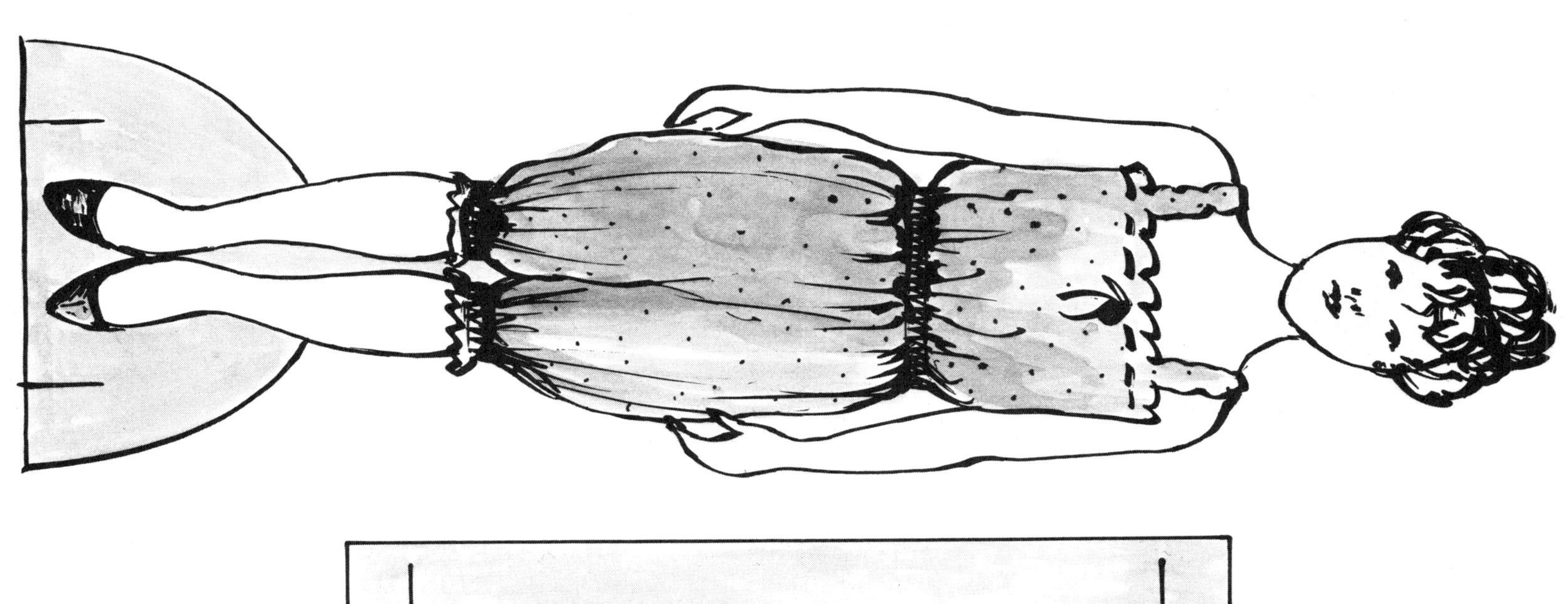

I have heard of shearers crawling on all fours to their beds after a heavy day of shearing. When a man was paid for every sheep shorn it was a case of "going hell for leather" to keep up your tally. Of course, the day was always ahead when age crept up and the tally starts to drop. This particularly sensitive song captures the thoughts of the shearer who "once was a ringer" but "can't do it now". The ringer was the fastest shearer on the board.

The old shearer will still point out that Jack Howe's great record of shearing three hundred and twenty sheep in a single day was made using hand blades. That was in 1892. It remained unchallenged for fifty-five years, and even now has been beaten only once.

Although Paterson included a version of this song in his Old Bush Songs *I have used the version collected by A. L. Lloyd in Cowra, New South Wales, around the 1920's. The tune is "Pretty Polly Perkins".*

I'm one of the has-beens, a shearer I mean,
I once was a ringer and used to shear clean,
I could make the wool roll off like the soil from the plough,
But you may not believe me, for I can't do it now.

CHORUS:
I'm as awkward as a new chum, and I'm used to the frown
That the Boss often gives me, saying, "Keep them blades down!"

I've shorn with Pat Hogan, Bill Bright and Jack Gunn,
Tommy Leighton, Charlie Fergus, and the great roaring Dunn.
They brought from the Lachlan the best they could find,
But not one among them could leave me behind.

Still it's no use complaining, I'll never say die,
Though the days of fast shearing for me have gone by,
I'll take the world easy, shear slowly and clean,
And merely have told you just what I have been.

G
D7
A7
Em

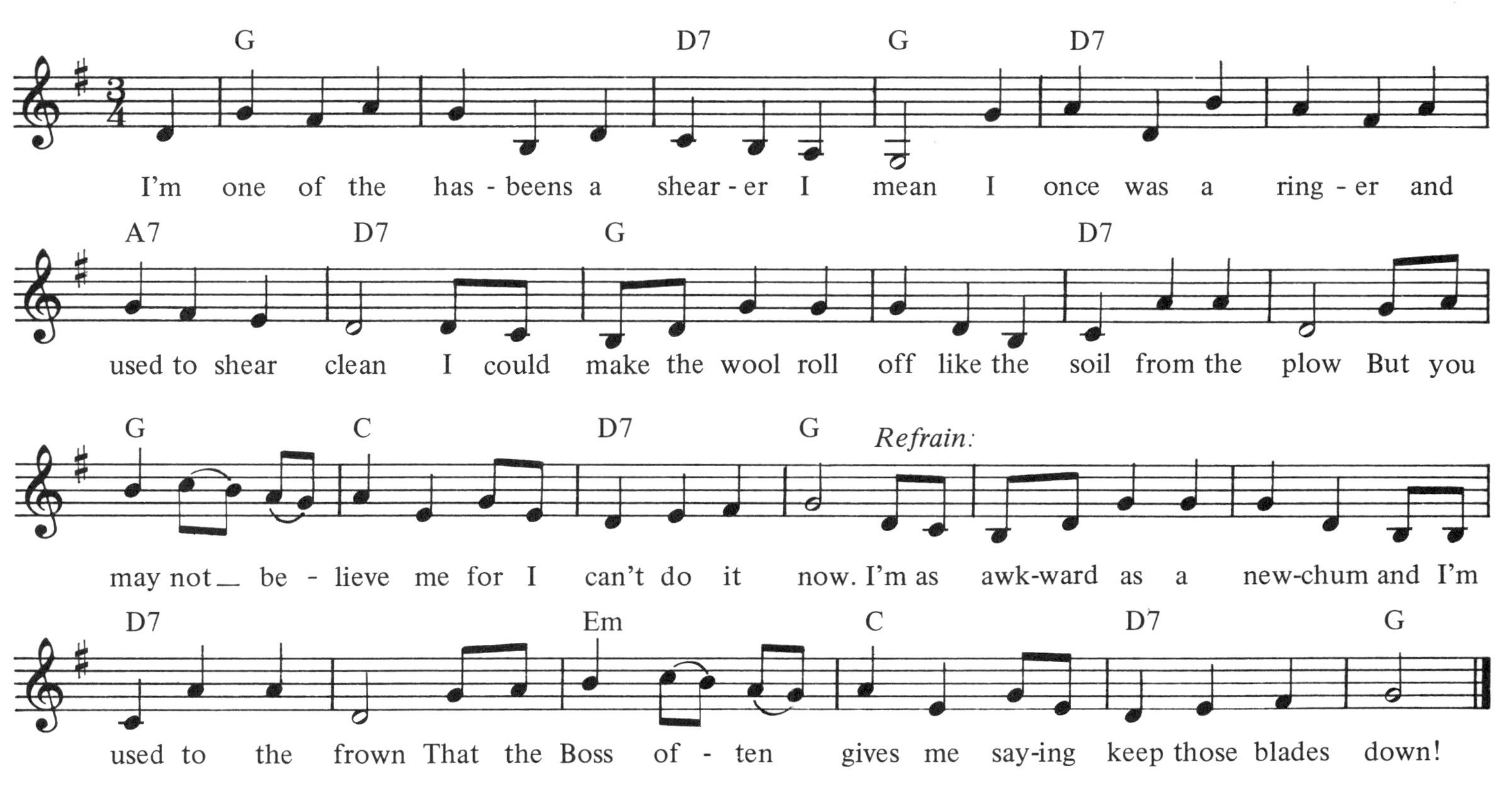
G D7 G D7
I'm one of the has - beens a shear - er I mean I once was a ring - er and
A7 D7 G D7
used to shear clean I could make the wool roll off like the soil from the plow But you
G C D7 G
Refrain:
may not — be - lieve me for I can't do it now. I'm as awk-ward as a new-chum and I'm
D7 Em C D7 G
used to the frown That the Boss of - ten gives me say-ing keep those blades down!

The Mustering Song

Tales of the supernatural are rare in Australian folk song. This story sees the station-owner dead and buried and then reappearing. Maybe it was the bush twilight, maybe the booze, or maybe . . .!

From the Hurd Collection, Brisbane Library. The tune is "So Early in the Morning". It is probably an adaptation of a minstrel song. Ron Edwards prints a version in his Big Book of Australian Folksongs, *Rigby, 1979.*

The old man came to the men's hut door
And said as he'd often said before:
"Tomorrow will be mustering day,
So boys be up and get away."

CHORUS:
So early in the morning
So early in the morning
So early in the morning
Before the break of day.

So up we got before sunrise
And off to breakfast with sleepy eyes;
The horses soon were caught and manned,
And on we jumped with whip in hand.

We found a mob not far away,
And started them off without delay.
A poley cow ran on the track;
The old man rode to fetch her back.

Now the mare he rode was fast and free,
And ran him against a bluegum tree.
She threw the old man on his head,
We picked him up and found him dead.

Next day I got the big draught horse
To take away the old man's corpse;
And in the dawn's uncertain light
I got a most tremendous fright.

For there I saw the old man's ghost
Sitting on the stockyard's corner post.
Smoking the very same old clay
He used to smoke on mustering day.

Where'er I go, where'er I stray,
I'll never forget that mustering day,
I'll never forget the old man's ghost
With his black dudgeen on the stockyard post.

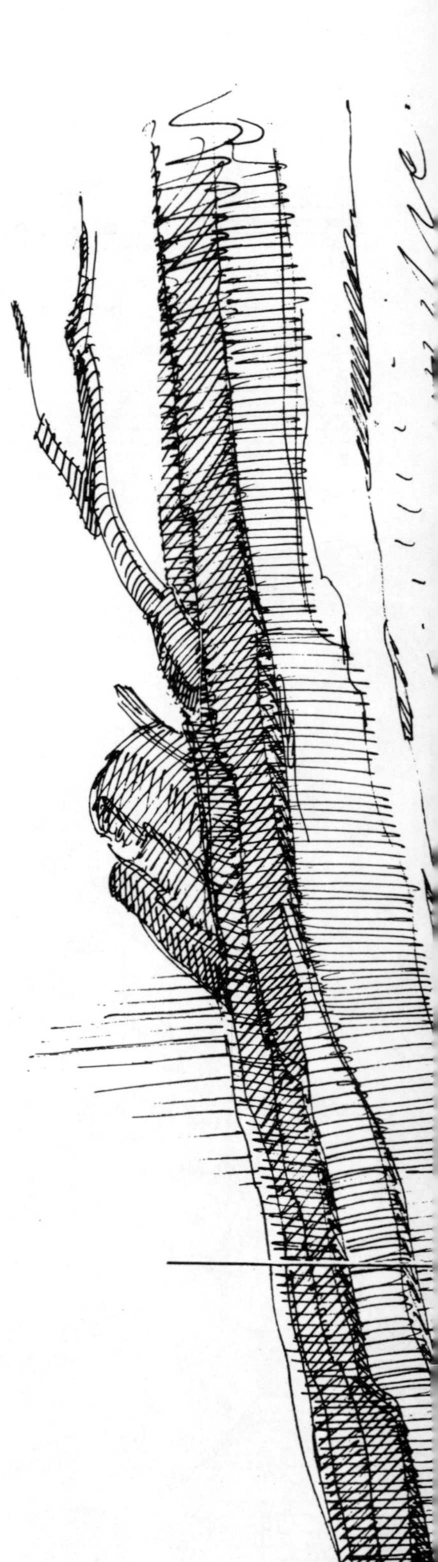

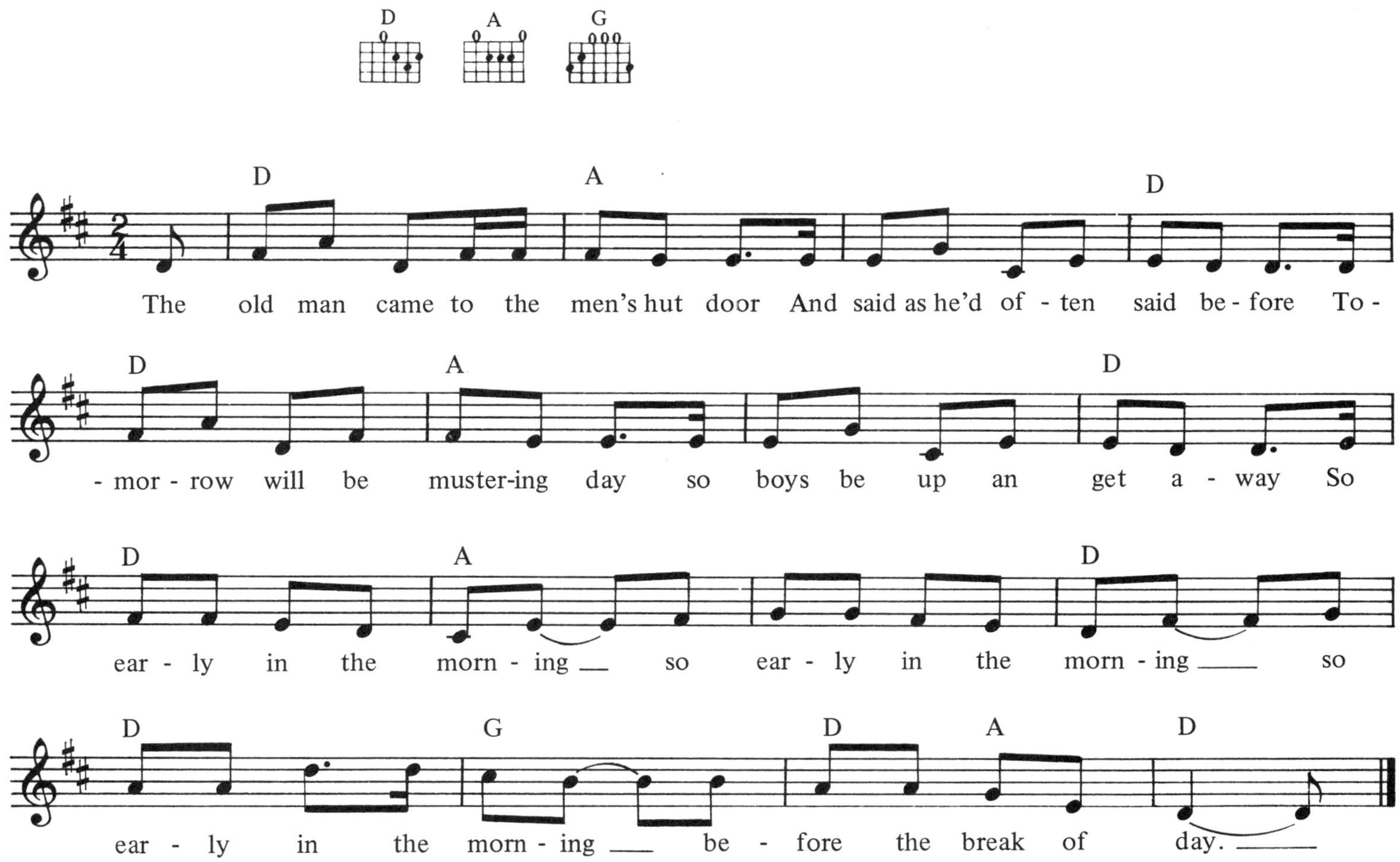

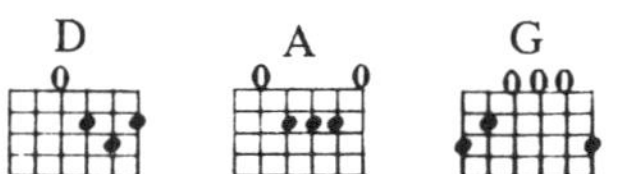

D A D

The old man came to the men's hut door And said as he'd of - ten said be - fore To -

D A D

- mor - row will be muster-ing day so boys be up an get a - way So

D A D

ear - ly in the morn - ing ___ so ear - ly in the morn - ing ___ so

D G D A D

ear - ly in the morn - ing ___ be - fore the break of day. ___

The Drover's Dream

This is a great song setting where many of the Australian bush creatures parade, play music and dance. It was a much-loved song and it found widespread popularity in the bush.

"Have you ever been droving out West,
Where the flies are a terrible pest,
And the mosquitoes at night, by Jesus, they bite,
And the bulldog ants in your blankets at night
By the Jesus you know, you're earning your dough,
When you take on droving out West!" *(Bush poem)*

From Mr Tom Grayson, Loch Lomond, Queensland. Collected in 1973, by Warren Fahey. Also collected from Mrs Blair of Ashfield, New South Wales, in 1974.

One night when travelling sheep, my companions lay asleep,
There was not a star to 'luminate the sky,
I was dreaming, I suppose, for my eyes were nearly closed,
When a very strange procession passed me by.

First there came a kangaroo, with his swag of blankets blue,
A dingo ran beside him for a mate;
They were travelling mighty fast, and they shouted as they passed,
"We'll have to jog along, it's getting late!"

The pelican and the crane, they came in from off the plain
To amuse the company with a Highland Fling;
The dear old bandicoot played a tune upon his flute,
And the native bears sat round them in a ring.

The drongo and the crow sang us songs of long ago,
While the frill-necked lizard listened with a smile,
And the emu standing near with his claw up to his ear
Said, "Funniest thing I've heard for quite a while!"

The frogs from out the swamp, where the atmosphere is damp,
Came bounding in and sat upon the stones;
They each unrolled their swags and produced from out their bags
The violin, the banjo and the bones.

The goanna and the snake, and the adder wide awake
With the alligator danced "The Soldier's Joy";
In the spreading silky oak the jackass cracked a joke,
And the magpie sang "The Wild Colonial Boy".

Some brolgas darted out from the tea-tree all about
And performed a set of Lancers very well,
Then the parrot green and blue gave the orchestra its cue
To strike up "The Old Log Cabin in the Dell".

I was dreaming, I suppose, of these entertaining shows,
But it never crossed my mind I was asleep,
Till the Boss beneath the cart woke me up with such a start,
Yelling, "Dreamy, where the hell are all the sheep?"

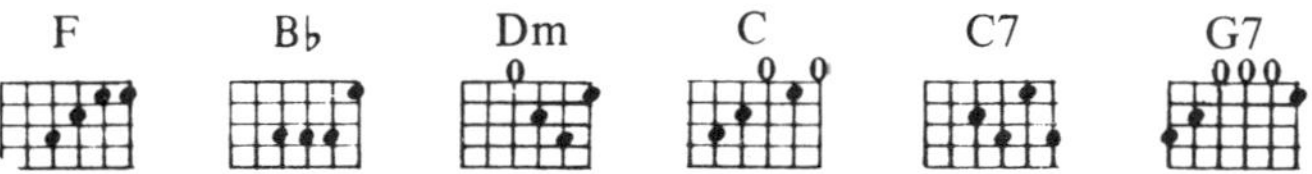

F B♭ F Dm
One night when trav - 'ling sheep My com-pan - ions lay a - sleep There was not a star to

C C7 F B♭
'lu - mi - nate the sky ___ I was dream-ing I sup - pose for my eyes were near - ly

F C7 F
closed When a ve - ry strange pro - ces - sion pas'd me by ___ First there

F Dm F
came a kan - ga - roo with his swag of blan - kets blue ___ A din - go ran be-

G7 C C7 F B♭
- side him for a mate ___ They were trav - 'ling migh - ty fast and they shou - ted as they

F Dm C7 F
passed ___ We'll have to jog a - long, it's get - ting late. ___

CASTON

Sometimes known as "Augathella Station" this song was apparently very popular with drovers who no doubt readily identified with the "ranting and roaring" drovers of the story. Typical of many boastful bush songs, the chorus has probably rattled a good many shanty rooftops over the years gone by.

This version of "Augathella Station" is the version popularised by the British collector and singer A. L. Lloyd. Another interesting text can be found in the Hurd Collection, Brisbane Library. Bob Michell produced an excellent study on this song. Published by Ron Edwards as a Folklore Occasional Paper.

Farewell and adieu to you Brisbane ladies,
Farewell and adieu to the girls of Toowong;
For we've sold all our cattle and have to be moving,
But we hope we shall see you again before long.

CHORUS:
For we'll rant and we'll roar like true Queensland natives,
We rant and we roar as onward we push,
Until we return to the old cattle station
What joy and delight is the life in the bush!

The first camp we make is called the Quart-pot,
Caboolture and Kilcoy, then Colinton hut;
We pull up at Stonehouse, Bob Williams' paddock,
And early next morning we cross the Blackbutt.

On, on! Past Taromeo to Yarraman Creek, boys!
It's there where we'll make a fine camp for the day,
Where the water and grass are both plenty and good, boys,
The life of a drover is merry and gay.

Now the camp is all snug and supper is over,
We sit round the fire enjoying a smoke,
And yarning of dogs and of cattle and horses,
Till all join in chorus to Grandfather's Clock.

Then it's right through Nanango, that jolly old township,
"Good day to you, lads" with a hearty shake-hands;
"Come on, this is my shout!", "Well, here's to our next trip,
And we hope you'll come back, boys, tonight to our dance."

Oh, the girls look so pretty; the sight is entrancing;
Bewitching and graceful they join in the fun,
The waltz, polka, first step and all other dancing,
To the old concertina of Jack Smith the Don.

Now fill up your glasses and drink to our lasses;
Come, sing the loud chorus, sing farewell to all.
Until we return to the old cattle station,
We'll always be pleased to give you a call.

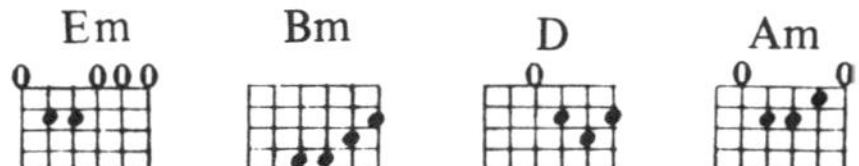
Em
Bm
D
Am

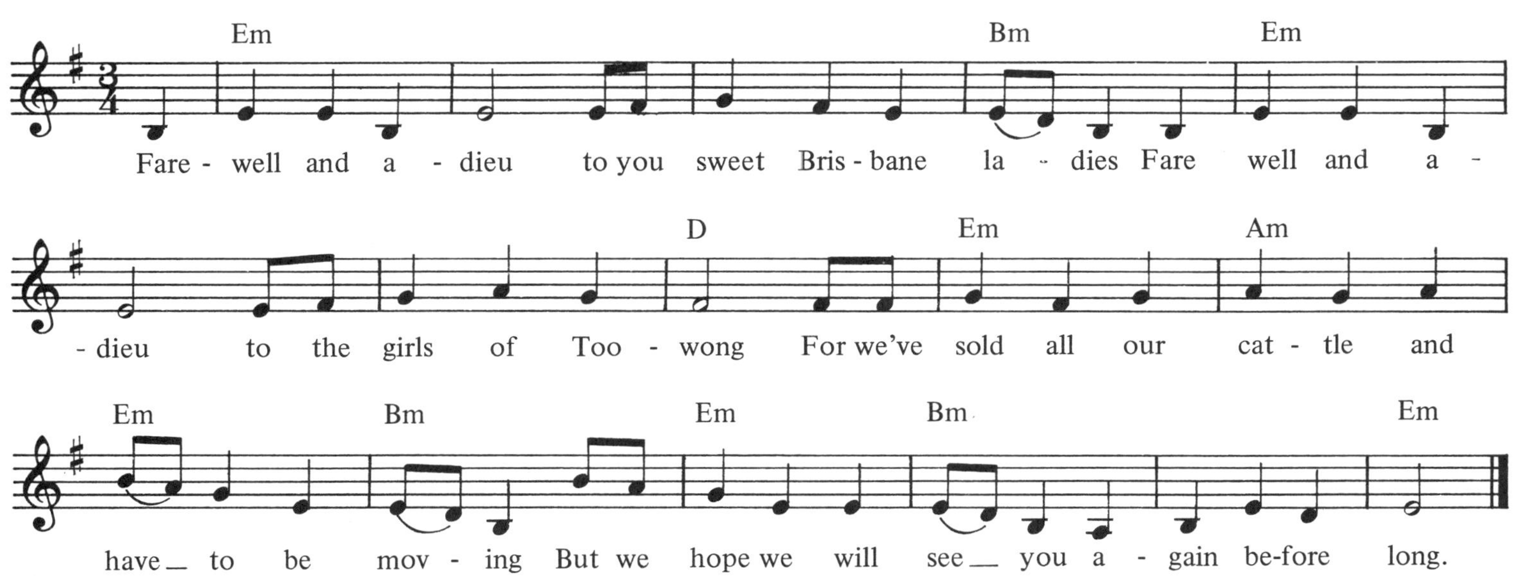
Em Bm Em
Fare - well and a - dieu to you sweet Bris - bane la - dies Fare well and a -
D Em Am
- dieu to the girls of Too - wong For we've sold all our cat - tle and
Em Bm Em Bm Em
have_ to be mov - ing But we hope we will see_ you a - gain be-fore long.

The Overlanders

The drovers were often called "overlanders" because of the unbelievably long journeys they would take to lead their bellowing herds from feeding spot to feeding spot. As with any itinerant and isolated bush worker, the end of the journey was a good enough reason for celebration. As the song says, "When we've earned a spree in town we'll live like pigs 'in clover' " – it also points out that often "the whole damn cheque pours down the neck of many a Queensland drover".

There seem to be two related tunes to this popular droving song. This is the standard setting, however. The tune as interpreted by A.L.Lloyd is quite handsome. A version appears on the record "The Great Australian Legend", Topic Records. The text is from the Joy Durst Songbook *published by the Victorian Folk Music Club.*

There's a trade you all know well; it's bringing cattle over –
On every track, to the Gulf and back, men know the Queensland drover.

CHORUS:
So pass the billy round, boys, don't let the pint pot stand there,
For tonight we drink the health of every overlander.

I come from northern plains where the girls and grass are scanty,
Where the creeks run dry or ten feet high and it's either drought or plenty.

There are men from every land, from Spain and France and Flanders,
They're a well-mixed pack, both white and black, the Queensland overlanders.

When we've earned a spree in town, we live like pigs in clover;
And the whole damn cheque pours down the neck of many a Queensland drover.

As I pass along the road, the children raise my dander,
Shouting, "Mother dear, take in the clothes, here comes an overlander."

There's a girl in Sydney Town, who said, "Please don't leave me lonely",
I said, "It's sad, but my old prad has room for one man only."

But I'm bound for home once more, on a prad that's quite a goer,
I can find a job with a crawling mob on the banks of the Maranoa.

C F G7 Am

C F C G7
There's a trade you all know well It's bring-ing cat-tle ov-er On
C F C G7 C
ev-'ry track to the Gulf and back men know the Queens-land dro-ver
Chorus:
So
Am F C G7
pass the bil-ly round, boys Don't let the pint-pot stand there For to
C F C G7 C
night we'll drink the health of ev-'ry Ov-er-land-er.
© VISKA

The Flash Stockman

*"The stockmen of Australia, what rowdy boys are they,
They will curse and swear a hurricane if you come in their way.
They dash along the forest on black, bay, brown or grey,
And the stockmen of Australia, hard riding boys are they!"*

(Traditional poem)

The life of the Australian stockman was one of routine and responsibility. The cattle herds were continually on the move with regular checks for strays and the menace of dingo attacks and cattle duffers. Life was levelled on the roadside for it was an endless series of nights around the campfire and early mornings in the saddle. When the stockman completed his run it was usually a case of "going on the rantan".

Collected by A. L. Lloyd c.1930 from an unnamed source. Steward and Keesing print a full text in Old Bush Songs *credited to Mr D. Carroll of Mosman, New South Wales.* Ben Bowyang Reciter, *1933, has another version.*

I'm a stockman by me trade
And me name is Ugly Dave,
I'm old and grey and I've only got one eye,
In the yard I'm good, of course,
But just put me on a horse
And I'll go where lots of others daren't try.

I can lead 'em through the gidgee,
Over country rough and ridgy,
I'll lose 'em in the very worst of scrub.
I can ride both rough and easy,
With a dewdrop, I'm a daisy;
And a right down bobby-dazzler in the pub.

You should see me with a whip,
I can give the dawdlers gyp,
I can make the flamin' echoes roar and ring,
With a branding iron well,
I'm a perfect flaming swell;
In fact, I'm duke of every bloody thing.

If it's fencing that you're after,
I'm a mighty flamin' grafter
I bar 'em from the bottom of the hole,
Clean-skin fleece they are a treat,
I can chuck 'em fifty feet;
But I wouldn't be a scab to save me soul.

Now see me skin a sheep,
It's so lovely you could weep,
I can act the silvertail as if me blood were blue.
Now strike me pink or dead!
If I stood upon me head,
I'd be just as good as any other two!

I've a notion in me pate,
That it's luck – it isn't fate,
That I'm so far above the common rung
For in anything I do,
You can cut me fair in two,
For I'm much too bloody good to be in one!

D7 G G7 C D

I'm a stock - man by me trade And me name is Ug - ly Dave. I'm

G Em Am D7 G

old and grey and I've only got one eye. In the yard I'm good of

G7 C D G D7 G

course. But just put me on a horse And I'll go where lots of oth-ers dare-n't try.

G7 C G

I can lead them through the gid-gee. Ov - er coun - try rough and rid - gy. I'll

Em Am D7 G G7

lose 'em in the ve - ry worst of scrub I can ride both rough and ea - sy. With a

C G D7 G

dew-drop I'm a dai - sy; And a right down bob - by - daz - zler in the pub.

Just as sailors like to be buried at sea and airmen like to have their ashes scattered through the skies, the stockman feels it right that his last resting place should be under the shade of the tall Australian gum trees with the fragrance of the native wattle. This song was known by "any stockman worth his salt".

From the singing of Mr Rad Dawson, Forrester's Beach, New South Wales, in 1973. Collected by Warren Fahey. Mr Dawson was a retired stockman and knew this song and "The Dying Stockman".

Be ye stockman or no, to my story give ear,
Alas for poor Jack, no more shall we hear
The crack of his stockwhip, his nag's lively trot,
His clear "Go ahead, boys", his jingling quart pot.

CHORUS:
For we laid him where wattles their sweet fragrance shed,
And the tall gum trees shadow the stockman's last bed.

When drafting one day, he was gored by a cow,
"Alas!" cried poor Jack, "It's all up with me now!
For I fear I shall never my saddle regain,
Or bound like a wallaby over the plain."

His whip, it is silent, his dogs they do mourn,
His horse waits in vain for his master's return,
No friends to bemoan him, unheeded he dies,
Save Australia's dark sons, none knows where he lies.

Now, stockman, if ever on some future day,
After wild cattle you happen to stray,
Tread softly the creek-bed where trees make a shade,
For it may be the spot where poor Jack's bones are laid.

FINIS
SM

The Dying Stockman

This song has many relatives – Dying Airmen, Dying Bagmen, Dying Cowboy, Dying Fettlers and, of course, the infamous Dying Harlot. One of the most popular of all the bush songs, "The Dying Stockman" relates the dying wishes of the stockman . . . No fancy graveyard for him – "wrap me up in my stockwhip and blanket and bury me deep down below . . . in the shade where the coolibahs grow."

From the singing of Rad Dawson, Forrester's Beach, New South Wales, recorded 1973. Collected by Warren Fahey.

A strapping young stockman lay dying,
His saddle supporting his head,
And his comrades around him were crying,
As he leant on his elbow and said:

CHORUS:
"Wrap me up in my stockwhip and blanket,
And bury me deep down below,
Where the dingoes and crows won't molest me,
In the place where the coolibahs grow.

"**T**hen cut down two stringybark saplings,
Place one at my head and my toe,
Carve on them crossed stockwhip and saddle,
To show there's a stockman below.

"**T**here's tea in the battered old billy,
Place the pannikins all in a row,
And we'll drink to the next merry meeting,
And say that a stockman lies low.

"**I**f I had the flight of a bronzewing,
Away to my true love I'd fly,
Straight to the home of my childhood
And there I would lay down and die.

"**B**ut hark! 'tis the wail of a dingo,
Watchful and weird – I must go,
For it tolls the death-knell of the stockman,
Who soon will be lying below."

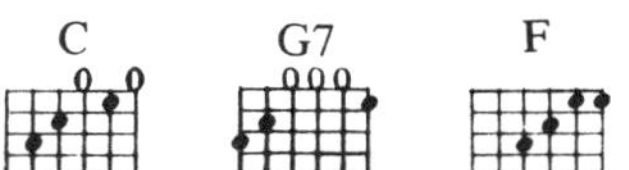
C
G7
F

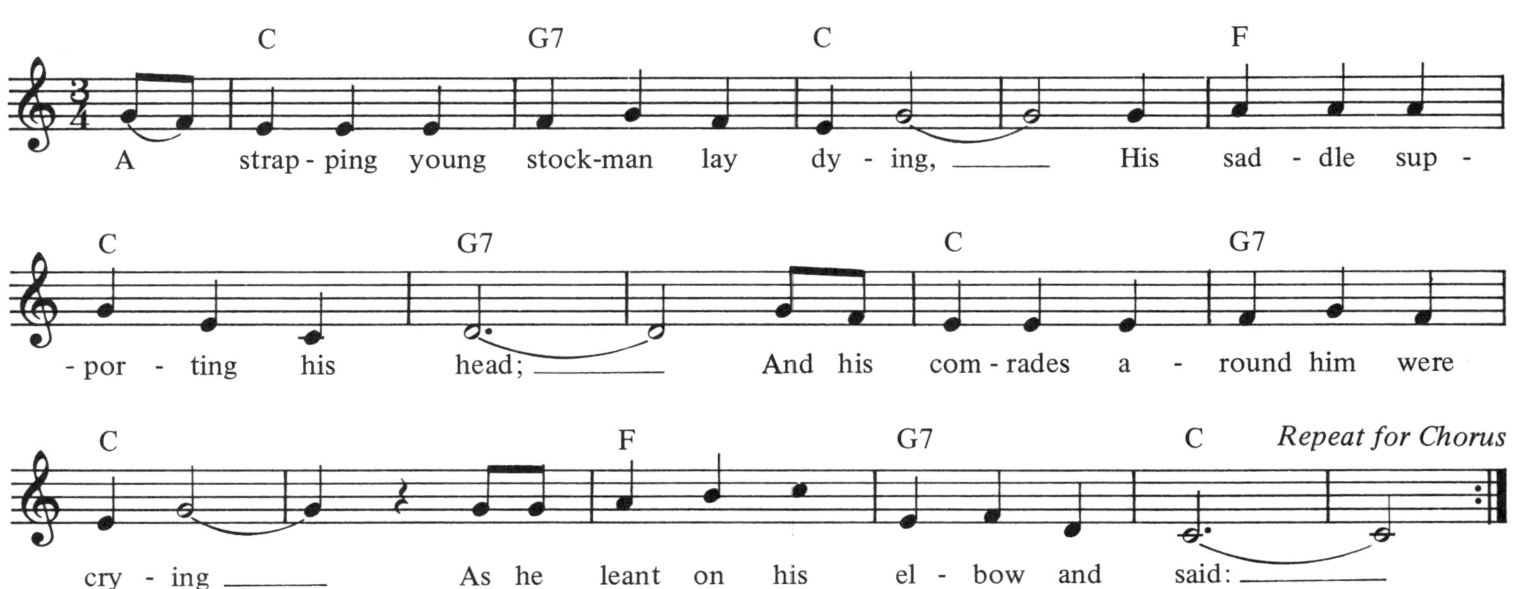
C G7 C F
A strap-ping young stock-man lay dy-ing, His sad-dle sup-
C G7 C G7
-por-ting his head; And his com-rades a-round him were
C F G7 C
Repeat for Chorus
cry-ing As he leant on his el-bow and said:

The Gumtree Canoe

A love song from the Australian bush. The mighty gum-trees are extremely solid and the Aboriginal people used them as dug-out canoes. In this song the mighty gum floats down the inland river like "a feather".

From the singing of Mr Jim Cargill, Randwick, New South Wales, in 1973. Collected by Warren Fahey. Mr Cargill can be heard singing this song on Larrikin record LRF007, "Bush Traditions", 1976, Sydney.

On a thorn bonny river, in a hut I was born,
Built of thorns and wild yellow corn,
It's there, I first met with Julia, so true,
And we went for a row in the gum-tree canoe.

CHORUS:
We will row, yes, we'll row
Over the waters so blue
Like a feather I'm afloat –
In my gum-tree canoe.

With my thumb on the banjo, my toe on the oar,
I'll sing to my Julia, I'll sing as I row
And the stars shone down on Julia, so true,
On the night we rowed out in my Gum-tree canoe.

'**T**was for three solid days we sailed out in the bay,
We could not get back, we were forced to stay.
Then we spied a large ship, flying the flag of true blue,
And she took us in tow, in my gum-tree canoe.

I once left the river, and went on the land
To set myself up as a cocky, so grand,
But the life didn't suit me, it made my heart sore,
So, back to the bonny river, boys, and Julia once more.

Chorus:

The Freehold on the Plain

"I cast my eyes on the plain before me, and saw my flock of sheep studding the plain, with my working bullocks at a little distance . . . As we sat at breakfast that morning in my rude cottage, with the bare walls of logs of trees and the shingle roof above us, all rough enough, but spacious, and a little too airy, I began to have a foretaste of that feeling of independence and security of home and subsistence which I have so many years enjoyed." (Memories of an early settler.)

With the joys of ownership came the problems of drought, flood, bushfires and economic disaster – sometimes all at once! Times were tough for the early settler and many were forced to walk off their treasured property "leaving it for the crows and 'roos".

Printed in Paterson's Old Bush Songs *and the Hurd Collection, Brisbane Library. The tune is identified as "The Little Old Log Cabin in the Lane".*

I'm a broken-down old squatter, my cash it is all gone,
Of troubles and bad seasons I complain;
My cattle are all mortgaged, of horses I have none,
And I've lost that little freehold on the plain.

CHORUS:
The stockyard's broken-down, and the woolshed's tumbling in
I've written to the mortgagees in vain;
My wool it is all damaged and it is not worth a pin,
And I've lost that little freehold on the plain.

I commenced life as a squatter some twenty years ago,
When fortune followed in my train;
But I speculated heavy and I'd have you all to know
That I've lost that little freehold on the plain.

I built myself a mansion, and chose myself a wife;
Of her I have no reason to complain;
For I thought I had sufficient to last me all my life,
But I've lost that little freehold on the plain.

And now I am compelled to take a drover's life,
To drive cattle through the sunshine and the rain,
And to leave her behind me, my own dear loving wife –
We were happy on that freehold on the plain.

I'm a bro - ken down old squat - ter my cash it is all gone Of
trou - bles and bad sea - sons I com - plain
My cat - tle are all mort-gaged of hor-ses I have none And I've lost that lit - tle free- hold on the plain.
The stock-yards bro - ken down and the wool-sheds trem-bling in I've
writ-ten to the mort-ga - ges in vain;
My wool it is all dam-aged and it is not worth a pin,
And I've lost that lit - tle free - hold on the plain.
MORTGAGEES AUCTION

The Man From Tumbarumba is a typical bush character. He has worked at nearly every job from rabbiter to shearer, drover to well-sinker . . . he's the man who has done nearly everything – a "jack of all trades". I once met a bushman just like our man – he'd done everything and I asked him what was the most difficult job he'd ever taken. "I was up Bundaberg way and a cockie farmer asked me to take on as a drover. He had five hundred eighteen-gallon kegs of rum he needed to go to Hobart in the island of Tasmania. He gave me a push start and the barrels rolled on down through Queensland, New South Wales, Victoria and finally to Hobart." I asked him about the great expanse of water known as Bass Strait. "Oh! Strike me blue, mate, I didn't go that *way!"*

A poem set to music by Warren Fahey. The adapted tune is of British origin and commonly known as "The Jack of All Trades".

He asked for work at muster-time,
We tried him as a rider,
We tried him out as the rousteabout,
And as the cook's offsider,
He had sailed the seven seas,
He'd been up in Alaska,
He'd been in every western state
From Texas to Nebraska.

CHORUS:
He said he'd shorn a sheep or two,
And cut a bit of lumber,
And waged war on the kangaroo,
At Tumba-bloody-rumba.

We had him in the shearing shed,
We put him on the stacker,
We tried him digging rabbits out,
He wasn't worth a cracker,
He had a shop in Singapore,
He owned a pearling lugger,
He was a champ at baccarat,
Australian rules and rugger.

He never showed his aptitude,
On work he was allotted,
But showed his skill upon the drinks,
And cigarettes he botted,
He said he'd climbed the Matterhorn,
He'd been a union leader,
And years ago in Adelaide
He was a pigeon breeder.

We tried him cutting fencing posts,
We tried to find his caper,
Until that happy pay-day when
He got his piece of paper.
I wonder what he's doing now,
Perhaps back on the lumber,
Or shooting kanga-bloody-roos,
At Tumba-bloody-rumba.

D A A7 C
D A
He asked for work at mus - ter time we tried him as a ri - der__ we
D A7 D
tried him as the rouse a - bout and as the cook's off - si - der.__ He
D C D A7
said he'd sailed the se - ven seas he'd been up in Al - as - ka __ he'd
D A7 D G D A7 D
been in eve - ry west - ern state from Tex - as to Neb - ras - ka __ He
D A7
said he'd shorn a sheep or two and cut a bit of lum - ber __ and
D A7 D
waged war on the kan - ga - roo at Tum - ba - bloo - dy - rum - ba.
PARK
NEIL McLEAN '84

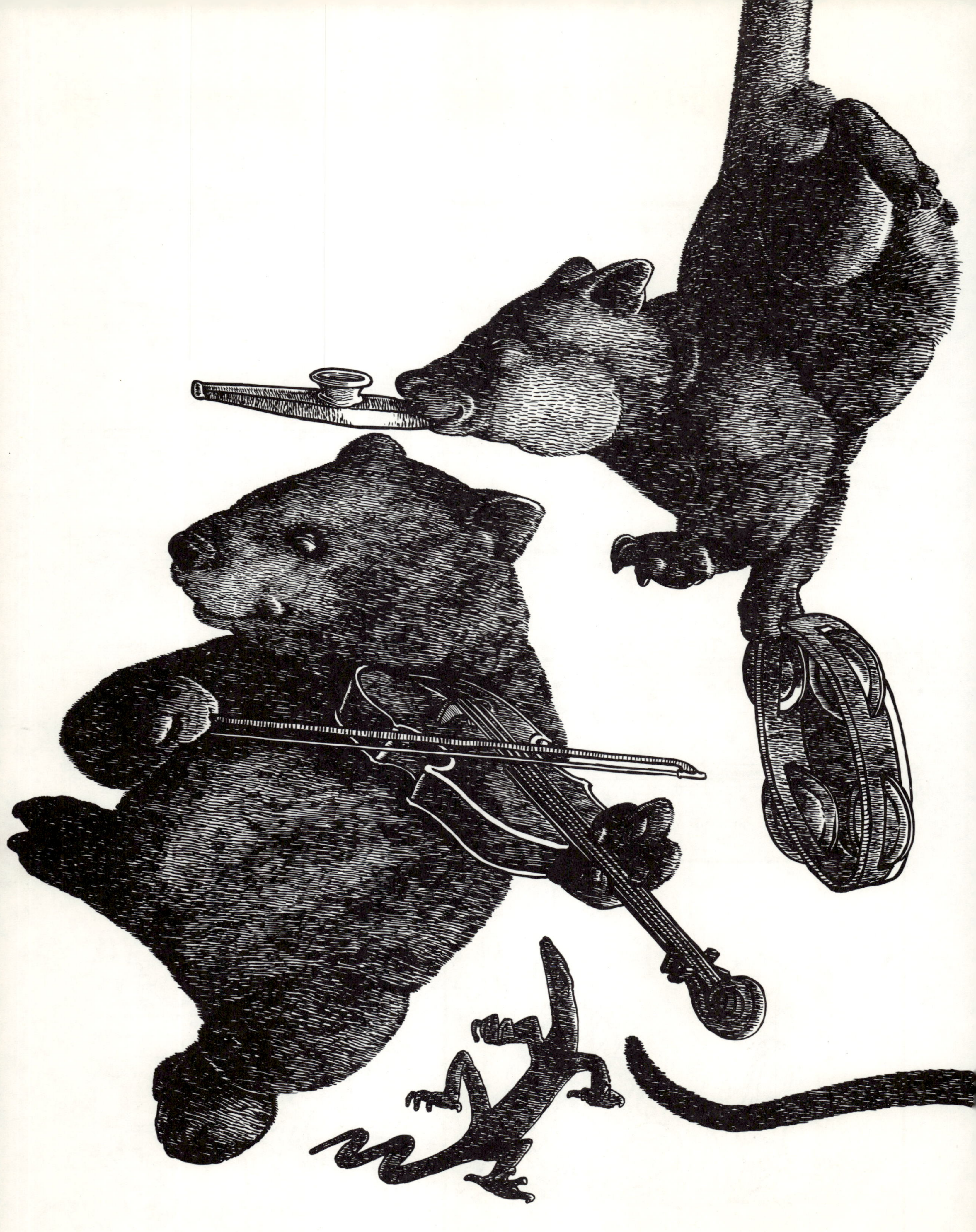

SWAGMEN, VICTORIAN EXPANSION SPORTING LIFE AND DISASTERS

By the year 1900 Australia had grown into a young adult. Gone were the gloomy days of its convict past. Gone too were the glorious days of gold that had attracted adventurers from the four corners of the globe. The heady days of pioneering were also past and wool, cattle and crops were now an accepted part of the economy. Here was Australia in the twentieth century – a rather brash and gawky young adult.

The world's largest island continent had seen some dramatic changes. It was no longer the "impenetrable bush" for railways and roadways now snaked their ways across mountains, down rivers and across plains. Telegraphic wires linked city to city and town to town. Waterways now boasted dams and programmes of irrigation were sending much needed water to thirsty lands "up the country". It was still a country of "bushwackers" but more and more people were settling in the cities, no doubt lured by the attraction of regular employment, cheaper housing, higher learning and the general excitement of urban living.

The 1890's had been a decade of bitter strikes followed by widespread rural unemployment. Men, women and even children were forced to uproot and travel the roadway, taking their chances "on the wallaby". There are desperate stories of pioneering families, forced by drought or economic circumstance, who simply walked off their properties "leaving the parched fields to the crows".

Desperation is often the mother of invention and many songs, poems and yarns were created to hold the national spirit together. Good times were ahead and new employment opportunities were soon found in the booming cities as well as in established industries such as coal mining and sugar which had now reached an international market.

The good times were shortlived for in the early days of the 1900's Australia declared its involvement as an ally in World War I. Men marched off to Europe in a scenario that was to be repeated in the 1940's when once again Australia found itself a participant in World War II. Once again songs were created to boost the spirits of those at the front and those at home.

In the 1930's Australia suffered yet another blow finding itself in a national economic depression the likes of which it could never have imagined. Once again men, women and children found themselves "on the wallaby". There was a general feeling of resentment – Australia, the land of riches, was bankrupt.

Wars and the Depression had forced Australia to "stand on its own legs" and the "down under" country was now an accepted and respected international contributor. Australia had paid its dues! The 1950's saw a quick recovery with vigorous programmes of economic development, housing and mineral booms and, most importantly, an aggressive programme of immigration that turned Australia into a vibrant multi-cultural society.

Although still tied to Britain as part of the Commonwealth, flames of independence have always been obvious. The republican calls of the Eureka Stockade still ring in the voices of many Australians who sing the national anthem of "Advance Australia Fair".

Australia is now hurtling towards the twenty-first century but as with any community of people we must look at our past for the keys to the future. We have a unique heritage, raised in the bush with a rare quality of independence and self-sufficiency. It is a heritage of mateship combined with a love of freedom and of country. Our history is told in our songs. Long may we sing!

Nails

It is interesting to see how tradesmen's tools are incorporated into a song text. This song offers the tools of trade of the building industry. In its way it is a nonsense song with a delightful "fal a riddy" chorus.

From the singing of Cyril Duncan, Hawthorne, Queensland. Collected by Warren Fahey, in 1973. Cyril learnt this song from his bullock driver father who had an extensive repertoire including "The Parson and The Clerk", "Trafalgar Bay" and "The Ship That Never Returned". Cyril's versions of these songs and fifty-three others are included in the "Australian Folklore Unit" tape collection.

Harry Cotter, bush musician

Oh, this world is like a bag of nails and some are very queer ones,
Some are sharp and some are flat, and some are very dear ones
Through sprigs and spikes and sparrables, some little, great and small, Sir
Some folk love nails with monstrous heads
And some love none at all, Sir.

CHORUS:
With me O dear O
Right fal a riddy iddy
O dear O

Now the doctor nails you with a bill
Which sometimes proves a sore nail
The undertaker wishes you as dead as any door-nail
You'll often find a client to be nailing his employer
And the Devil knows the lawyer
But the lawyer knows the Devil.

Now French monsieurs will get some clouts
If here they cause to roam, Sir,
Us Englishmen like hammers . . .
Will be sure to drive them home, Sir.

Now if I've gained your kind applause
For what I've sung and said, Sir,
I'm sure you will agree I've hit
The right nail on the head, Sir.

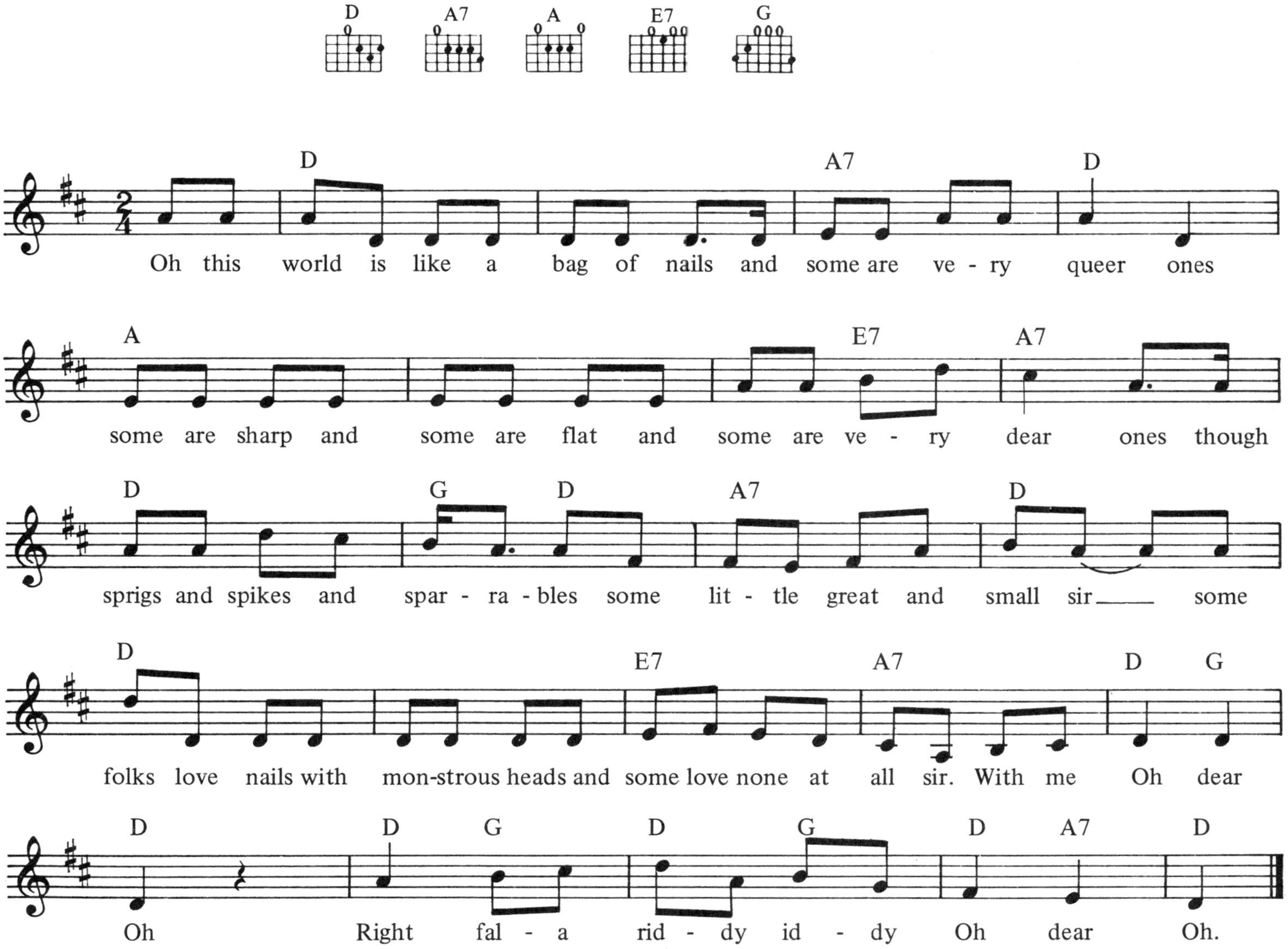

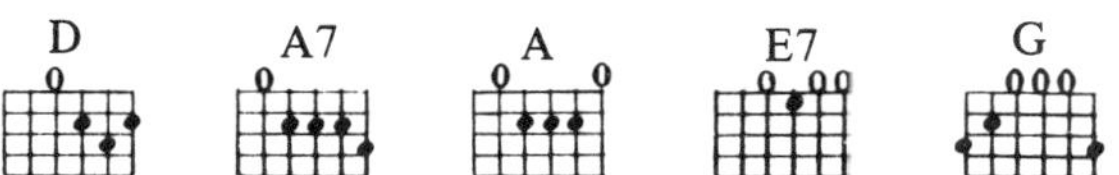

D A7 A E7 G
D A7 D
Oh this world is like a bag of nails and some are ve - ry queer ones
A E7 A7
some are sharp and some are flat and some are ve - ry dear ones though
D G D A7 D
sprigs and spikes and spar - ra - bles some lit - tle great and small sir some
D E7 A7 D G
folks love nails with mon-strous heads and some love none at all sir. With me Oh dear
D D G D G D A7 D
Oh Right fal - a rid - dy id - dy Oh dear Oh.

J. BALLCOCK
PLUMBER
OVERDUE
BUTCHER

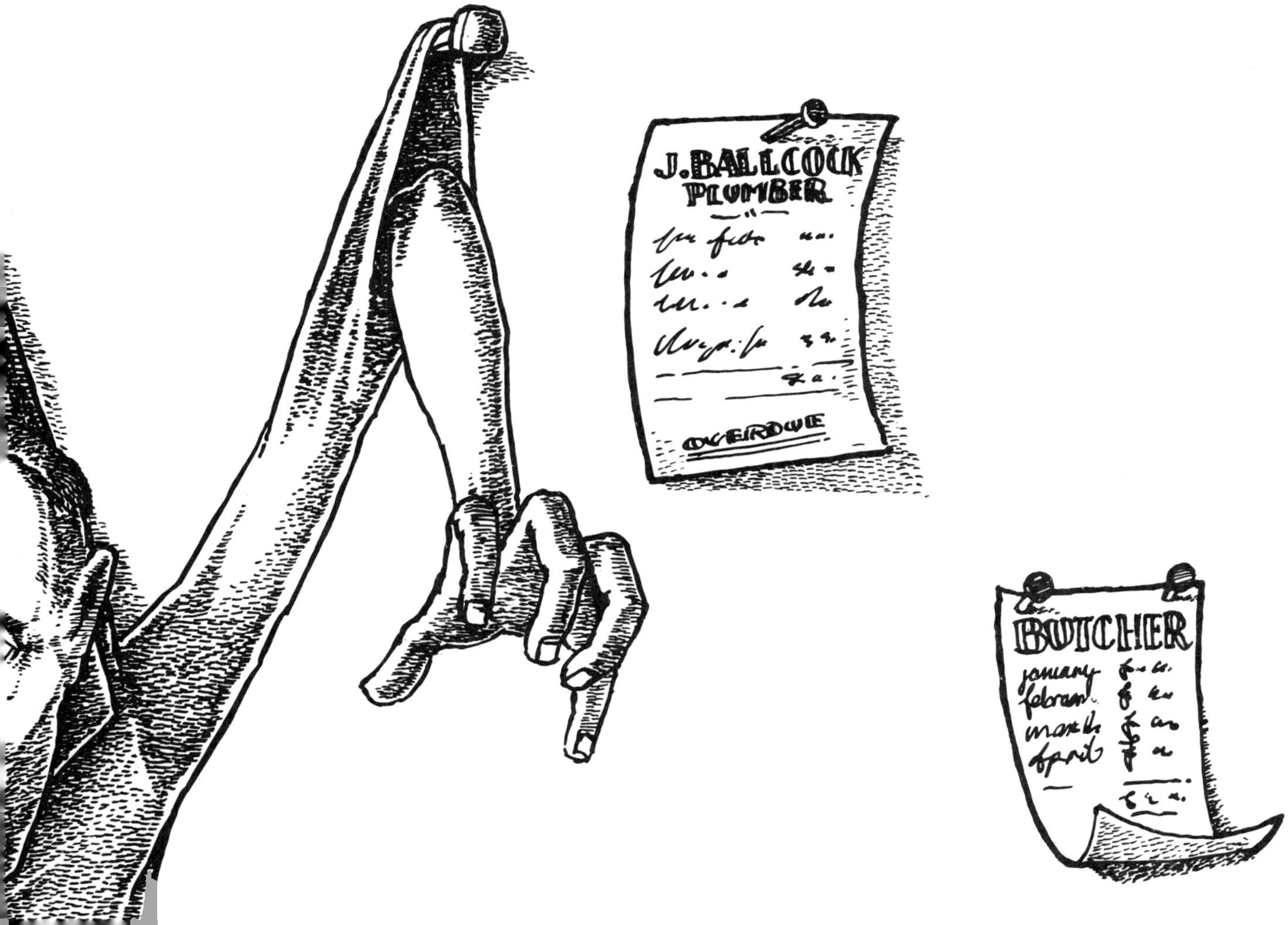

Nine Miles from Gundagai

The now famous tourist town of Gundagai claims that the trusty dog was simply sitting on the tucker box. Folklore has it that the dog had other ideas!

From swagman Jack Pobar, Toowoomba, Queensland. Collected by Warren Fahey, in 1973. Mr Pobar claims that Dan Sheehan sent him the poem "a long time ago".

I'm used to punching bullock teams across the hills and plains,
I've teamed outback these forty years in blazing droughts and rains;
I've lived a heap of trouble down without a bloomin' lie,
But I can't forget what happened to me nine miles from Gundagai.

'Twas getting dark, the team got bogged, the axle snapped in two,
I lost my matches and my pipe – ah, what was I to do?
The rain came on, 'twas bitter cold, and hungry too was I –
And the dog sat in the tucker-box nine miles from Gundagai.

Some blokes I know have stacks of luck no matter how they fall,
But there was I, lor' luvva duck, no blessed luck at all;
I couldn't make a pot of tea nor get my trousers dry,
And the dog sat in the tucker-box nine miles from Gundagai.

I can forgive the blinking team, I can forgive the rain,
I can forgive the dark and cold and go through it again,
I can forgive my rotten luck, but hang me till I die –
I can't forgive that bloomin' dog, nine miles from Gundagai!

But that's all dead and past and gone, and I've sold the team for meat,
And where I got the bullocks bogged, now there's an asphalt street.
The dog, ah well, he took a bait, and reckoned that he'd die;
So I buried him in the tucker-box, nine miles from Gundagai.

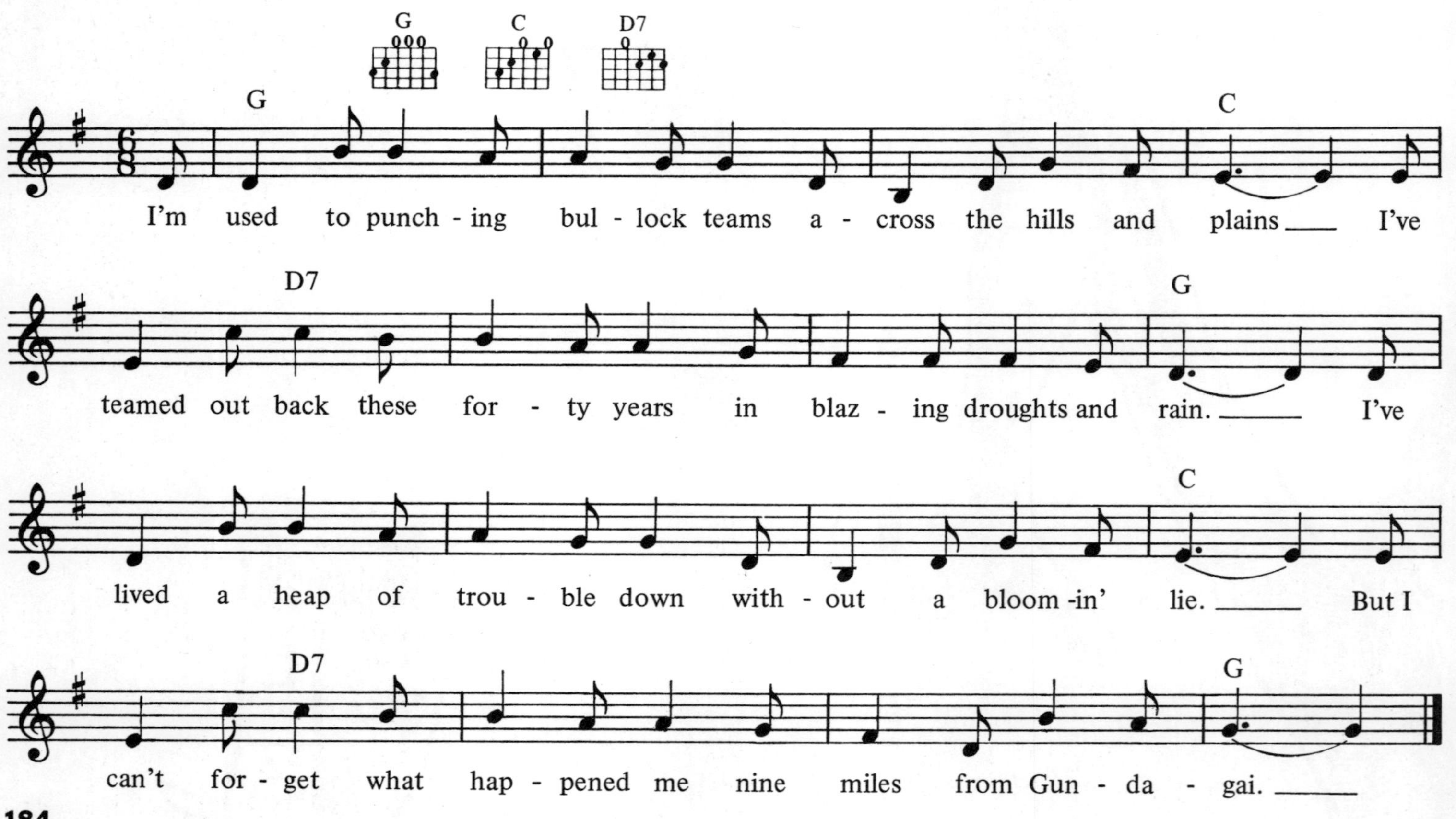

The Wallaby Brigade

"The swagman had to live off his wits and although he usually looked on his fellow travellers as equals he certainly had to show a great deal of respect for those who had battled the ranks to be elevated to the position of a 'professional swagman'. The professional had to serve an apprenticeship, learn off his mates, absorb the code of ethics – he'd have to be downright clever, outsmart everybody and out cadge anyone he met ... be they policeman, store keeper, train stationmaster or fellow swagman." (Bart Saggers, swagman, recorded 1973.)

From the singing of Cyril Duncan, Hawthorne, Queensland. Collected by Warren Fahey, in 1973. Also appears in Paterson's Old Bush Songs. *This version is a compilation to the tune of "Tramp, Tramp, Tramp".*

You often have been told of the regiments of old,
But we are the bravest in the land,
We're called the Tag-Rag Band, and we rally in Queensland,
We're the members of the Wallaby Brigade.

CHORUS:
Tramp, tramp, tramp across the borders,
The swagmen are rolling up I see,
When the shearing's at an end we'll go fishing in the bend,
Then hurrah for the Wallaby Brigade.

When you are leaving camp you must ask some brother tramp,
If there are any jobs to be had,
Or what sort of a shop that station is to stop
For a member of the Wallaby Brigade.

You ask if they want men, you ask for rations then,
If they don't stump up a warning should be made,
To teach them better sense, why, "Set fire to their fence"
Is the war cry of the Wallaby Brigade.

The squatters thought us done when they fenced in all their run,
But a prettier mistake they never made,
You've only to sport your dover and knock a monkey over,
There's cheap mutton for the Wallaby Brigade.

Now when the shearing's in our harvest will begin,
Our swags for a spell down will be laid,
But when our cheques are drank we will join the Tag-Rag rank,
Limeburners in the Wallaby Brigade.

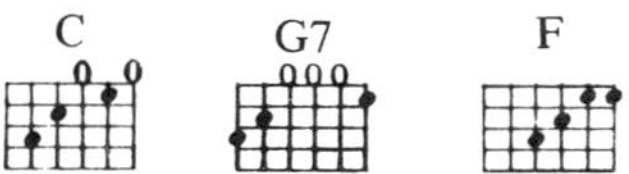

C C
You often have been told of the regiments of old But we are the bravest in the

G7 C F
land We're ___ called the Tag-Rag Band and we rally in Queensland we're the

G7 C
members of the Wallaby Brigade.

Chorus:

C
Tramp, tramp, tramp across the

G7 C G7 C
borders The swagmen are rolling up I see, When the shearing's at an end we'll go

F G7 C
fishing in the bend, Then hurrah for the Wallaby Brigade. ___

The Tent Poles Are Rotten

This song invites all the imagery of the Australian bush. Despite the seemingly hostile nature of the outback the true bushman will soon discover the crispness of the air, the intensity of the evening skies, the sounds, smells and wildlife. As the song says "there's joys to be had on the wallaby still". To "be on the wallaby" was a popular saying describing life on the move.

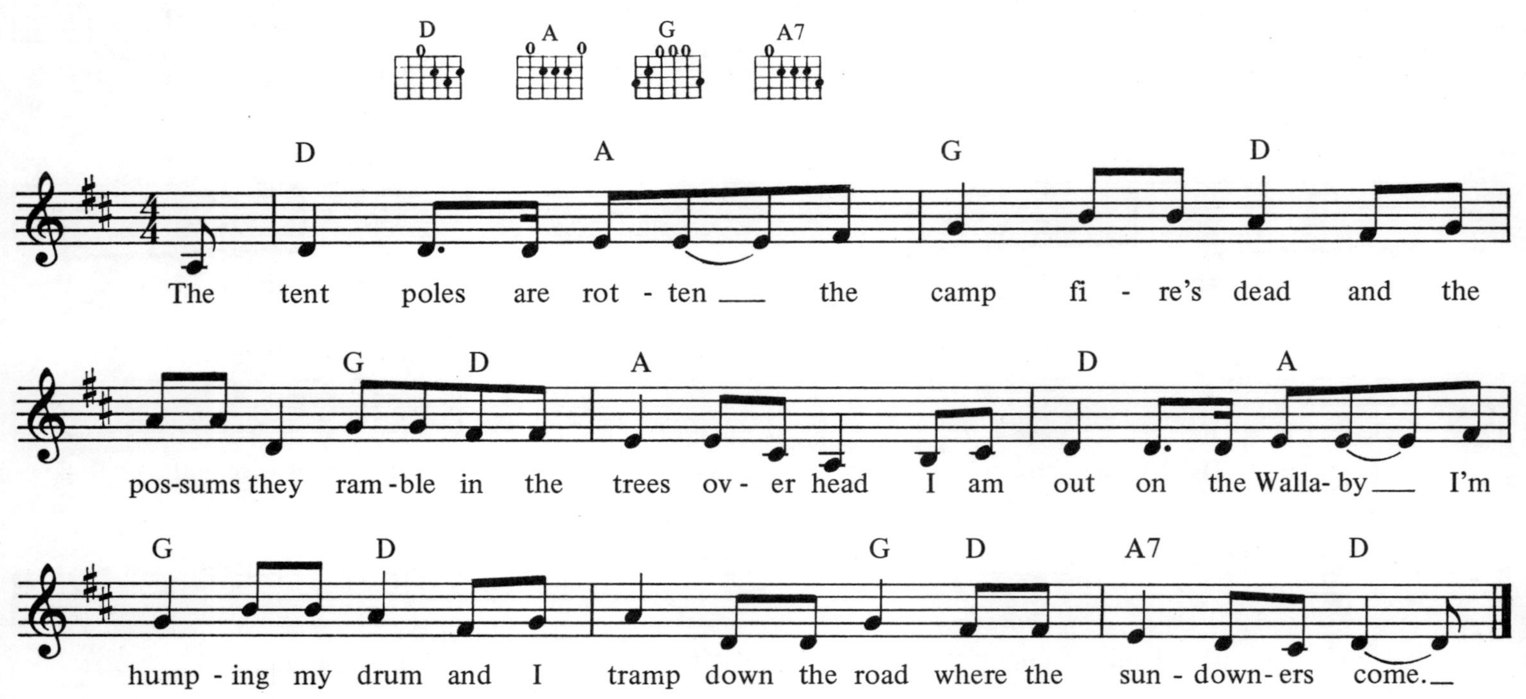

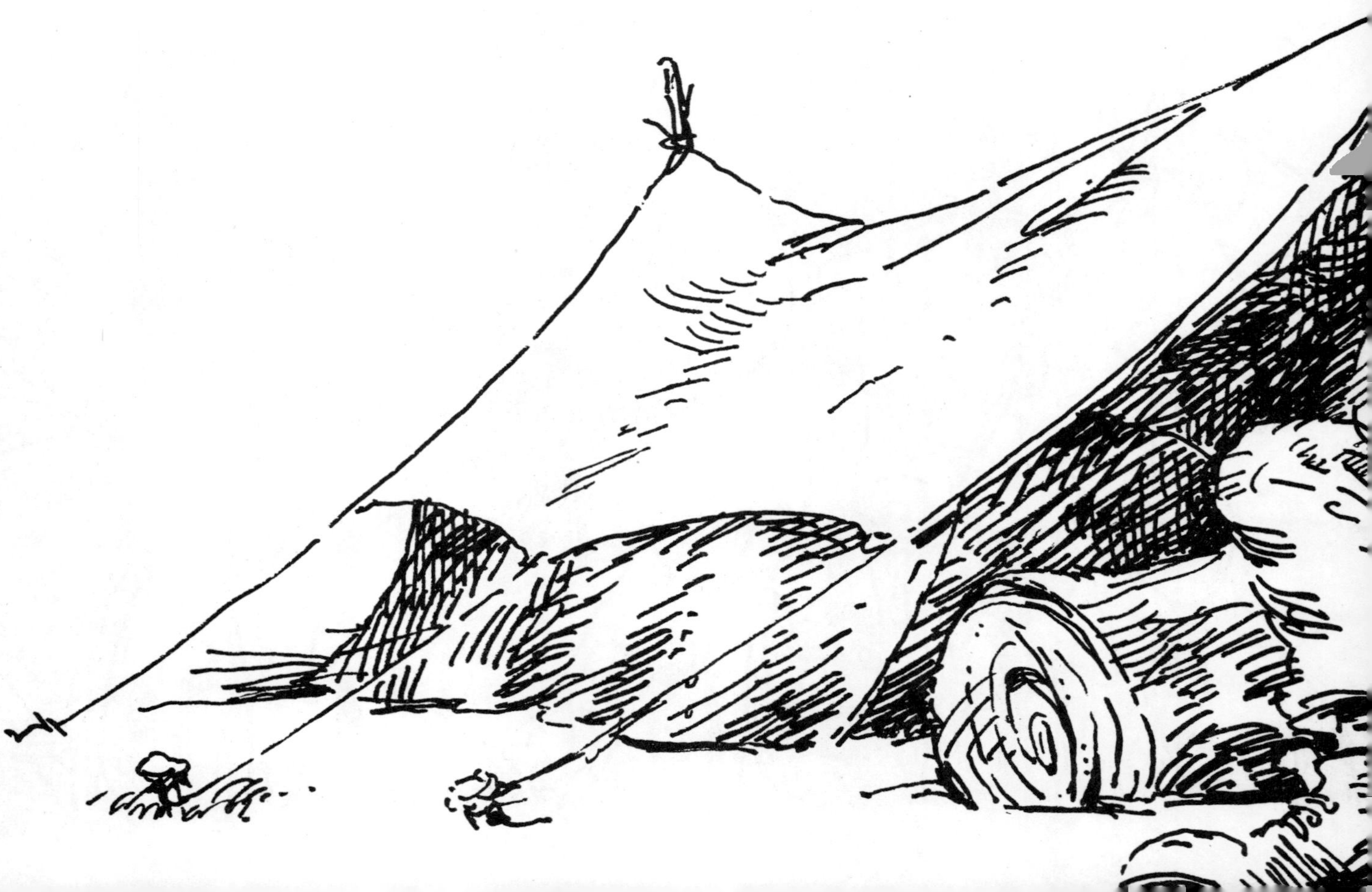

From a poem by Henry Lawson. Adapted and arranged by Dave de Hugard.

Dave de Hugard, bush musician

The tent poles are rotten, and the campfires dead
And the possums they ramble in the trees overhead
I'm out on the wallaby, I'm humping my drum
And I tramp down the road where the sundowners come.
And it's north west by west over ranges and far
To the plains where the cattle and the sheep stations are
With the sky for my roof and the earth for my bunk
And the calico bag for my damper and my junk.
And scarcely a comrade my memory reveals
But the spirit still tingles in my toes and my heels.
Now my tent is all torn and my blankets are damp
And the fast-rising waters still flow by the camp
And the cold water rises in jets from the floor
As I lie on my bed and I listen to it roar
And I think of tomorrow how my foot-steps will lag
As I tramp beneath the weight of a rain-sodden swag.
But the way of a swagman is mostly uphill
But there's joys to be found on the wallaby still
When your day has gone by with its tramp and its tail
And your campfire you build and your billy it can boil
Oh, there's comfort and peace in the bowl of your clay
Or the yarn of a mate who is tramping that way.
But beware of the city where it's poison for years
And there's always a danger in drinking long beers
For a bushman gets bushed in the streets of the town
And he loses his friends when his cheque's all knocked down
He's alright 'til his pockets are empty and then
He must hump his old bluey up the country again.

The Bald-Headed End of the Broom

A song with a warning! From the 1930's Depression, this song enters the field of nonsense verse but still it makes its point – "the butcher comes around to collect his bill ... with a dog and a double-barrelled gun!".

From the singing of Mr Herb Green, St Lucia, Queensland. Collected by Warren Fahey, in 1973. Mr Green refers to the song as "The Honeymoon Song". An American version exists under the title of "Lines of Love" (collected Chicago, 1885). This appears to be the only Australian version of the song.

O love it is a funny funny thing
It affects both young and old
It's like a plate of boarding house hash
And many's the man that is sold
It makes you feel like a fresh-water eel
Causes your head to swell
You'll lose your mind 'cause true love is blind
And it empties your pocket-book as well.

CHORUS:
So boys, keep away from the girls, I say
And give them lots of room
For, when that they are wed, they will bang you on the head
With the bald-headed end of the broom

When a man is gone on a pretty little girl
He'll talk to her as gentle as a dove
He'll spend all his money and he'll call her his honey
All for fun and love
When his money's all spent and his clothes all rent
He'll find that the old story's true
That a mole in the arm's worth two on the leg
And what is he going for to do?

With a wife and sixteen half-starved kids
You'll find it is no fun
When the butcher comes round to collect his bill
With a dog and double-barrelled gun
With a cross-eyed baby on each knee
And a wife with a plaster on her nose
You'll find true-love doesn't run so very smooth
When you have to wear second-hand clothes.

So now, my boys, take my advice
And don't be in a hurry to wed
You'll think you're in clover till the honeymoon is over
And then you'll wish you were dead
When the rents are high and the children cry
For want of a hash to chew
You'll call on your son to load up his gun
And shoot your old mother-in-law.

C G7 Em Am

C G7 C G7 C

O love it is a fun-ny fun- ny thing It af - fects both young and old. It's

C Em C G7 C G7 C

like a plate of board-ing house hash And ma - ny's the man that is sold, It

C G Am Em Am G7 C

makes you feel like a fresh wa-ter eel Caus - es your head to ___ swell. You'll

C Em C G7 C G7 C

lose your mind 'cause true-love is blind And it emp - ties your poc-ket-book as well

C G Am Em Am G7 C

So boys, keep away, from the girls I ___ say And give them lots of ___ room For,

C Em C G7 C G7 C

when that they are wed, they will bang you on the head With the bald - head - ed end of the broom.

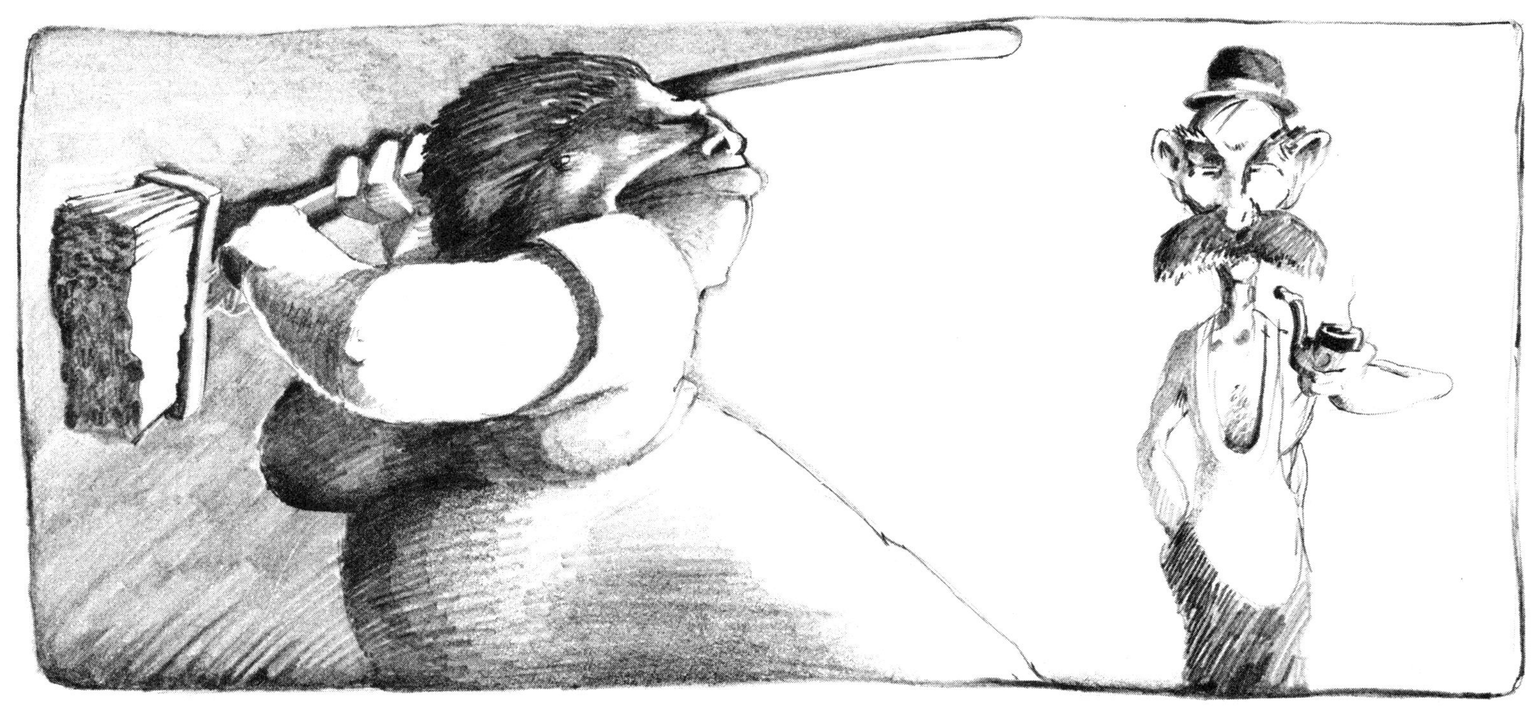

The Two Professional Hums

To be on the "hum" is a euphemism for "bum" – a swagman term.

"In the old days the swagman was pretty right to get the standard ration handout. We used to call it the 8, 10, 2 and a half. Eight pounds of flour, ten of meat, two of sugar and half a pound of tea. Today you still get 8, 10, 2 and a half ... eight minutes to get off the property, ten yards start on the dog, two reasons why you could be had up for trespassing and only half a chance to explain yourself!"

From the singing of Mr Harry Chaplin, Broken Hill, New South Wales. Collected by Warren Fahey, in 1975. Recorded by the Australian Broadcasting Commission. The song seems to be a re-working of the "Haywire Mack" Harry McClintock "Three Jolly Bums".

Come all you jovial fellows and listen to me chums,
And I'll relate to you the story of two professional hums,
Who travelled England, Ireland; all over Scotland too,
And took an oath in Bendigo, no more work they would do.

No more work they would do boys, troll old army dough boys,
Humming a drink where 'ere we could, sing fol the righty-o,
For we are hums and jolly good chums, we live like Royal Turks,
And if we've luck we'll hum our cheques and shoot the man who works.

We asked a lady, the other day, for something for to eat,
A little bit of chicken or a little bit of meat,
A little bit of turkey or a little bit of ham,
A half-a-dozen loaves of bread and a bucket full of jam.
Or anything at all, Mam, for we're nearly starving,
Anything to help a poor joker on his way,
For we are hums and jolly good chums, we live like Royal Turks,
And if we've luck we'll hum our cheques and shoot the man who works.

A farmer asked me the other day, "If I would go to graft?"
Says I, "What is the work?", says he, "A-cutting of some chaff."
Says I, "What is the payment?" – "A dollar and a half's the sum"
Says I, "Why don't you go shoot yourself! For we would rather hum
Than work upon the harvest and let the cockies starve us."
Humming a drink where 'ere we go, singing fol the righty-o,
For we are hums and jolly good chums, we live like Royal Turks,
And if we've luck we'll hum our cheques and shoot the man who works.

So to conclude and finish, the remainder of my song,
The song that was proposed, me boys, by two professional hums.
Who travelled England, Ireland; all over Scotland too,
And took an oath in Bendigo, no more work they would do.

No more work they would do boys, troll old army dough boys,
Humming a drink where 'ere they could, sing fol the righty-o
For we are hums and jolly good chums, we live like Royal Turks,
And if we've luck we'll hum our cheques and shoot the man who works.

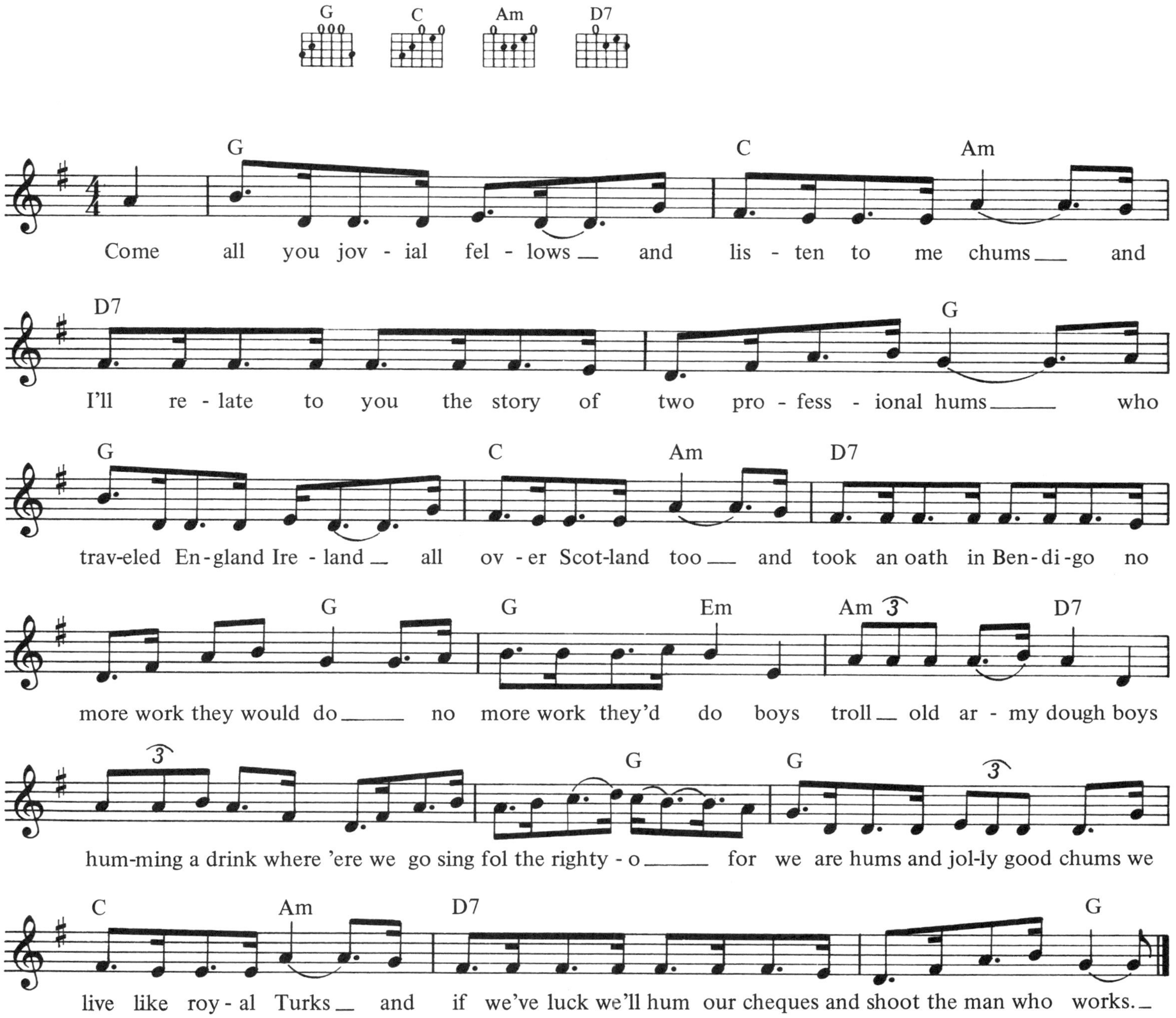

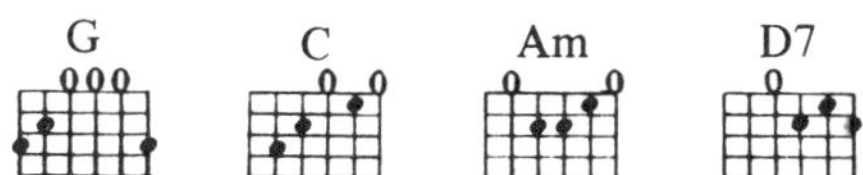

G C Am D7
Come all you jov - ial fel - lows and lis - ten to me chums and
I'll re - late to you the story of two pro - fess - ional hums who
trav-eled En-gland Ire - land all ov - er Scot-land too and took an oath in Ben-di-go no
more work they would do no more work they'd do boys troll old ar - my dough boys
hum-ming a drink where 'ere we go sing fol the righty - o for we are hums and jol-ly good chums we
live like roy - al Turks and if we've luck we'll hum our cheques and shoot the man who works.

TEA
Billington

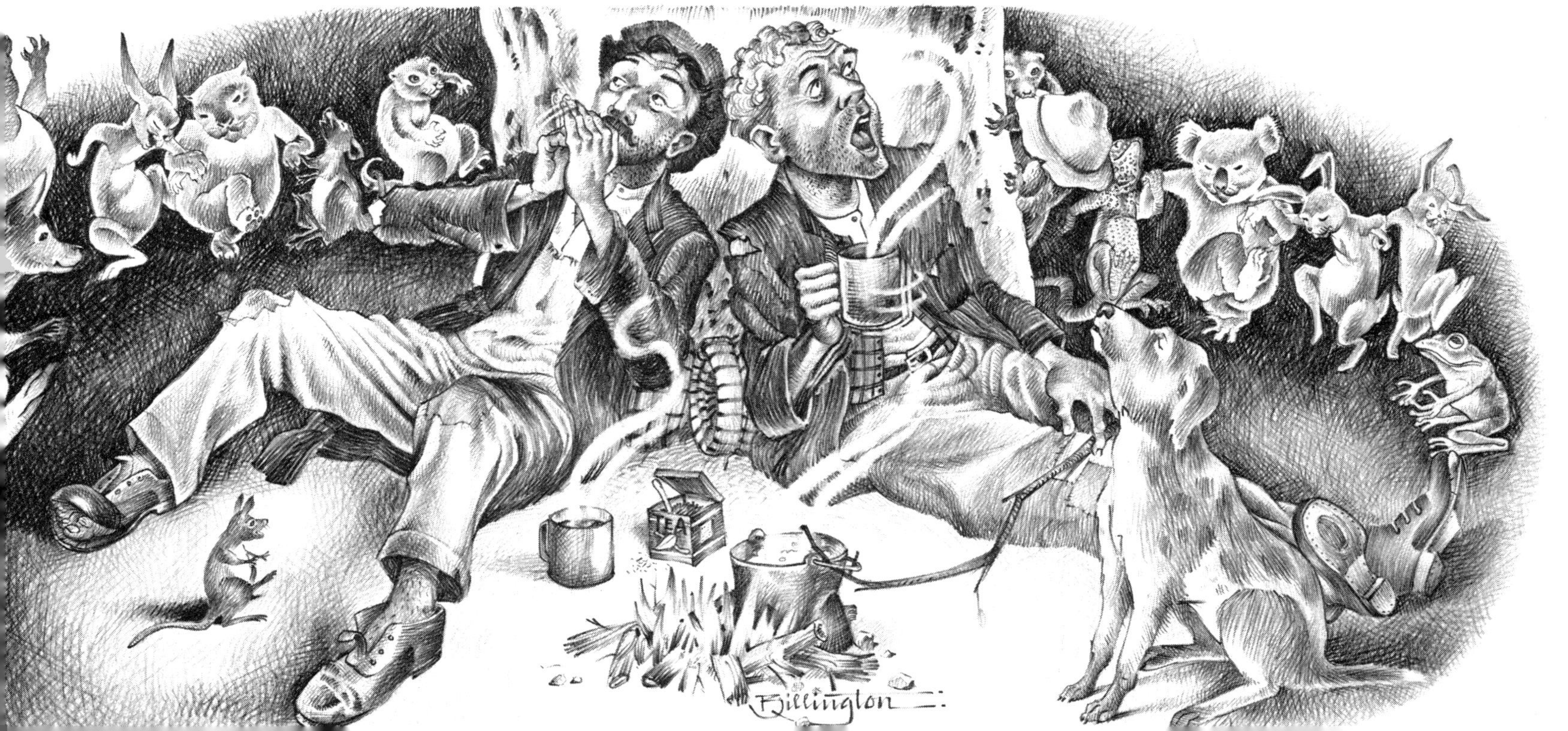

Sydney was the home of the Larrikin. It was here that the character of the big cities was being decided at the turn of the century. Woolloomooloo is an inner-city suburb of Sydney and attracted its own "larrikin push" that gave the suburb a rather unsavoury reputation. Today it is a modern inner-city residential complex retaining much of its old charm.

"Up and down the Sydney Road,
In and out of the Weasel.
That's the way the money goes.
Pop goes the Weasel.

Half a pound of bread and cheese,
Half a steak and kidney.
That's the way the money goes.
Half living down in Sydney."

From the singing of Mrs Susan Colley, Bathurst, New South Wales. Recorded by Warren Fahey, in 1973. Mrs Colley sings this and several other songs on the Larrikin record LRF007 "Bush Traditions". The parody of "Pop Goes The Weasel" was also collected from Mrs Colley.

I happened to be born on a very frosty morn
Quite contagious in the town of Woolloomooloo,
And it was in Riley Street where folks first heard me bleat,
For at the time I'd nothing else to do.

Every time my dad got tight, then mother and him would fight
Half their time they used to spend in jail,
They were known to the police for they always broke the peace
And not a soul would ever go their bail.

When I grew up a lad I went straight into the bad
And soon became a most accomplished thief.
But the Government was kind, and didn't seem to mind
For in Darlinghurst they granted me relief.

I was watched with constant care and they used to cut my hair
For six months I wasn't allowed to roam.
But my visits I'll renew 'twixt there and Woolloomooloo
And in either place I'll find a welcome home.

For my name it is McCarty I came from the old Dart-y
My father drives a cart-y 'cause he's nothing else to do.
Some folk say he's crazy but he don't work 'cause he's lazy,
All gone wrong with the boozy throng that hangs 'round Woolloomooloo.

I hap - pened to be born on a ve - ry fros - ty
morn quite con - ta - gious in the town of Wool - loo - ma - loo.
And it was in Ri - ley Street where folks first heard me
bleat for at the time I'd noth - ing else to do.

The theme of this old tearjerker song is that of the prodigal son. After leading a wild life there is remorse, regret and the familiar "I won't do that again" warning to others. This is the type of song that would reduce grown men to tears as they sat in the hotel bar and gave thought to their own lives and distant family.

From the singing of Mrs Sally Sloan, Lithgow, New South Wales. Recorded by Warren Fahey and Graham Seal, in 1976. It is a relative of the popular "The Wild Rover".

Oh, my father he died and he left me his estate,
I married a lady whose fortune was great,
And through keeping bad company I've spent all my store.
I have been a wild boy, but I'll be so no more.

Oh, there was Bill, Tom and Harry and Betsy and Sue
And two or three others belonged to our crew;
We sat up till midnight and made the town roar.
Oh, I've been a wild boy, but I'll be so no more.

I was always too fond of treating ladies to wine,
Till my pockets grew empty too soon I would find;
Twenty pounds in one night, oh, I've spent them and more.
Oh, I've been a wild boy, but I'll be so no more.

Oh, it's first down to Newgate a prisoner I went;
I had on cold irons, I had to lament,
And I had to find comfort as I lay on the floor.
Oh, I've been a wild boy, but I'll be so no more.

Oh, the next down to Newgate a prisoner I stand,
And what I have longed for is now out of hand,
And if ever I gain my liberty, as I've had before,
I will be a good boy and go roaming no more.

Oh, bad luck to all married men who visit strange doors,
I've done so myself but I'll do so no more;
I'll go back to my family, I'll go back to my wife,
And I'll be a good boy all the days of my life.

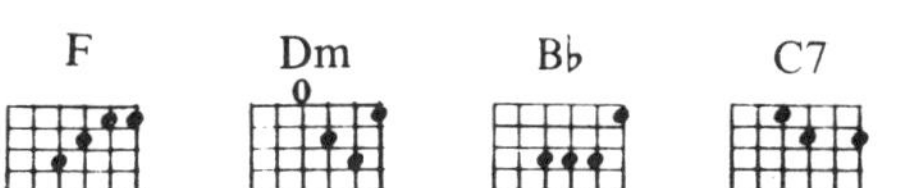
F
Dm
B♭
C7

F Dm B♭ F
B♭ F C7 F C7
Dm F C7 Dm C7
F Dm B♭ F

Sign On Day

As with many seasonal jobs the opening up of the season starts with "signing up" the labour. Men might go fruit picking in the Riverina for three months and then head up north for the cane-cutting season. The sign-on usually took place in a local church or school hall – as it was usually the venue for the weekly or monthly dance it is mentioned in the song as the "Dance Palais".

"Like it or not you had to work. You'd get paid for what you hacked. No cutting no money! You're up before dawn to load up yesterday's harvest and then you cut cane all day till dusk and then you burn off the cane for the next morning. Hard yakka, still, next season you end up coming back and you sign-on." (Jim Whaley, cane-cutter, 1973.)

From Bill Oliver, Redlynch, Queensland, in 1960. Collected by Ron Edwards.

It's sign-on day at the Dance Palais,
And we're down to a quid or two,
But we'll cut a quick ton if you give us the run,
And we'll see the season through.

CHORUS:
You can have Maria,
Sophia and Madelaine,
But we'll take the sugar,
That comes from sugar cane.

We've cut down on the rivers,
And up at Mosman too,
But give us the cane with the Herbert strain
And we'll see the season through.

The ganger is a gun, me boys,
The cook can make a stew,
If he drops the cane inspector in
We'll see the season through.

Our hands are raw, but two bob more
Will make them seem like new,
If we get enough pay we'll cut all day,
Till we see the season through.

There's grog of sorts in other parts,
But Cairns has got the brew,
That we'll drink and drink and drink and drink,
When we've seen the season through.

WOOLGOOLMOOLOOGA
DANCE PALAIS
CUTTER WANTED APPL WIT
DANCE
THIS SATURDAY NIGHT · DUSK
NO ANIMALS HORSES OR DOGS
SIMON

"Cutting cane isn't a living – no, it's a living hell. I've worked the fields for twenty-six years and I'm telling you … it's no work for a white man, a black man, or for that matter a man of any colour – orange included!." (Jim Whaley, cane-cutter, 1973.)

This song is sung as a sea shanty but instead of yanking sail-ropes and winches the work effort is in swinging a cane-cutter's blade.

Written by Merv Lilley with music set by Chris Kempster. Printed in Singabout Vol 1, No. 1, *Bush Music Club, Sydney. This song has stood the test of time!*

SOLO:
I was a cane-cutter, but now I'm at sea;
CHORUS:
Stool it, and top it, and load it, my boys;
SOLO:
Once Cain killed Abel, but it won't kill me;
CHORUS:
Stool it, and top it, and load it, my boys.

There was an old seaman who sang this refrain,
He stood at the bar and he filled up again.

I rose every morning about half past three,
To cook my own breakfast, my dinner and tea.

I worked very hard until I went to sea;
Once Cain killed Abel, but it won't kill me.

This cutting of cane, it isn't much fun,
They melt it all down and make Bundaberg rum.

I was a cane-cutter, but now I'm at sea,
Once Cain killed Abel, but it won't kill me.

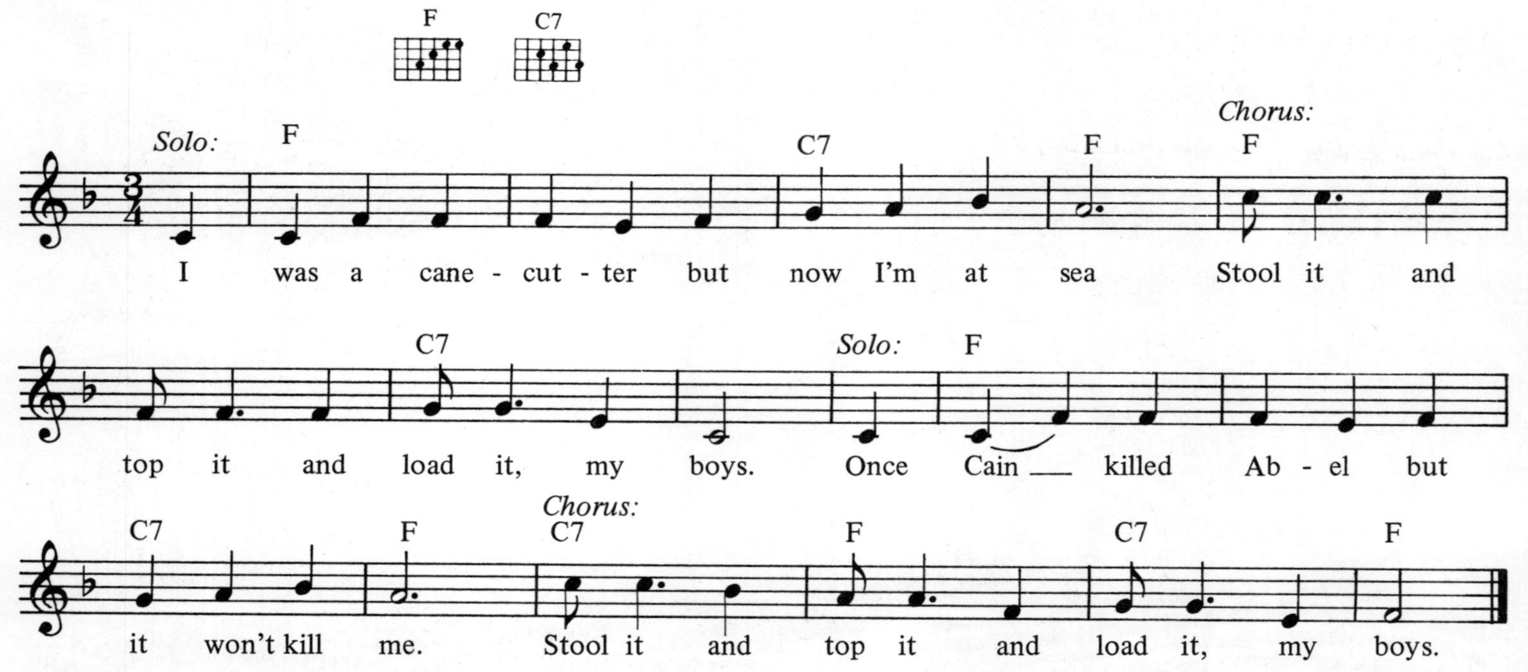

A rather earthy song from the Queensland canefields. Cane-cutting like most seasonal work attracted a particular type of worker. The cook was always a prime target for the odd curse. It was a common belief "that in Queensland a cook was a man too old and too dirty to be anything else!". There was another old saying that went:

"To the North!, To the North!
The last place God made.
The contract unfinished,
Lost, stolen or strayed."

A widespread song from the Queensland canefields. This version from cane-cutter and seasonal fruit picker Jim Whaley of "no fixed address" collected by Warren Fahey in Bundaberg, Queensland, in 1973. Incomplete verses have been patched from the version collected by Stan Arthur and printed in Bill Scott's Complete Book of Australian Folk Lore *(Ure Smith, 1976). Compare with "The Shearer's Lament" which tends to be much more bawdy.*

How we suffered grief and pain
Up in Queensland, cutting cane.
We sweated blood, we were black as sin
For the ganger, he drove the spur right in.

The first six weeks, so help me Christ
We lived on cheese and half boiled rice,
Doughy bread and cat's-meat stew,
And corn beef that the flies had blew.

The Chinese cook with his cross-eyed look
Filled our guts with his corn-beef hashes,
Damned our souls with his halfbaked rolls
That'd poison snakes with their greasy ashes.

The cane was bad, the cutters were mad,
The cook had shit on the liver,
And never again will I cut cane
On the banks of the Queensland river.

Now I'm leaving this lousy place,
I'll cut no more for this hungry bugger,
He can stand in the mud that's red as blood
And cut his own blasted sugar.

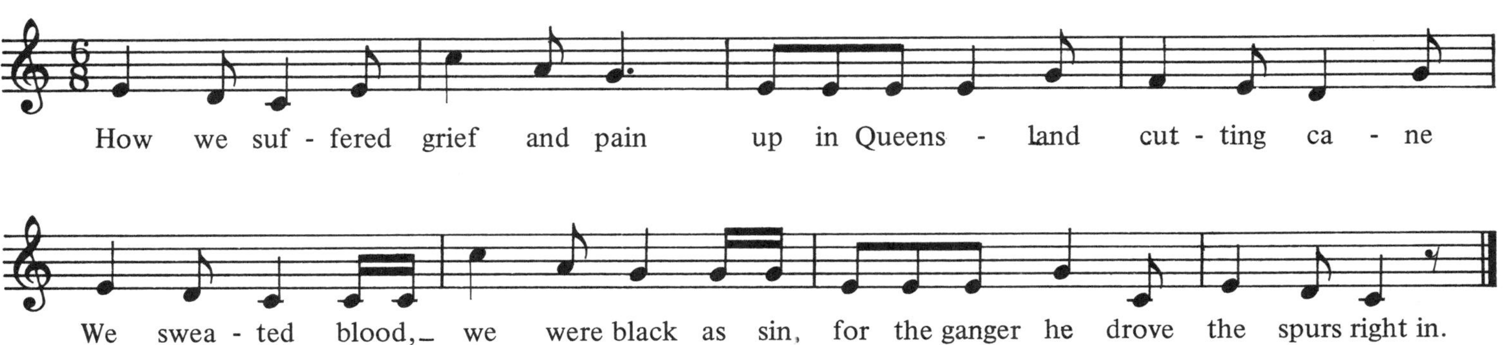
How we suf - fered grief and pain up in Queens - land cut - ting ca - ne
We swea - ted blood, we were black as sin, for the ganger he drove the spurs right in.

The face of mining is continually changing. From the fossicking days of the goldrush era we have dug deeper and deeper into the earth. This song relates the life of a pit miner in the Hunter Valley coalfields and reflects on the bitter struggles the mining unions faced to bring about changes in the mining industry. "There was blood on the coaldust but the changes came." (Jock Graham, miner and poet.)

Written by the bard of the coalfields, Jock Graham, of Kurri Kurri, near Cessnock, New South Wales. Jock was a miner, unionist and poet. He was extensively recorded by Warren Fahey, in 1974, and is included in the "Australian Folklore Unit" tape collection.
... The tune was worked by Phyl Lobl, Sydney, in 1975.

By profession and birth I'm a man of the earth,
I burrow in it like a mole;
I dig it and drill it, and blast it and fill it
For that great commodity coal.

To some I'm a brave man, to others a knave man
Who's putting the land in a hole;
A strike and attack man, a black man and slack man
Who plunders the country of coal.

It's narkin' at times to be blamed for their crimes,
And placed in the villainous role
Invented by story, press-jury and tory,
The profit-made agents of coal.

No story of men who are suffering pain;
Of heroes who starve on the dole;
Nought written or spoken of hearts that are broken:
The widows and orphans of coal.

The court is the gauge which determines my wage,
The parson looks after my soul;
My hands are my boss's, his gains are my losses;
My body is bartered in coal.

The gaps in our lines: "Red roll of the mines",
Show death has been takin' his toll,
While snipers at maimed men and dead men and famed men
Grow fat on the blood on the coal.

Yet through muck and mire and lung-dust and fire,
More clearly I'm seein' my goal:
Of diggin' and drillin' and blastin' and fillin';
Supplyin' a socialised coal.

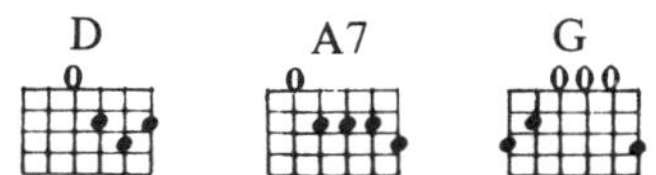

D

By pro - fes - sion and birth I'm a man of the earth I bur-row in

A7

it like a mole. I dig it and drill it and

D

blast it and fill it for that great com - mo - di - ty coal. To

A7 D A7

some I'm a brave man to oth - ers a naive man who's put - ting the

D G

land in a hole. A strike and a tack man a

D A7 D

black man a slack man plun-ders the coun-try of coal.

The Eldorado Mining Disaster

In July 1895, the Eldorado Mine near Chiltern, Victoria, collapsed, entombing the miners. Before they faced their death from suffocation the miners scraped messages on their blackened billycans. Ches Dawkins wrote: "I am getting faint. No air. God protect me for the sake of my poor children and my wife, Lizzie. Look after them and bring them up good. The money I have in my box and bank be divided with the little ones. Make the best of what I have saved. Kiss them for their poor father's sake. I forgive all. My love to all that are dear to me. Goodbye, my dearest children."

From a broadside printed by James Purtell and sold for one penny through newsagencies. The tune is given as "Balaclava." Collected in Lithgow, in 1973, by Warren Fahey. Ron Edwards gives a short collected version under the title of "Poor Dorkins" in his Big Book of Australian Folksongs, *Rigby, 1976.*

With sorrow we remember, the middle of July,
When those six noble miners were all destined to die.
Hemmed in beneath the surface, no power on earth could save,
For no one could approach them, down in their living grave.

CHORUS:
Oh, 'tis a touching story; the loss we all bewail;
Extremely sad to hear it, this true pathetic tale,
How those poor fellows perished on that eventful day,
We mourn in sorrow for them all, now silent in the clay.

Poor Kneebone suffered dreadful, crushed up against the wall
(Beyond all recognition) – the saddest fate of all
Oh God, he must have struggled, for freedom, all in vain!
But death soon lent a kindly hand, relieving all his pain.

Oh, how they must have suffered, locked in that dismal tomb;
All huddled close together, they met their fearful doom.
Just contemplate their feelings, all raving in despair,
As they were slowly dying for want of food and air.

Their thoughts of home and mother, their friends so true and kind,
Their wives and little children, whom they would leave behind.
Their last words were in prayer, all praising God above,
As each one wrote upon his can a message full of love.

REPEAT CHORUS:

Poor Dawkins died a hero, a brave courageous man;
Just listen to the touching words he wrote upon his can:
God help my little children, and keep them from all strife;
And God be kind to Lizzie, my fond and loving wife.

What money I have in my box, please go to it and take,
And kiss my little ones for me, their own dear father's sake.
Give love to my poor mother, and tell her not to cry;
And write and tell that dear old soul the cruel death I die.

CHORUS:

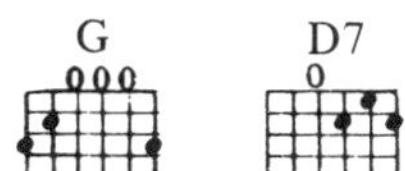

With sor-row we re-mem-ber the mid-dle of Ju-ly when those six no-ble mi-ners were all dest-ined to die. Hemmed in be-neath the sur-face no power on earth could save for no-one could ap-proach them down in their liv-ing grave.

Chorus:

Oh, 'tis a touch-ing sto-ry, the loss we all be wail ex-treme-ly sad to hear it this true, pa-thet-ic tale. How those poor fel-lows per-ished on that e-vent-ful day, we mourn in sor-row for them all now si-lent in their tomb.

The coalfields of Lithgow, New South Wales, were the setting for many a bitter strike battle. In 1911, Charles Hoskin of the Hoskin Mine retaliated to a request for a pay rise of two pennies in the load by reducing the coal rate by two pennies. The strike was on! Hoskin transported scab labour from Victoria and after verbal and eventually physical attacks the strike was broken. The miners had won. This strike song was written and sung at the time of the struggle.

From "champion" Jack Mays. Collected by Warren Fahey, Lithgow, New South Wales, in 1973. The tune is indicated as "When The Sheep Are In The Fold Jenny Dear". However, I have preferred to use the version from "Man of The Earth", Larrikin record, LRF001.

It is strike time in the dear old Lithgow Valley,
The men on strike intend to do their best,
A few scabs round the tyrant seem to rally –
But there's not a spark of manhood in their breast.
When the tyrant said he'd take them down for tuppence
Like a spirit each man seemed to disappear
As they said, "Farewell, they added, we'll return again
When you give that tuppence back Charlie dear."

CHORUS:
When you give that tuppence back, Charlie, dear,
We can then return to work with conscience clear.
But as heaven's sky is blue
We will never work for you
'Til you give that tuppence back, Charlie, dear.

As we wander up and down old Lithgow Valley,
The scenes of strife and want must give us pain,
Standing for their rights like men of honour –
Let us hope the struggle will not be in vain.
Then we wander down the roadway to the furnace,
And it makes us sad to see scabs working there –
They'd be better in the churchyard safely sleeping
Instead of being scabs for Charlie, dear.

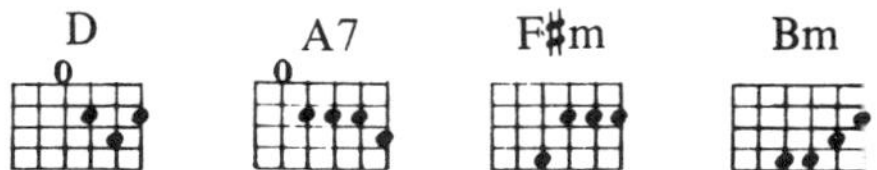

D
It is strike-time in the dear old Lith-gow Val-ley, the

A7
men on strike in-tend to do their best, a few scabs round the ty-rant seem to

D A7 D
ral-ly, but there's not a spark of man-hood in their breasts: ___ When the

A7 D
ty-rant said he'd take them down for tup-pence, like a spi-rit each man seemed to dis-a-

A7 D F♯m Bm F♯m
-pear as they said fare-well they ad-ded,'We'll re-turn a-gain When you

D A7 D A7
give that tup-pence back Char-lie dear. *Chorus:* When you give that tup-pence back Char-lie

D A7
dear, we can then re-turn to work with con-science clear but as

D F♯m Bm F♯m D A7 D
hea-ven's sky is blue we will ne-ver work for you, 'til you give that tup-pence back Char-lie dear.

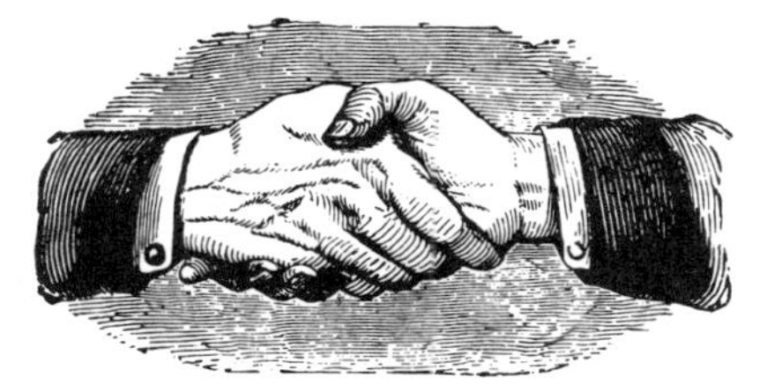

The Sunshine Railway Disaster

"On Easter Monday, 20 April 1908, one of the most deplorable catastrophes in Australian railway history occurred at Sunshine, seven miles from Melbourne. The 6:50 pm 'up' Bendigo crashed into the rear of the 7:15 pm 'up' Ballarat, which was standing at Sunshine station platform. Both trains, crowded with holiday-makers returning to Melbourne, were running late. Forty-four passengers in the Ballarat train were killed and over four hundred on both trains were injured." *(From* Victorian Railways to '62.)

From the singing of Mrs Peg Collins of Perth, Western Australia, and collected by Warren Fahey, in 1974. The tune is that melodramatic "If Those Lips Could Only Speak" and belongs to a song-type that prolificated between the period 1840-1910 when emotional expression was all the rage. Mrs Collins learnt the song from her mother in New Zealand.

He was driving a Bendigo engine,
The train was running all right.
It was going along as usual
Till Sunshine came in sight.
He put on his brakes and he whistled,
For the signal was against the train;
He applied his brakes for emergency,
But alas! It was all in vain.

CHORUS:
If those trains had only run
As they should, their proper time,
There wouldn't have been a disaster
At a place they call Sunshine.
If those brakes had only held
As they did a few hours before
There wouldn't have been a disaster
And a death-roll of forty-four.

The doctors and nurses arrived there
And the sight it caused them pain
To see all the wounded and dying
In the wreck of that fateful train.
The people of Sunshine ne'er faltered,
But assisted with all their power
To help the doctors and nurses
In that awful painful hour.

CHORUS:

If those brakes had only gripped,
As they did a while before,
There would be no Sunshine disaster
Or deaths numbering forty-four.
If that guard had only seen,
That danger lay ahead,
There would be no widows or orphans
But happier homes instead.

CHORUS:

G D Am Bm F Em D7 C Gm A E7

G D
He was dri-ving a Ben-di-go en-gine ___ the train was running all right ___ It was

Am Bm F Em
go-ing a-long as us-ual ___ till Sun-shine came in sight ___ He

G D7 C
put on his brakes and he whist-led. ___ For the sig-nal was a-gainst the train ___ He ap-

G D7 C G
-plied his brakes for e-mer-gen-cy ___ but a-las it was all in vain. ___

Chorus:

Gm G D C
If those trains had on-ly run ___ As they should their pro-per time ___ There

A E7 D Gm G
would-n't have been a dis-ast-er at a place they call Sun-shine ___ If those

Gm G D C
brakes had on-ly held ___ as they did a few hours be-fore ___ There

D7 G
would-n't have been a dis-ast-er ___ and a death roll of for-ty-four. ___

The Albury Ram

A rather amusing song related to the ancient Derby Ram linked with British mythology and the reborn harvest king. The formula of the song introduces various parts of the ram's anatomy and, of course, they all are of king size! I collected a very bawdy version of this one that went by guise of "The Wattle Flat Ram". Albury is a large rural city on the border of New South Wales and Victoria.

From the singing of Tom Newbound, Rutherglen, Victoria, and published in the Joy Durst Collection, *Folk Lore Society of Victoria.*

Tom Newbound

As I was going to Albury along the other day,
I saw the finest sheep, sir, that ever fed on hay.

CHORUS:
Singing, blow ye winds to (till) morning,
Blow, ye winds, heigh-ho,
Blow away the morning dew,
Blow, boys, blow!

The sheep, he had four feet, sir, on which he used to stand,
And every one of them, sir, it covered an acre of land.

The sheep, he had two horns, sir, they grew so mighty wide,
They're going to make a bridge, sir, from Albury to Clyde.

The sheep, he had a tail, sir, it grew so mighty long,
They're going to make a telegraph from Sydney to Geelong.

The wool upon his belly, it bore him off the ground,
Was sold in Melbourne the other day for a hundred thousand pound.

The wool upon his back, sir, it grew so mighty high,
The eagles built their nest there, for I heard the young ones cry.

A hundred gallons of oil, sir, were boiled out of his bones,
Took all the girls in Albury to drag away his frame.

Oh, the man who owned this sheep, sir, he must have been mighty rich,
The man who made this song, sir, was a lying son of a ... gun!

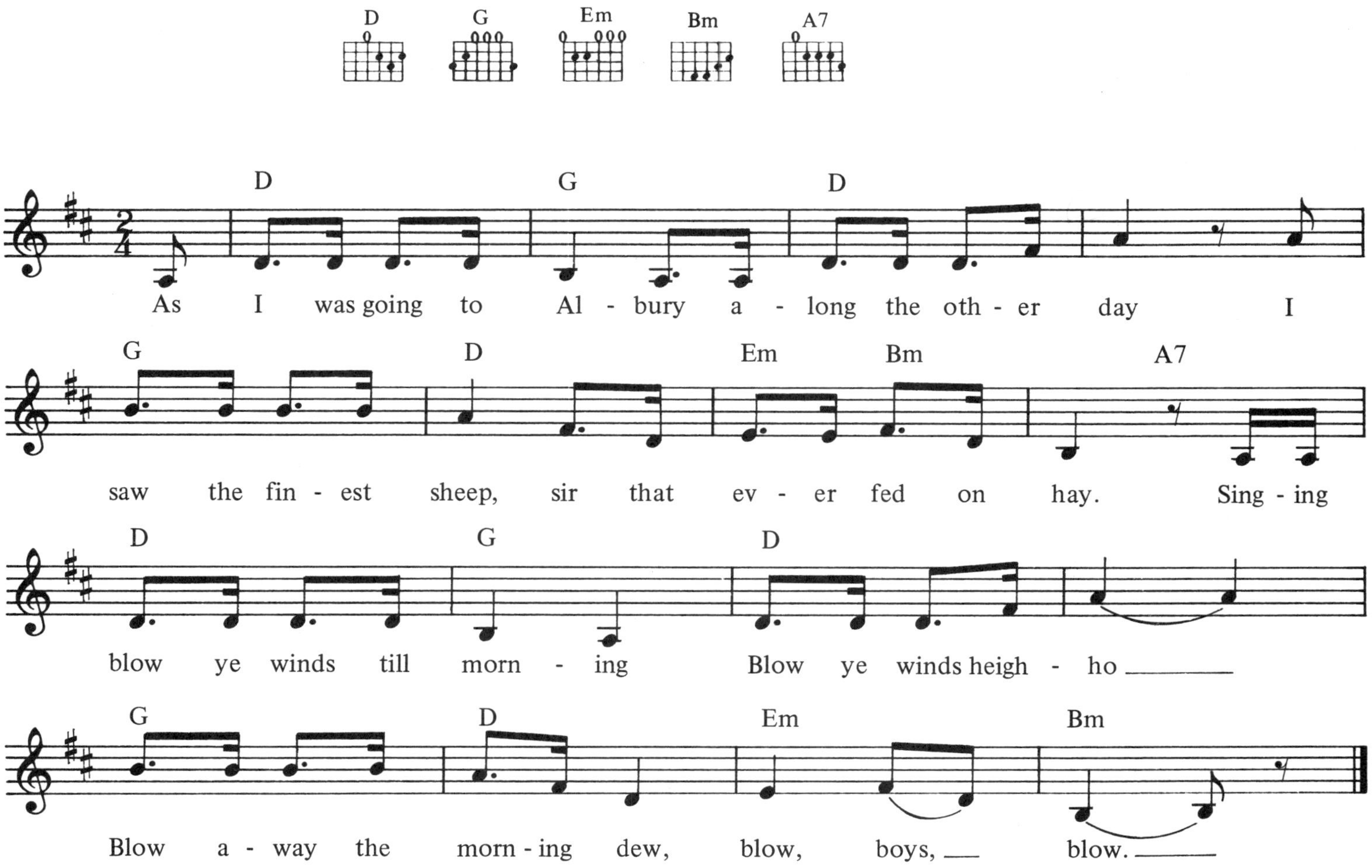

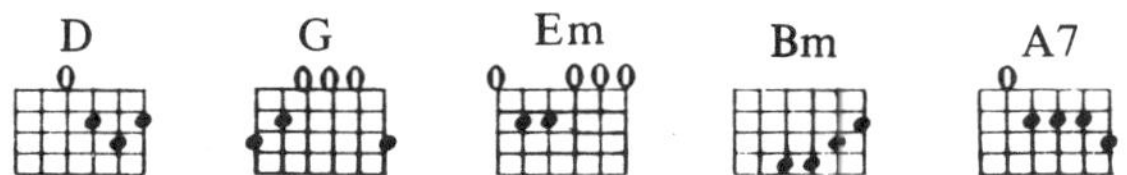

D G D

As I was going to Al - bury a - long the oth - er day I

G D Em Bm A7

saw the fin - est sheep, sir that ev - er fed on hay. Sing - ing

D G D

blow ye winds till morn - ing Blow ye winds heigh - ho

G D Em Bm

Blow a - way the morn - ing dew, blow, boys, blow.

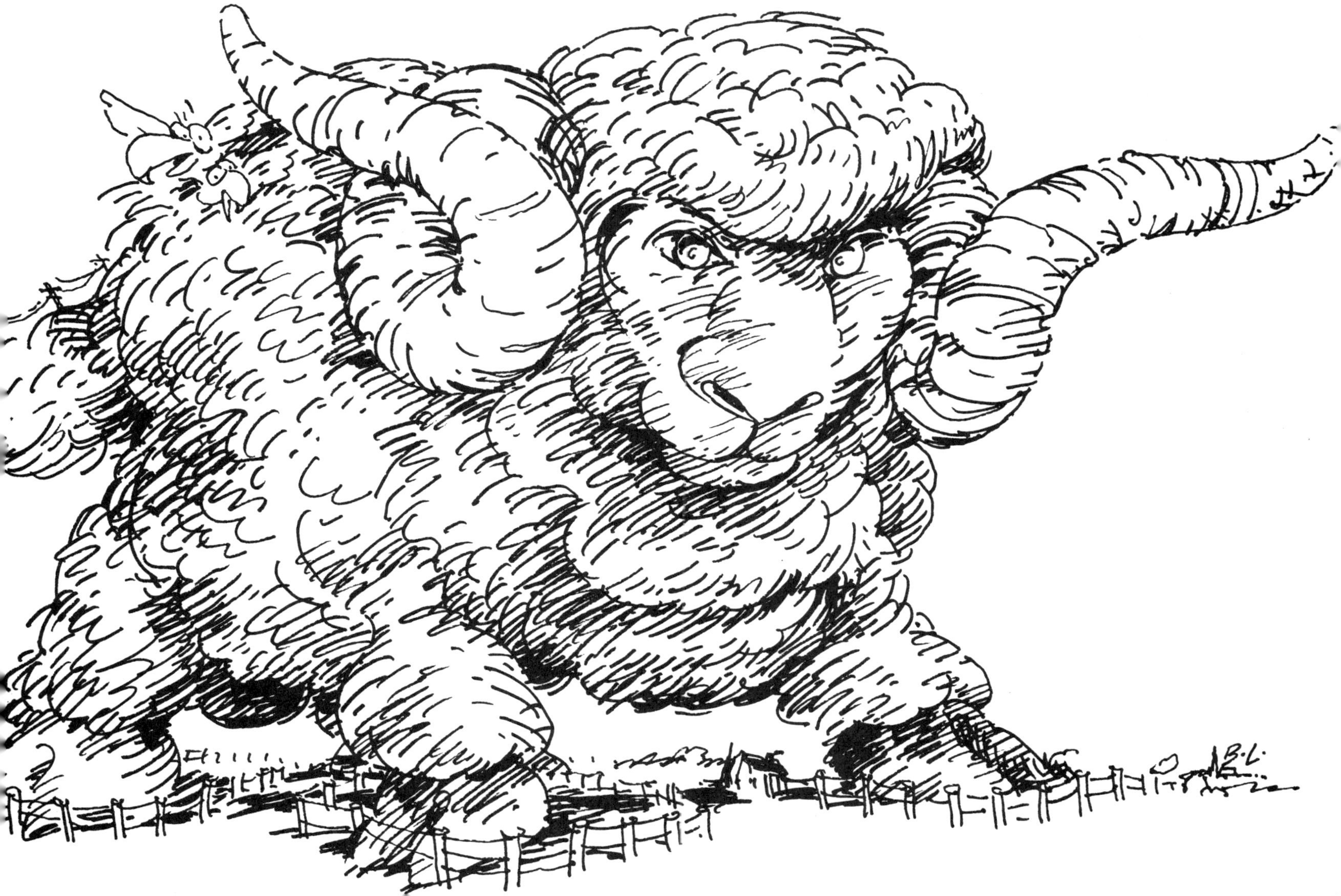

Heenan and Sayers

A fisticuffs fight took place between the Irish-American boxer John Heenan, known as the "Benicia Boy" and Tom Sayers, the British and European champion, at Farnsborough, Hampshire, on 17 April, 1860. According to the song the fight went on for over an hour until Heenan could no longer see and Sayers had a broken arm. At this point the crowd rushed into the ring and the fight was declared a draw.

Recalled by Cyril Duncan of Hawthorne, Queensland, and sent to Warren Fahey in 1974. Cyril had the song from his father who operated bullock teams in the Nerang District. This version reconstructed by the collector.

You ranting lads and sporting blades, well listen to my song
It's just a little ditty and it won't detain you long
On the seventeenth of April thousands waddled with joy
When they saw their English champion fight that bold Benicia Boy.

It was in the town of Farnsborough all in the blooming spring
When the burly English champion, he stripped off in the ring,
He stripped to fight young Heenan, that jolly son of Troy
And to try his English muscle on the bold Benicia Boy.

It was early in the morning before the cocks did crow
Like tigers into battle well, these jolly lads did go
The blood did flow in torrents, and never a strike they missed
For they carried a bunch of thunder bolts well fastened to each fist.

It's two to one on Sayers, yes, the English cried with joy
As they saw their burly champion fight that bold Benicia Boy
But the tiger rose within him, and lightning flashed his eye
Saying: "Roar away old England, but, Tommy mind your eye."

They fought for two hours and a half, each proved himself a man,
Till neither of these jolly lads did have a leg to stand,
The fight was all in favour of that bold Benicia Boy
When the bobbies batted in the ring their hopes they did destroy.

Tom Sayers said he soon would lick that bold Benicia Boy
But he soon found out at Farnsborough, he'd have to mind his eye
Well, his friends they were all shaken when they heard of this glorious battle
But Heenan cooked Sayers bacon and made his daylights rattle.

There never were two better lads and none could be more game
They were both honest heroes of honour and of fame
Tom Sayers trained with cannon-balls and he was good and strong
But Heenan played with lightning when his day's work was done.

Dm

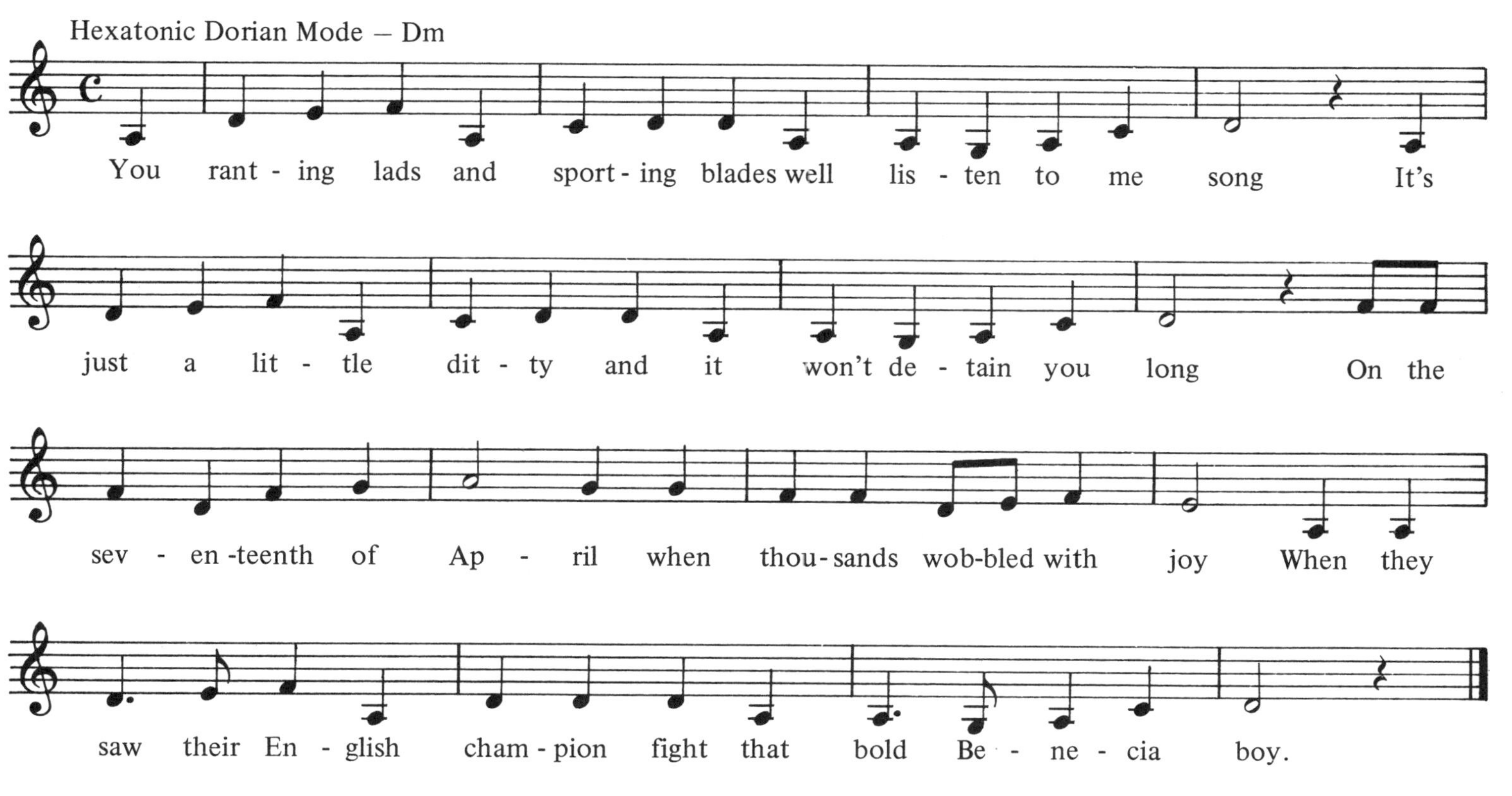
Hexatonic Dorian Mode – Dm
You rant - ing lads and sport - ing blades well lis - ten to me song It's
just a lit - tle dit - ty and it won't de - tain you long On the
sev - en - teenth of Ap - ril when thou - sands wob - bled with joy When they
saw their En - glish cham - pion fight that bold Be - ne - cia boy.

Morrissey and the Russian Sailor

Another international boxing contest that found itself in the repertoire of the Australian bushman's "songbag". John Morrissey was a "jack of all trades" – prize fighter, gambler and politician who became a State Senator and a Member of Congress. This fight took place in the 1860's after Morrissey had successfully beaten John Heenan. It took Morrissey a staggering thirty-eight rounds to defeat the unnamed Russian Sailor.

C F B♭ Gm Dm

C F B♭ F
Come __ all you gal - lant Ir - ish - men wher - ev - er you may be I

B♭ F Gm Dm F
hope you'll pay at - ten - tion and lis - ten un - to me I'll

B♭ Am B♭ F
sing a - bout a bat - tle that took place the oth - er day Be -

Gm C B♭ F
- tween a Roos - ian sail - or and gal - lant Mor - ris - sey.

As sung by Mr Joe Watson, Caringbah, New South Wales. Collected by Warren Fahey in 1975. Mr Watson recalled that this song was very popular whenever it was performed to illustrate his magic lantern slide series on "the big fight".

Come all you gallant Irishmen wherever you may be
I hope you'll pay attention and listen unto me
I'll sing about a battle that took place the other day
Between a Roosian sailor and gallant Morrissey.

'Twas in Tierra del Fuego in South Amerikay
The Roosian challenged Morrissey and these words to him did say
I hear you are a fighting man and wear a belt I see
Indeed I wish you would consent to have a round with me.

Then out spoke brave Morrissey with heart both brave and true:
"I am a valiant Irishman that never was subdued
For I can dare the Yankee, the Saxon bull and bear
In honour of old Paddy's land I still the laurel wear."

Those words enraged the Roosian all upon the Yankee land
To think he should be beaten by any Irish man
Says he: "You are too light in frame and that without mistake
I'll have you to resign the belt or else your life I'll take."

To fight upon the tenth of March those heroes did agree
And thousands came from everywhere this battle for to see
The English and the Russians their hearts were filled with glee
They swore the Roosian sailor would kill brave Morrissey.

These heroes stepped into the ring most gallant to be seen
And Morrissey put on the belt bound round with shamrock green.
Full sixty thousand dollars then as you may plainly see
Was to be the champion's prize for him who'd gain the victory.

They shook hands and walked around the ring commencing then to fight
It filled each Irish heart with pride for to behold the sight.
The Roosian he floored Morrissey up to the eleventh round
With Yankee, Russian, Saxon cheers the valley did resound.

A minute and a half he lay before that he could rise.
The word went all about the field: "He's dead," were all their cries
But Morrissey worked manfully and rising from the ground
From then unto the twentieth round the Roosian he put down.

The Irish offered four to one that day upon the grass
No sooner said than taken up and down they brought the cash
They parried away without delay to the twenty-second round
When Morrissey received a blow that brought him to the ground.

Up to the thirty-seventh round 'twas fall and fall about
Which made the foreign tyrants to keep a sharp look-out
The Roosian called his seconds for to have a glass of wine
Our Irish hero smiled and said: "This battle will be mine".

The thirty-eighth round decided all, the Roosian felt the smart
And Morrissey with a dreadful blow struck the Roosian on the heart
The Doctor he was called in to open up a vein
He said: "It was quite useless for he'll never fight again."

Our hero conquered Thompson and the Yankee Clipper too
The Benicia Boy and Sheppard he proudly did subdue
So let us fill our flowing glass and here is health galore
To noble Johnny Morrissey and Paddies evermore.

And Mr Watson, the singer, added a final toast:

"Here's the good health of John Morrissey that fighter of fame.
For he's conquered those bruisers from over the main.
He's never been beaten, by black, white or brown
That's well known to the country in Erin all 'round."

From the singing of Cyril Duncan, Hawthorne, Queensland. Collected by Warren Fahey, in 1973. Also collected from swagman Jack Pobar, Toowoomba, Queensland, in the same year. The song is an obvious parody on "My Home in Tennessee". It is thought the poem was written by P. F. Collins under the name of "Percy the Poet".

Many Australians believed Les Darcy to be the best middleweight boxer in the world. When he died of pneumonia in America in 1917 he was at the height of his boxing career. Soon after his untimely death a rumour spread that he had been poisoned and another that he had died of a broken heart.

Way down in Tennessee
There lies poor Les Darcy,
His mother's pride and joy
Yes Maitland's fighting boy.
All I can think of tonight
Is to see Les Darcy fight,
How he beats them,
Simply eats them,
Every Saturday night.

And people in galore
Said they had never saw,
The likes of Les before
Upon the stadium floor.
They called him a skiter
But he proved to them a fighter,
But we lost all hope
When he got that dope
Way down in Tennessee.

C G7 Em C7 D7

Way down in Tenn-ess-ee There lies poor Les Dar-cy His
moth-ers pride and joy yes Mait-lands fight-ing boy. All I can think of to
night is to see Les Dar-cy fight. How he beats 'em sim-ply eats 'em
ev-'ry Sat-ur-day night and peo-ple in gal-ore said they had ne-ver saw the
likes of Les be-fore up-on the Sta-dium floor They called him a skit-er but he
proved to them a figh-ter and he gave up hope when he got that dope way down in Tenn-ess-ee.

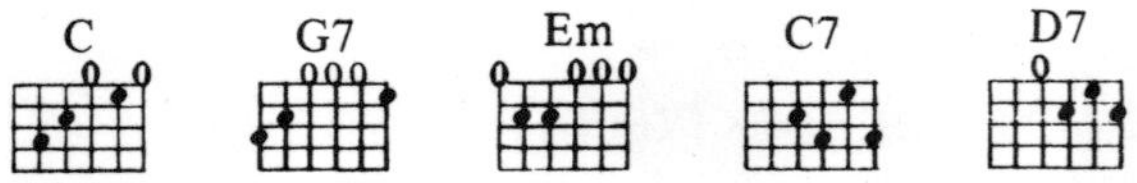

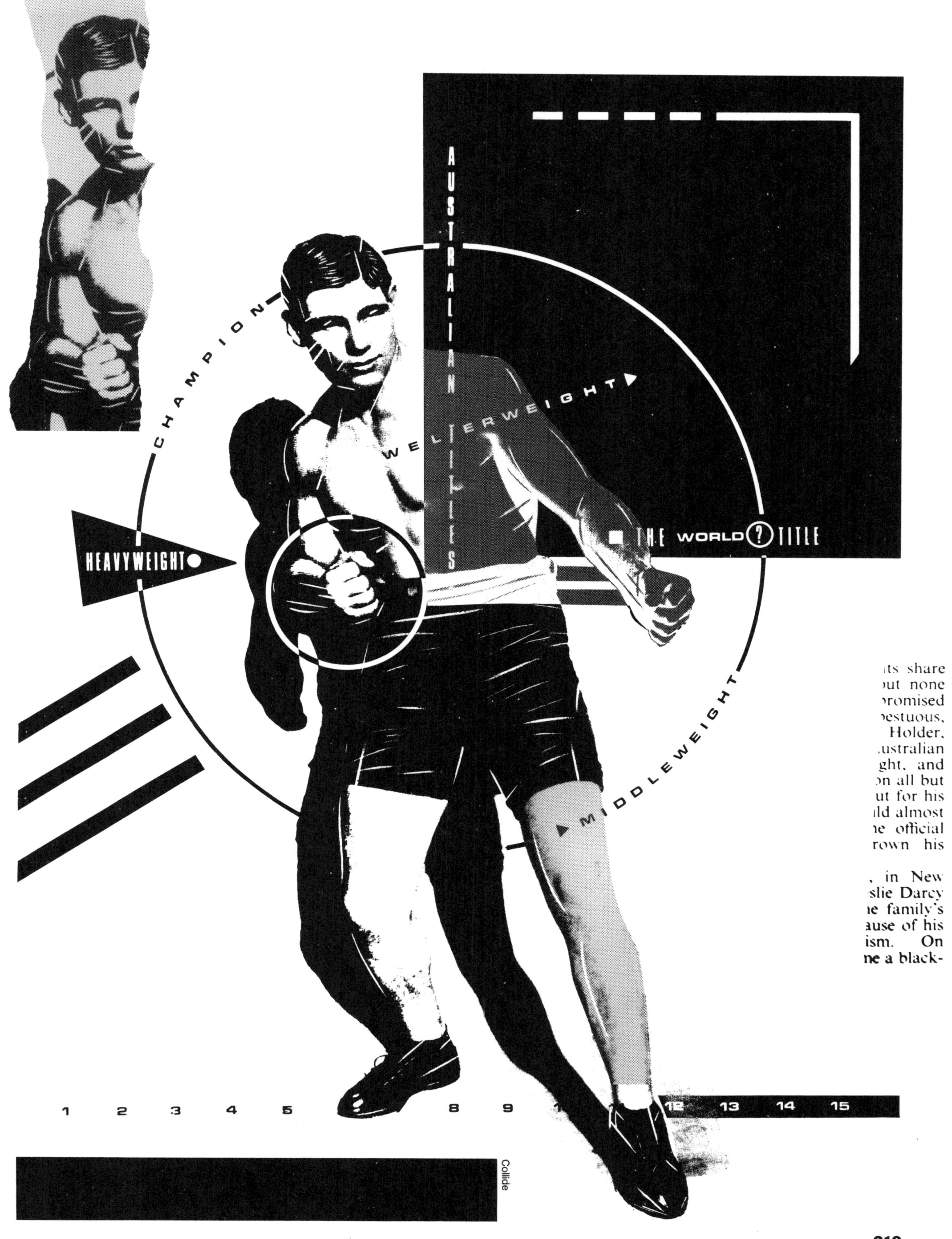

AUSTRALIAN TITLES
CHAMPION
WELTERWEIGHT
HEAVYWEIGHT
THE WORLD ? TITLE
MIDDLEWEIGHT
1 2 3 4 5 8 9 12 13 14 15
Collide
ıts share
ɔut none
promised
ɔestuous,
Holder,
ustralian
ght, and
on all but
ut for his
ıld almost
ıe official
rown his
, in New
slie Darcy
ıe family's
ause of his
ism. On
ne a black-

Alec Robertson was a jockey participating in the Caulfield Cup in the 1890's. According to the songs he was involved in a severe accident when fourteen horses collided. Robertson and his horse, Silvermine, were both killed.
Another song on the event commences:

"A good man has gone, he has drawn his last breath,
Cut down in the midst of his prime,
Poor Alec Robertson met his sad fate,
From his own favourite horse, Silvermine."

From the singing of swagman Jack Pobar, Toowoomba, Queensland. Collected by Warren Fahey in 1973. Another version was collected from Mr Joe Watson in 1975. Compare the version as collected by Bob Michell, 1961, and printed in Ron Edward's Big Book of Australian Folksongs *(Rigby).*

Kind friends, come gather 'round me
And a song I'll sing to you
It's about poor Alec Robertson
A sportsman brave and true.

Some say it was young Doolin's fault
But now it is too late
For on that Caulfield Day
Poor Alec met his fate.

Poor lad, his mother was not there
To bid him last goodbye
But his stable-mate stood near
With sad tears in his eye.

Go tell my dear old mother
Who resides now in Geelong
That I've been badly injured
By those jockeys who rode wrong.

My head does ache, my side does pain
I feel myself insane
God spare me just a little
'Til I see her once again.

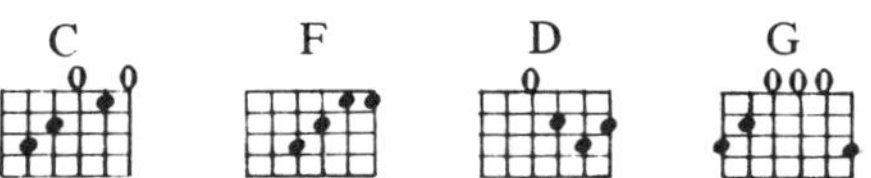

C F G7
Kind_ friends come gath - er round me and a song I'll sing to you, It's

C F G7 D G
about poor Al - ec Ro - bert - son, A sports-man brave and true. Some_

C F G
say it was young Doo-lins fault, But ___ now it's too late. For

C F C F C G7 C
on ___ that Caul - field day poor Al - ec met his fate.

Repeat for Chorus

MY HEAD DOES ACHE, MY SIDE DOES PAIN

McGOWAN

Australians have always respected the horse. In a country where endless bush tracks snake their way over mountains, down mighty rivers and across sunburnt plains the horse is the only way to travel. When work is completed it is not unusual to see outback workers with their horses. The rough saddle riding was replaced by short strip racing, rodeo and stunt riding. "Going to the races" is an integral part of Australian recreation.

Who was Musselman? Nobody seems to know but somebody cared enough to write a song about his last resting place.

From the singing of Mr M. Sullivan of Toowong, Queensland. Collected by Warren Fahey, in 1975. Mr Sullivan thought the song could have been written by "Cyclone" Jimmy Connors. Mr Sullivan also knew "Willie Stone" and "Laurel'll Have it!".

Where the summer winds blow, and the buttercups grow,
Near the swamp by Casino's old course,
Where the wild curlew flies, Jimmy's favourite lies,
An honest and trustworthy horse.

He came from a breed that could stay and had speed,
His trainer and jock loved him well
And you never would find a charger so true,
Than the son of Warlike and Gazelle.

Wherever he strayed each sweet little maid
Would call him by some pretty name
And he stepped, proud and light, with his coat shining bright,
They envied his long flowing mane.

For they could not compare their own silken hair
With the locks that fell down from his crest;
He was the pride of the whole countryside,
The king of all chargers, the best.

How the crowd on the course gathered round that old horse,
When they saddled him up for a race,
And Jim dressed so neat, stepped into his seat,
With a confident smile on his face.

He ran true and straight, and he ne'er came too late,
He smothered the field with his run,
When the ships were drawn out, backers would shout,
"Hurrah! For old Musselman won."

Then his name ever fresh in our memories we'll keep,
For he rests where the wildflowers wave;
Ye horsemen tread light, let the old hero sleep,
For here lies old Musselman's grave.

F Bb C7

F Bb F Bb
Where the sum - mer winds blow: And the but - ter - cups grow, Near the

C7 F Bb F
swamp by Cas- in - o's old course, Where the wild cur - lew flies Jim - my's

Bb C7 F tune B
fa - vour - ite lies An ___ hon - est and trust - wor - thy horse, He

C7 Bb F
came from the breed, That could stay and had speed, His

G C Bb F
ow - ner and jock- ey loved him well, And ne - ver would you find, A ___

Bb C7 F
char - ger so true, As the son of old War - like and Gaz - elle.

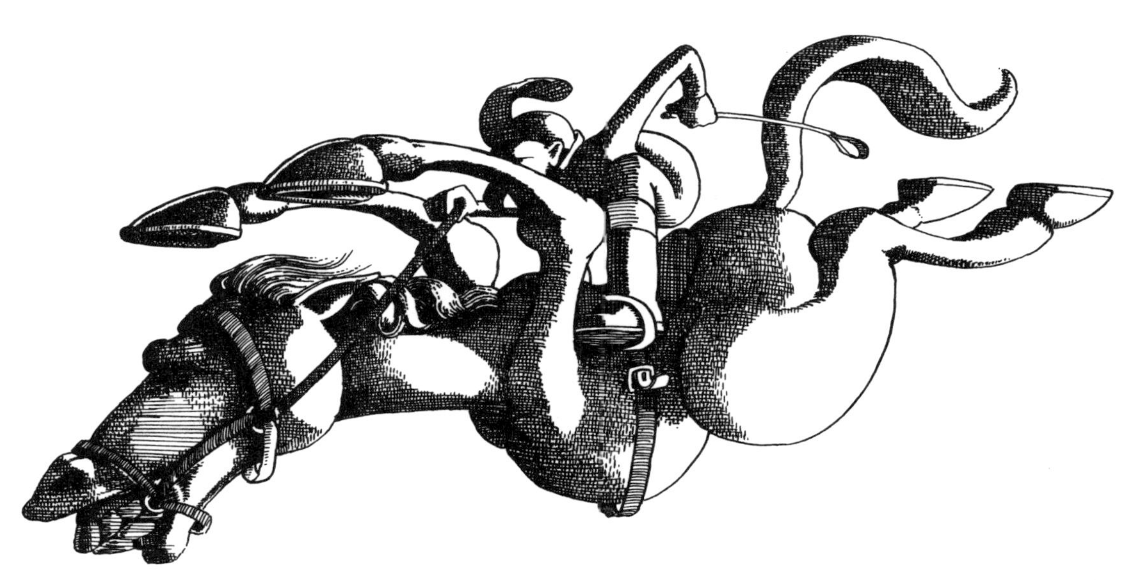

Another "tragedy" song from Australia's horse-racing history. Willie Stone was a Brisbane jockey who was accidentally thrown from his horse when it shied during a practice run on the Brisbane track. The Stone family were well known and highly respected Queensland racing identities. One of his brothers, John Stone, won renown as a leading trainer.

From Mr M. Sullivan, Toowong, Queensland. Collected by Warren Fahey, in 1975. Mr Sullivan also feels this could be the work of "Cyclone" Jimmy Connors. "When requested to perform, 'Cyclone' Jimmy, after exclaiming 'Dash it all!,' would inevitably commence with 'The Bushman's Farewell to Queensland' followed immediately by one of his most popular items – 'On the After Life.' Later he would sing or recite 'Willie Stone,' also frequently requested."

In the graveyard at Toowong, where the river rolls along,
Lies Willie Stone a trusted man and true,
With his saddle and his wreath, we laid him down beneath,
And the lilies they're all growing o'er his grave.

Oh tell it far and wide, a lad we loved has died,
His mission on this earth is at an end;
My eyes are wet and dim, today I think of him,
The one I was so proud to call my friend.

Ye jockeys on the turf, in the southland o'er the surf,
In our sorrow and our grieving take a share;
Ye sportsmen one and all, regret his fatal fall,
The loss of such as he is hard to bear.

CHORUS:
In the graveyard at Toowong, where the river rolls along,
Lies Willie Stone a trusted man and true,
With his saddle and his wreath, we laid him down beneath,
And the lilies they're all growing o'er his grave.

Oh bosom friend of mine, no other could outshine
Your cleverness or courage in a race,
Where silken jackets flash, how gallant you would dash
Courageously through every open space.

Left and right and roundabout, "Come on Willie Stone" they shout
And your horse would feel the steel spur in his side;
Then he would do his best and you would do the rest
And ride as only clever jockeys ride.

In the solemn silent bush, in the dreamland of the bush,
Where I love to wander night and day,
The voices on the breeze come floating through the trees
And this is what the voices seem to say:

"**A**h, cry not brothers, he is well off, sisters three,
Cease grieving, for your brother is at rest;
Oh father dry that tear, stop weeping mother dear,
'Twas God's decree and He alone knows best."

Where Silken Jackets flas
How Gallant You woul

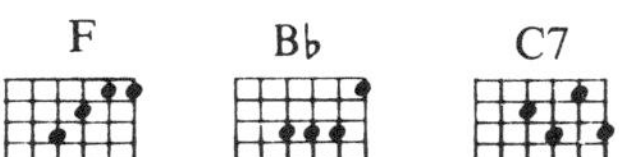

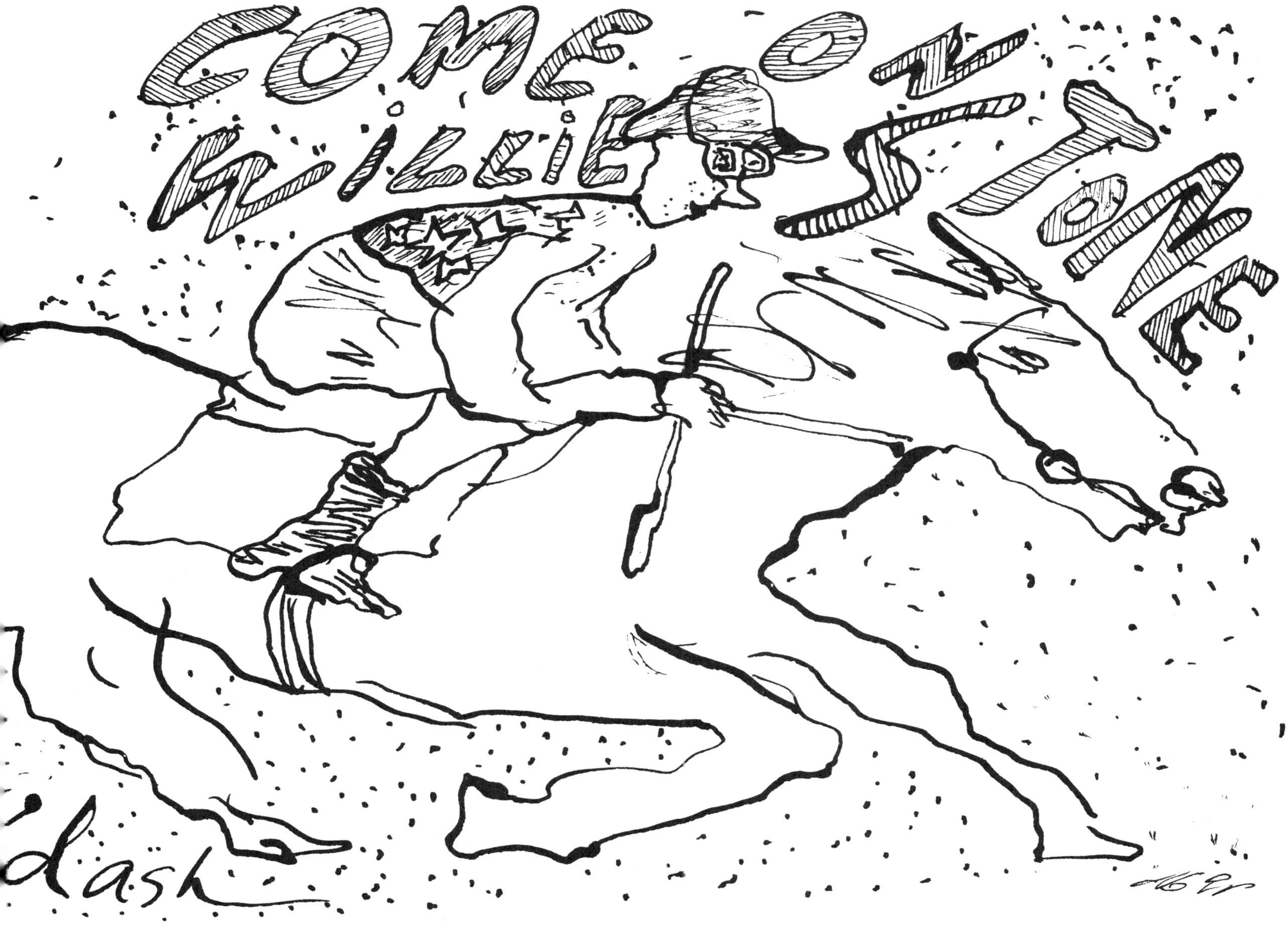

COME ON WILLIE STONE

dash

"At last daybreak came and in its light we saw the battlefield in all the ghostliness. In the long rank grass that covered 'No Man's Land' were lying the dead and wounded. The men looked about as if waking from a nightmare – only it wasn't a nightmare – it was war." (A soldier remembers.)

From Mrs Rollinson, Brisbane. Collected in 1973 by Warren Fahey.

8 little cylinders sitting facing heaven
One blew its head off
Then there were 7.
7 little cylinders used to playing tricks
One warped its inlet valve
And then there were 6.
6 little cylinders working all alone
One got a sooted plug
And then there were 5.
5 little cylinders working all the war
One overworked itself
And then there were 4.
4 little cylinders flying over the sea
One shot a piston ring
Then there were 3.
3 little cylinders wondering what to do
One over-oiled itself
Then there were only 2.
2 little cylinders very nearly done
One broke a valve stem
Then there was 1.
1 little cylinder trying to pull round seven
At last gave its efforts up
And ascended up to heaven.

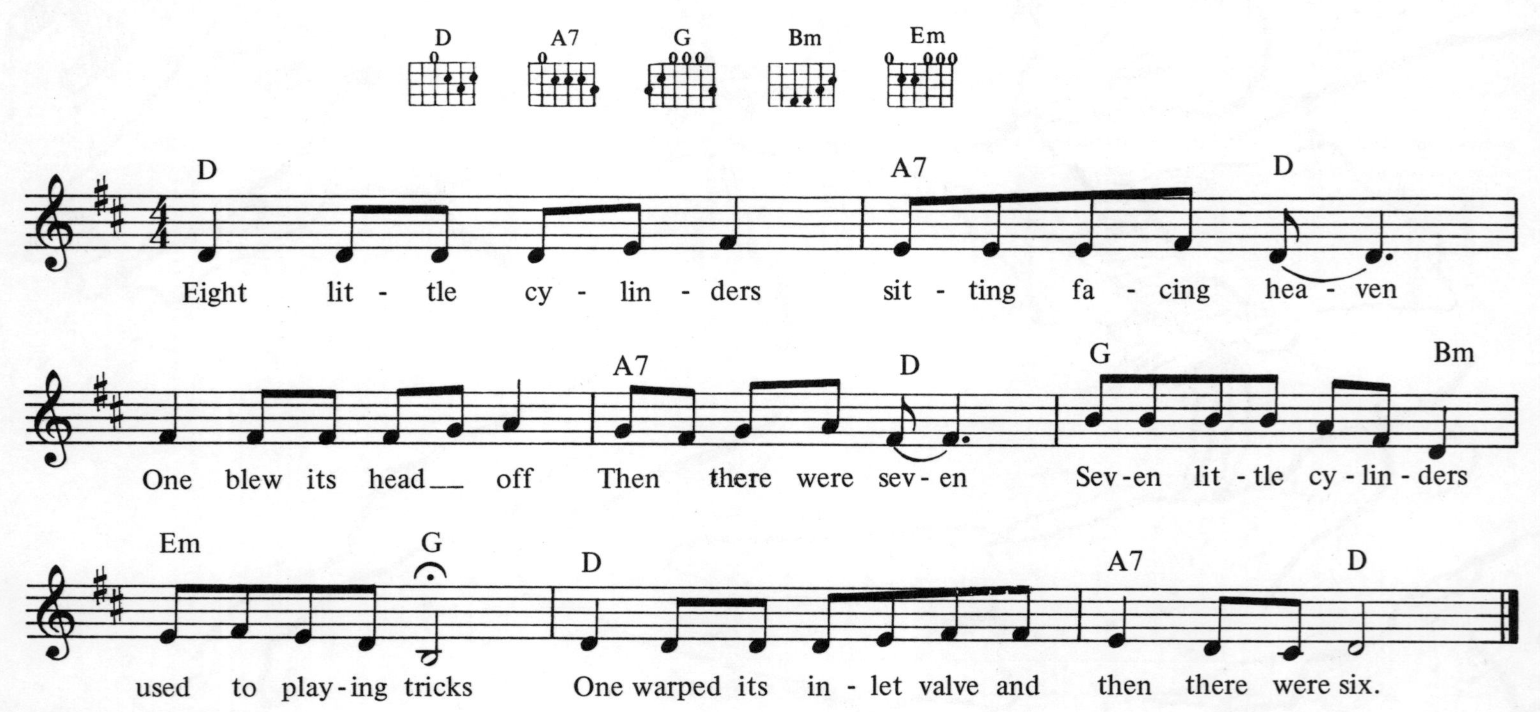

Stroke	Direction	Intake Valve	Exhaust Valve	Gas
Intake	Down	Open	Closed	Enters
Compression	Up	Closed	Closed	Compressed
Power	Down	Closed	Closed	Burnt
Exhaust	Up	Closed	Open	Expelled

"Hush a-bye radar, up in the blue,
Watched all the time by Archibald Screw,
When the shell bursts, the radar will fall,
Down comes observer, pilot and all."
(Wartime ditty)

From Mrs Rollinson, Brisbane. Collected by Warren Fahey in 1973.

Wrap me up in my old flying jacket
The one in which I used to soar
Give me my Mae West, my map and my goggles
And I'll feel once again as of yore.

Fasten up the jacket around me
Lift me into my place
For never would we say I would wind up
I've still got enough for the pace.

Wrap me up in my old flying jacket
Give me the joy stick to hold
Let me fly once again over targets
Thus shall my exploits be told.

Oh it's good to put on the old jacket
To hear the propeller go whirr
To sit by the engine is warming
And wait for the engine's sweet purr.

We're off over the line we will travel
To straff and to bomb is our aim
To win or to lose in a combat
But the game must be played just the same.

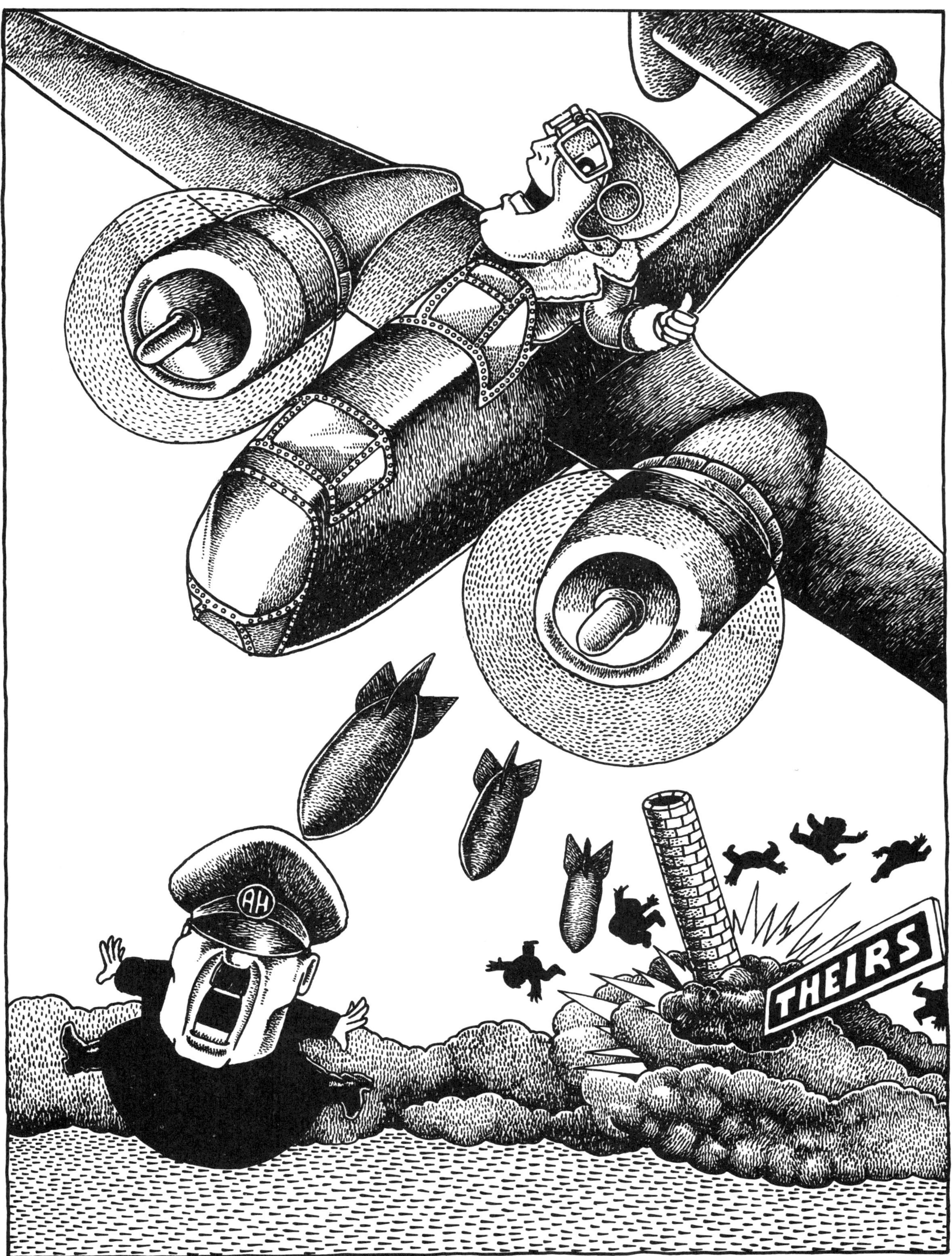
AH
THEIRS

The Tattooed Lady

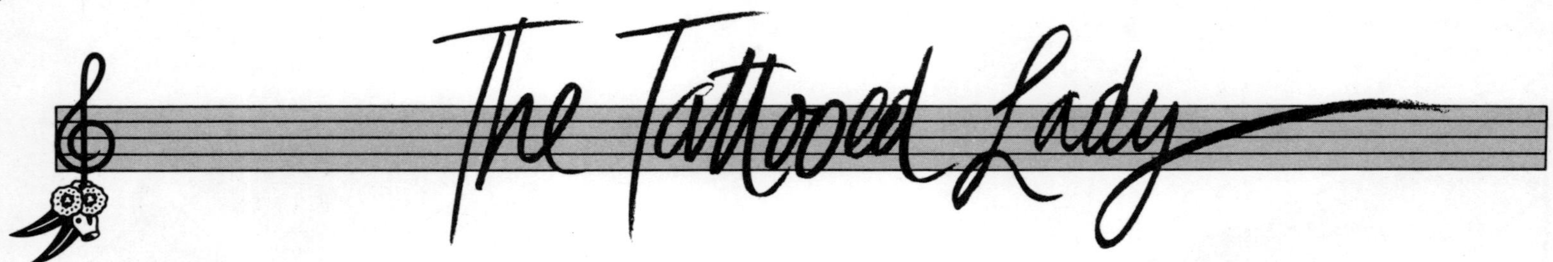

From the First World War we have a parody on the popular song "My Home in Tennessee". Songs exploring the anatomy are usually unprintable!

"Here's to the tree of Life,
Long may it stand.
It grows upon two rocks,
Upon the isle of man.
Here's to that little plant,
That doth around it twine.
It comes in flower every month
And bears fruit once in nine."
(Traditional toast)

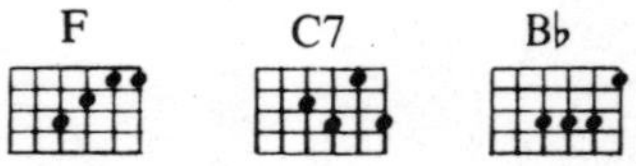
F
C7
B♭

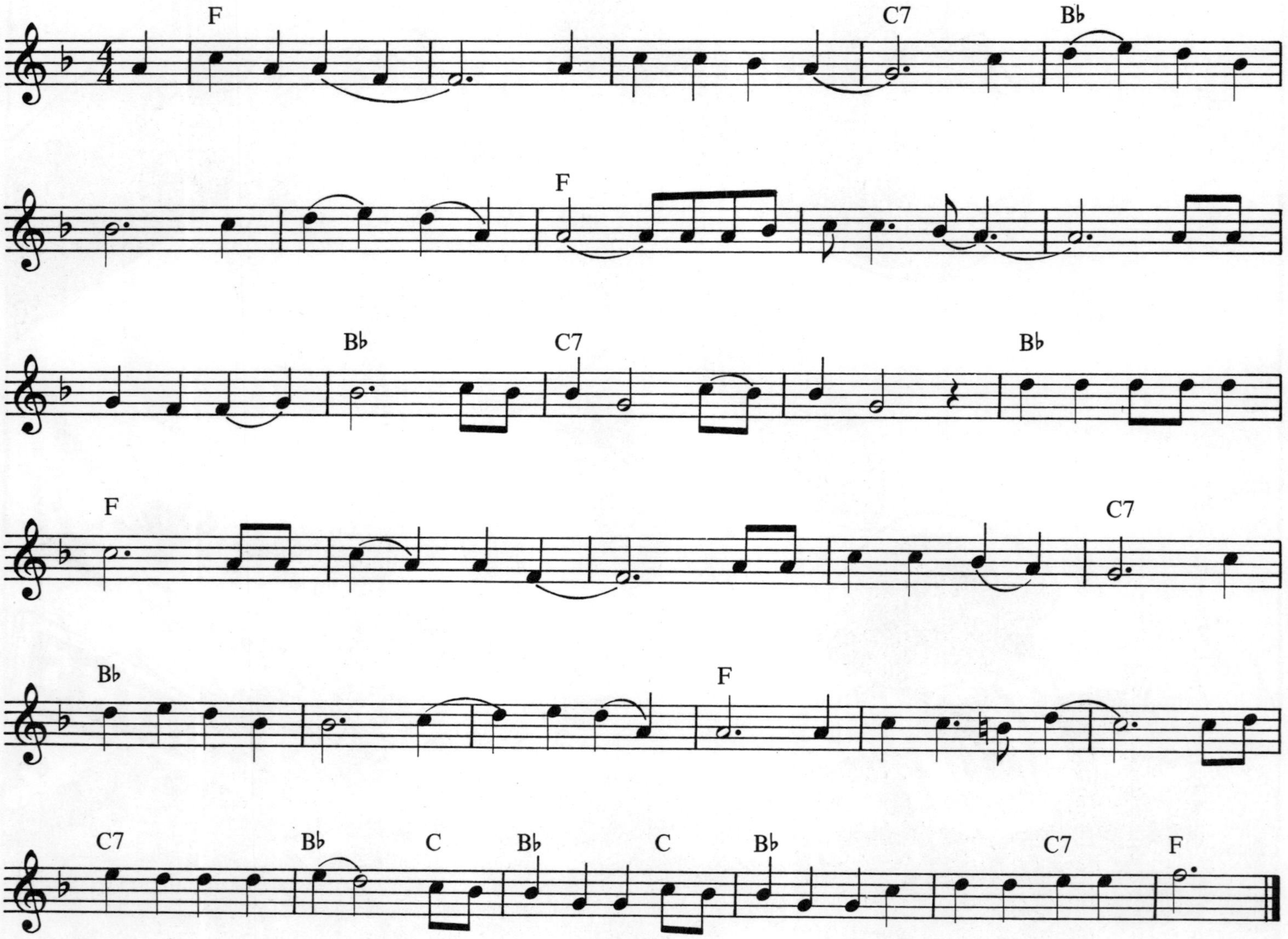
F
C7
B♭
F
B♭
C7
B♭
F
C7
B♭
F
C7
B♭
C
B♭
C
B♭
C7
F

From the singing of Jean and Moss Phillips, Ramsgate, New South Wales. Collected by Warren Fahey, in 1975. Parody on "My Home in Tennessee". Compare with "Les Darcy". The toast was collected by Warren Fahey from Dick Wyoming, Forbes, New South Wales, in 1973.

I paid a franc to see a fair tattooed lad-y
And right across her jaw, were the words great Anzac Corp
And on her chest was a possum and a great big kangaroo
And on her back was a Union Jack, coloured red, white and blue.
A map of Germany, was where I couldn't see
And right across her hips, was a line of battleships.
And on her kidney, and on her kidney
Was a birds-eye view of Sydney
And 'round the corner, 'round the corner,
Was my home in Woolloomooloo!

"Here's to you as good as you are
And here's to me as bad as I am
And as good as you are
And as bad as I am
I'm as good as you are
As bad as I am!"
(Traditional toast)

From the singing of swagman Jack Pobar, Toowoomba, Queensland. Collected by Warren Fahey, in 1973. This song is a parody on "Rose of No Man's Land". The toast was collected by Warren Fahey from Mr Clarrie Peters, Austinmer, New South Wales, in 1973.

Oh, It's the nose that grows
on my old man,
And it's wonderful to see,
Though it's stained with beers —
it will live for years
In my garden of misery

For it's the one red nose
that the boozer knows,
And it's the work of a barmaid's hand.
Amid the drink and curse
There can be no worse,
Than the nose on my old man!

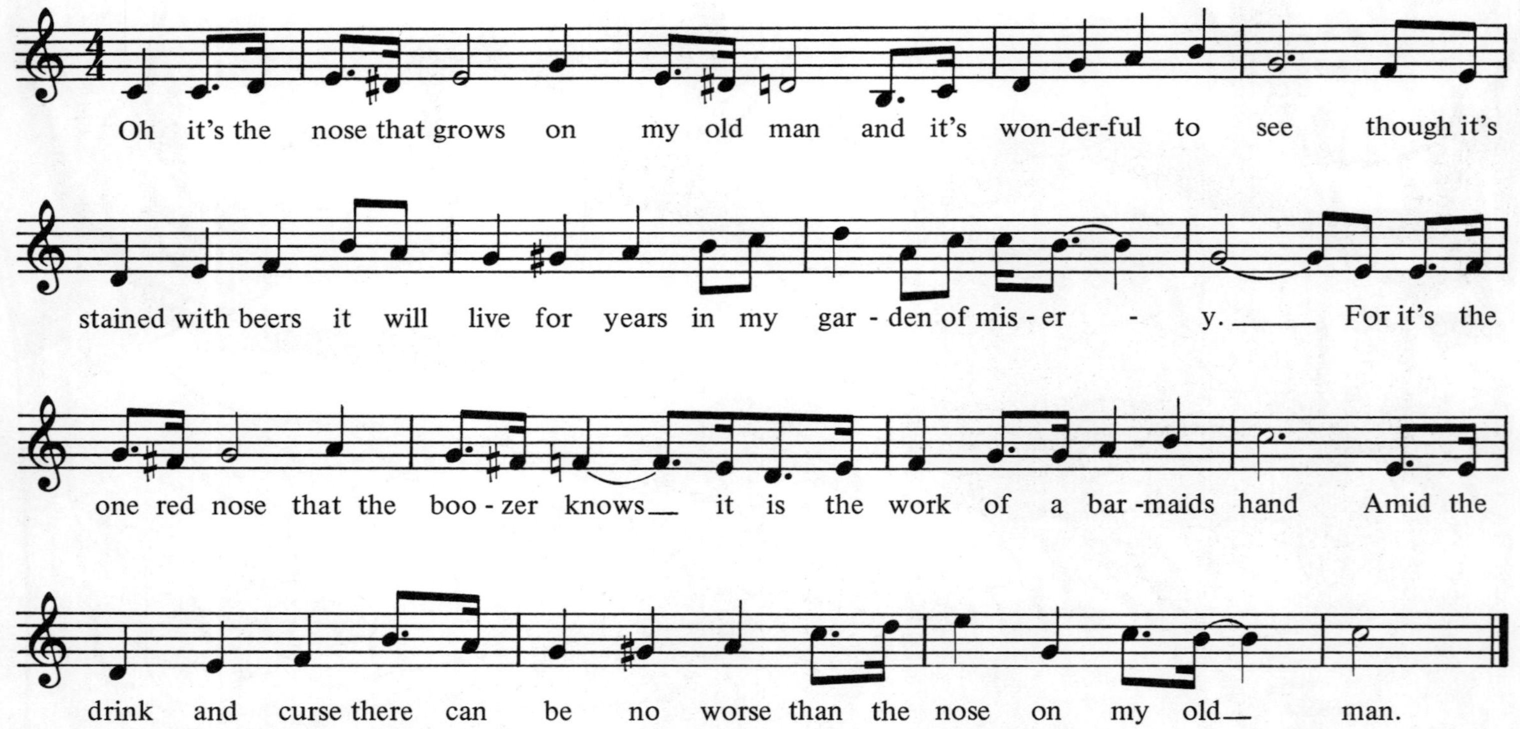

The Blackboy's Waltzing Matilda

"Waltzing Matilda" has been accepted as the "unofficial" Australian national anthem. Here's a version chock full of Aboriginal slang. The jumbuck sheep becomes a jimbuck, waltzing becomes walkabout and the coolibah tree becomes the big fella tree.

From the singing of Mr Herb Green, St Lucia, Queensland. Collected by Warren Fahey, in 1973. An Aboriginal pidgin-English parody on "Waltzing Matilda".

Old fella bagaman camp alonga billybung
Sitta longa shade big fella tree
Singum watchum old billy boiling
You'll come walkabout tildalonga me.

You'll come walkabout
Big fella roundabout
You come walkabout tildalonga me
Leadum dillybag meat froma tuckabag
You carry plurry swag tildalonga me.

Up come a jimbuck to drink at the waterhole
Bagman tallem comalonga me
Singum shovim longa tuckabag
You coma walkabout jimbuck longa me.

Down come the troopie mounted on their prads
Down come a troopie one, two, three
Where's that jimbuck you got in tuckabag
You coma walkabout comalonga me.

Bagman benup jumpa longa waterhole
Drown plurry self near big fella tree
Ghost him be seen all night by waterhole
You come walkabout tildalonga me.

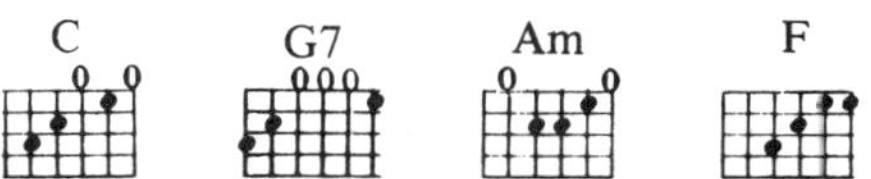
C
G7
Am
F

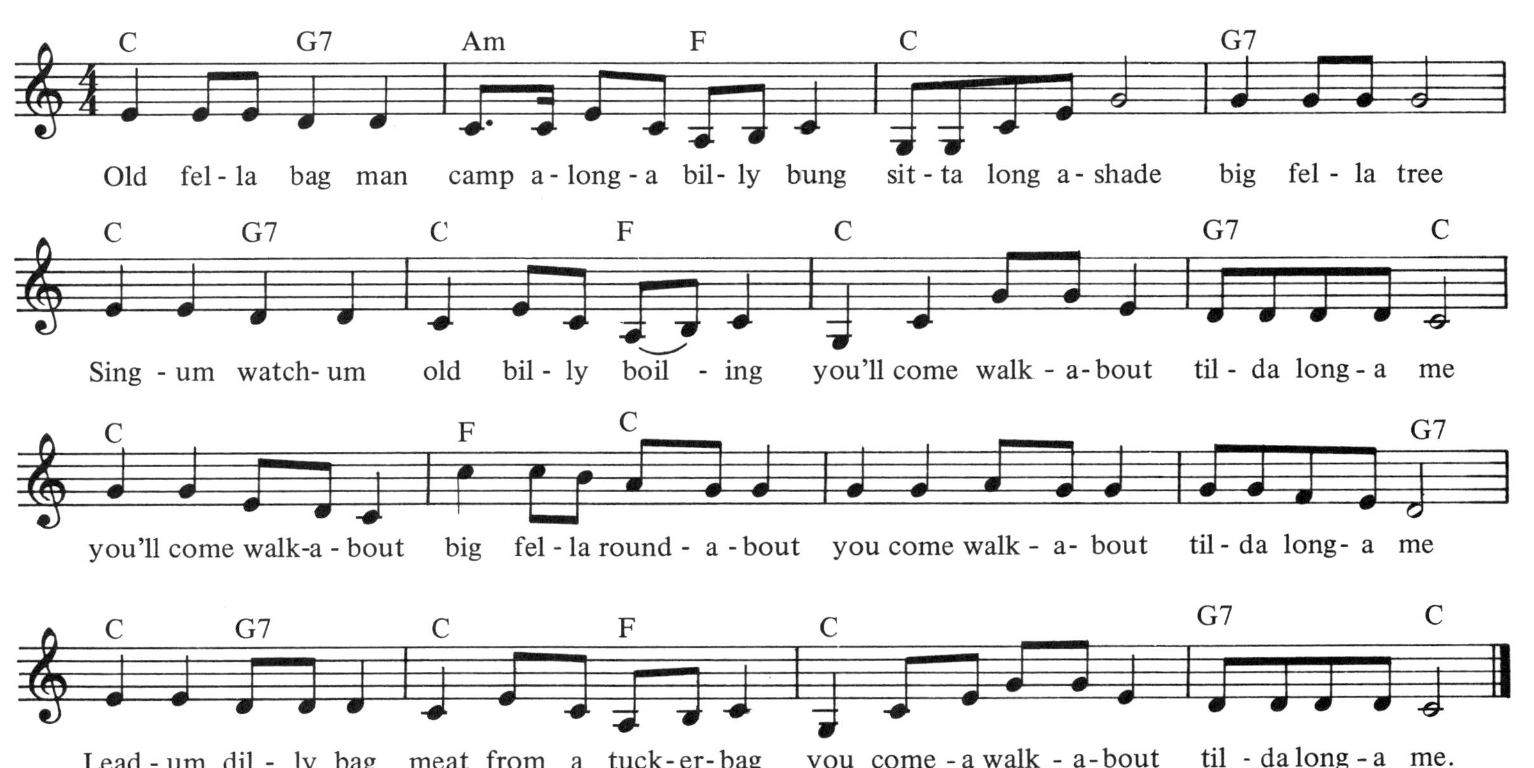
Old fel-la bag man camp a-long-a bil-ly bung sit-ta long a-shade big fel-la tree
Sing-um watch-um old bil-ly boil-ing you'll come walk-a-bout til-da long-a me
you'll come walk-a-bout big fel-la round-a-bout you come walk-a-bout til-da long-a me
Lead-um dil-ly bag meat from a tuck-er-bag you come-a walk-a-bout til-da long-a me.

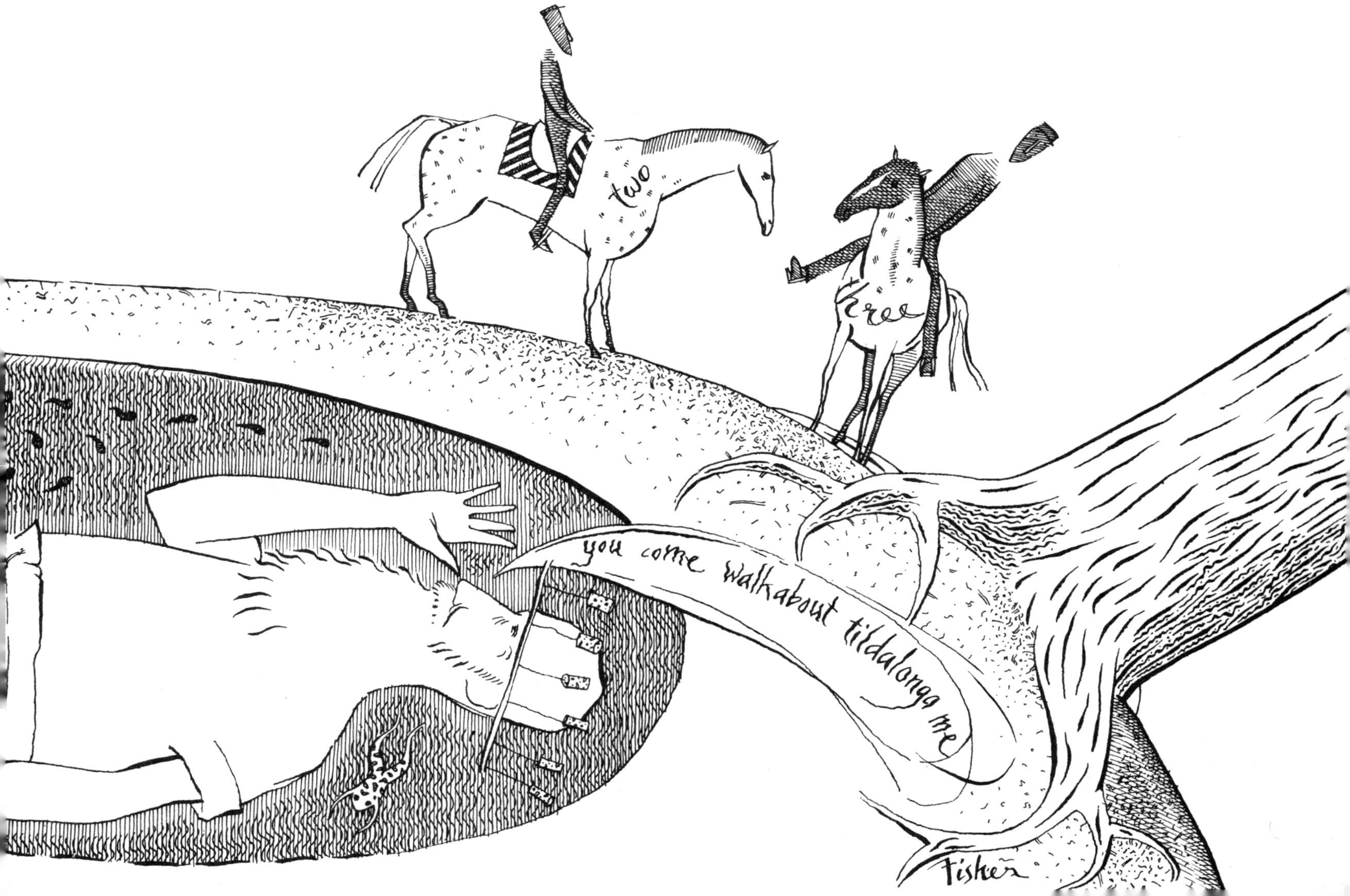

two
three
you come walkabout tildalonga me
Fisher

Compiling this book was hard yakka!
Here's a further toast to the many Australians who have sung their songs into my tape-recorder for the past fifteen years – you are the "song carriers" and the key to the noble tradition of the folksong.

I would also like to toast my fellow folklore collectors. The songs in this collection belong to the people of Australia but it is our work that preserves the past for the future.

And finally a toast to Mimmo Cozzolino who designed the book, and to the fine band of illustrators who added their interpretations to the songs. Your work is also part of a noble and continuing tradition. (The illustrators are listed in order of first and subsequent spread appearances.)

Neil **C**urtis: 2, 6, 12, 32, 38, 62, 80, 116, 120, 132, 144, 178, 182, 190, 202, 222, 228, 236; **S**hane **M**cGowan: 10, 22, 36, 210, 220; **G**eoff **C**ook: 14, 138; **P**eter **V**iska: 16, 56, 106, 164; **C**on **A**slanis: 18, 48, 58, 88, 104, 134, 196; **M**urray **W**alker: 20, 74, 84, 224; **D**ougal **R**amsay: 24; **J**eff **F**isher: 26, 82, 136, 184, 234; **S**tephen **B**irch: 28; **V**ictoria **R**oberts: 30, 194; **R**ay **C**ondon: 34, 86, 96, 146; **C**hris **P**ayne: 40, 108, 128, 170; **M**elissa **W**ebb: 42, 232; **M**eg **W**illiams: 44, 68, 158, 206; **C**hris **G**rosz: 46, 52, 78, 114, 162, 214; **N**eil **M**cLean: 50, 92, 126, 176, 186; **D**avid **D**oyle: 54, 166; **S**imon **M**cLean: 60, 124, 156, 198; **M**ichael **L**eunig: 66, 118, 150, 174; **B**ruce **L**auchlan: 70, 152, 188, 212; **K**en **U**chida: 72, 204; **S**teve **M**alpass: 76, 168, 208, 226; **P**hilip **E**llett: 90, 172; **B**etty **G**reenhatch: 94, 142; **S**tuart **B**illington: 98, 102, 112, 140, 192; **M**eg **B**roadbent: 100; **D**avid **H**ughes: 130; **R**ocky **R**usso: 148; **M**egan **S**tone: 154; **G**aston **V**anzet: 160, 216; **J**ane **T**anner: 200; **C**lyde **T**erry: 218; **B**ruce **W**eatherhead: 230.